Prophetic Christianity

Series Editors

Bruce Ellis Benson
Malinda Elizabeth Berry
Peter Goodwin Heltzel

The Prophetic Christianity series explores the complex relationship between Christian doctrine and contemporary life. Deeply rooted in the Christian tradition yet taking postmodern and postcolonial perspectives seriously, series authors navigate difference and dialogue constructively about divisive and urgent issues of the early twenty-first century. The books in the series are sensitive to historical contexts, marked by philosophical precision, and relevant to contemporary problems. Embracing shalom justice, series authors seek to bear witness to God's gracious activity of building beloved community.

PUBLISHED

Bruce Ellis Benson, Malinda Elizabeth Berry, and Peter Goodwin Heltzel, eds., *Prophetic Evangelicals: Envisioning a Just and Peaceable Kingdom* (2012)

Jennifer Harvey, *Dear White Christians: For Those Still Longing for Racial Reconciliation* (2014)

Peter Goodwin Heltzel, *Resurrection City: A Theology of Improvisation* (2012)

Johnny Bernard Hill, *Prophetic Rage: A Postcolonial Theology of Liberation* (2013)

Grace Ji-Sun Kim, *Embracing the Other: The Transformative Spirit of Love* (2015)

Randy S. Woodley, *Shalom and the Community of Creation: An Indigenous Vision* (2012)

Embracing the Other

The Transformative Spirit of Love

Grace Ji-Sun Kim

WILLIAM B. EERDMANS PUBLISHING COMPANY

GRAND RAPIDS, MICHIGAN / CAMBRIDGE, U.K.

Published 2015 by

Wm. B. Eerdmans Publishing Co.

2140 Oak Industrial Drive N.E., Grand Rapids, Michigan 49505 /

P.O. Box 163, Cambridge CB3 9PU U.K.

Printed in the United States of America

21 20 19 18 17 16 15   7 6 5 4 3 2 1

Library of Congress Cataloging-in-Publication Data

Kim, Grace Ji-Sun, 1969-

Embracing the other: the transformative spirit of love / Grace Ji-Sun Kim.

pages   cm.   — (The prophetic Christianity)

Includes index.

ISBN 978-0-8028-7299-9 (pbk.: alk. paper)

1. Women — Religious aspects — Christianity.

2. Sex role — Religious aspects — Christianity.

3. Women — Social conditions.

4. Race discrimination — Religious aspects — Christianity.

5. Racism — Religious aspects — Christianity.

I. Title.

BT704.K471255   2015

230.082 — dc23

2015017965

www.eerdmans.com

Dedicated to my husband,
Perry Y. C. Lee,
for twenty years of marriage and partnership
in the transformative Spirit of love

Contents

Acknowledgments		ix
Introduction		1
1.	Foreign Women in the Hebrew Bible	11
2.	The Lives of Asian American Immigrant Women	31
3.	Women as the Other: A Postcolonial Perspective	59
4.	Overcoming the Gendered Division of Humanity	91
5.	Spirit God and Shalom Justice	115
6.	The Transformative Spirit of Love	140
	Conclusion	165
	Postscript	170
	Index	174

Acknowledgments

Every book is written in community. *Embracing the Other* is no different, growing out of many conversations with colleagues and friends. During the autumn of 2011, Peter Goodwin Heltzel invited me to write a book for the *Prophetic Christianity Series* at Eerdmans. I would like to thank each of the editors of the series — Bruce Ellis Benson, Malinda Berry, and Peter Heltzel — for their insight and encouragement. I am especially grateful to Peter Heltzel, for his constant enthusiasm, words of wisdom, and earnest prayers throughout the writing of the book. Much thanks is also extended to David Bratt, Executive Editor at Eerdmans, who helped ensure that each stage of the production went smoothly and efficiently.

I am always thankful for my theological dialogue partners who helped me sort through some of my theological struggles for this book. My deep thanks to Joseph Cheah, Dwight Hopkins, Jesse Jackson Sr., Jeffrey Kuan, Donald K. McKim, Kwok Pui Lan, and Miguel De La Torre, who have supported me during the time of my writing. They have been both spiritually and theologically encouraging to me as I wrote the book.

I would also like to thank my friends who read and edited parts of this book. I am thankful to Barbara Lucia, Katie Mulligan, and Mark Koenig for reading parts of the manuscript. I am deeply grateful to my research assistant, Bruce Marold, for reading it with a careful eye and catching errors and problems. His advice improved this manuscript and I am deeply thankful for his help.

Parts of the book have appeared elsewhere, notably in *Feminist Theology* and *Insights,* and are used here with permission. I am particularly in-

ix

debted to Peter Phan for the generous resources and critical exchange that I was provided as a Visiting Research Scholar at Georgetown University, where I was able to research, write, and complete the manuscript. I will forever be grateful for his kindness, encouragement, affirmation, and generosity. I thank him for encouraging me to develop my own Asian American constructive theological vision.

Lastly, I thank my family for standing by me during the vicissitudes of writing and editing; my sister, Karen, and brother-in-law, Bruce, for feeding me when I was in desperate need of Korean food; my niece and nephew for making me laugh countless times and making me realize that breaks are needed when writing a book.

I am deeply grateful to my husband, Perry, for taking on extra work around the house and for handling our children's activities during the writing of my book. I thank my son, Theodore, for studying hard at school and excelling in every subject and extracurricular activity. I also thank Theo for being involved in church activities like youth band and aiding in Sunday school. I thank my daughter, Elisabeth, with whom I have shared my deepest hope for the next generation of women leaders in the church. She knows that any girl can find space in the church to grow, mature, and even lead. I thank my youngest, Joshua, who has made my life joyful with his constant mimicking of his own mom to make my rather serious life a little more lighthearted and enjoyable. To the communities of church, friends, and family that nourished and helped me, I give my heartfelt thanks.

Introduction

My Story: Being an Immigrant in North America

As an Asian American woman growing up in North America, I have experienced alienation, discrimination, and racism. Because of the color of my skin and the shape of my eyes, (some) people in the white dominant society think of me as different, and treat me that way.

Our family immigrated to Canada in 1975 and that year I started kindergarten. I still remember the pain I felt at the racial slurs directed toward me and other Korean friends at my school. Children ganged up against me and my Korean friends; they called us names and bullied us racially. Since we looked different and spoke with a distinct accent and in "broken" English, we became easy targets of their racism. This type of bullying continued through much of elementary school.

First as a teenager and now as an adult, I see that these overt forms of racism have become more subtle and covert. When racism becomes institutionalized, it feels much more difficult to call it racism. Institutionalized racism percolates in our society under different guises, including such terms and behaviors as the "model minority," "honorific whites," and being under "white privilege." It is vital to unpack these forms of racism, prejudice, and subordination so that we as a society can work towards dismantling them.

Why, as a society, do people tend to treat those who are different with suspicion, discrimination, and trepidation?

Racism and Sexism in Transatlantic Context

During a recent trip to South Africa, I visited Cape Town and witnessed many positive developments in politics, history, and culture. But when I visited Khayelitsha Township which is the fastest-growing township in South Africa, it was as though time had stood still. The world has heard of the end of apartheid. We have heard of the political ascendancy of the African National Congress (ANC), of the election of Nelson Mandela and several of his successors to the presidency, and of a "New South Africa." This makes it all the more astonishing to see the poor, unsanitary living conditions that persist among Black Africans in townships such as Khayelitsha. They live in tiny metal shacks cobbled together out of scrap metal they find lying around. The roofs of these tiny homes usually leak during the rainy season, and therefore people can go days without sleeping on something dry. The government has built toilets throughout the township. But many homes and many people share each toilet, and each one is dirty, neglected, and unsafe. Water pumps are scattered throughout the township, but people have to go out of their shacks to get it and bring it home. Life in these townships is harsh compared to the lavish communities of wealthy whites.

The townships that still exist today convey the impression that apartheid has never been dismantled. How could such an evil system have been eliminated and yet leave in its wake millions of Black Africans living in abysmal conditions? This systemic mistreatment of people of color occurs because of our own preconceived notions of who the "foreigners" are. The Black Africans lived in South Africa first, while it was the Dutch and the English who colonized the country. The power that a few white people could gain over the many colored people in a short period of time is astounding and tragic.

Unfortunately, this process of racial discrimination has its roots in Christian theology. The racism and prejudice that exist in South Africa was shaped in part by a Dutch Calvinist theology that was used to maintain the colonial status quo. The Afrikaners were predominantly Dutch settlers who first arrived in South Africa in the seventeenth and eighteenth centuries. The Afrikaners believed that God made a special covenant with them, one that essentially gave them a "Promised Land" and in so doing excluded the indigenous population. The distortion of Christian theology is the idea that God has specially elected a particular ethnic or racial group at the expense of others — something that John Calvin himself would have found incomprehensible. The separation of Afrikaners from "others" was not limited to those of color such as the native Africans or Indians. It also included the South Africans of British descent, and this division became part of the basis for the Anglo-Boer Wars.[1]

The logic of Calvinist "chosenness" was applied not only to religious life, but also to economic life. As Max Weber would unveil, economic productivity becomes a sign of election within certain Calvinist worldviews.[2] The sovereign God not only dictates who can and who cannot be saved, but also who should and should not succeed within the socioeconomic order. People who cannot make money are doomed, while people who make money are saved, in this life and the next. The biblical logic of election can easily be distorted into an ethic, not of compassion and service, but rather of exclusivity, discrimination, and domination.

Christian theology was central to the production of race in the "New World." In Puritan New England, the Calvinist doctrine of election was also used by the European colonists to justify racial discrimination against Native Americans. While indigenous people were racialized as "Indians," enslaved Africans were racialized as "black." Within this racial hierarchy, Native Americans and African Americans were seen as subhuman. The "white masculine," exported from Europe, was believed to be the ideal for all humanity.[3]

This "white masculine" ideal unveils not only the problem of racism, but the problem of patriarchy. While there is an inordinate amount of injustice and oppression towards people of color in our societies, women and girls are often the most vulnerable victims of oppression. Women are continually mistreated, abused, and discounted because of the patriarchal pathology that judges women by different moral rules than men. Again, the roots of patriarchy are often theological, as male clergy seek to keep women in subordinate

---

1. For an introduction to the struggle for racial justice in South Africa with reference to Dutch Calvinism see Allan Boesak, *Black and Reformed: Apartheid, Liberation, and the Calvinist Tradition*, ed. Leonard Sweetman (Maryknoll, NY: Orbis, 1984).

2. Max Weber, *The Protestant Ethic and the Spirit of Capitalism* (London: G. Allen & Unwin, 1930).

3. For recent accounts of race as a theological problem in the Americas see J. Kameron Carter, *Race: A Theological Account* (Oxford: Oxford University Press, 2008); Jennifer Harvey, *Dear White Christians: For Those Still Longing for Racial Reconciliation* (Grand Rapids: Eerdmans, 2014); Peter Goodwin Heltzel, *Jesus and Justice: Evangelicals, Race and American Politics* (New Haven: Yale University Press, 2009); Willie Jennings, *Christian Imagination: Theology and Origins of Race* (New Haven: Yale University Press, 2011); Reggie L. Williams, *Bonhoeffer's Black Jesus: Harlem Renaissance Theology and an Ethic of Resistance* (Waco, TX: Baylor University Press, 2014).

positions, quoting the Apostle Paul, "I permit no woman to teach or to have authority over a man; she is to keep silent" (1 Tim. 2:12), without considering the cultural context and worship practices of the early Christian movement. Christian theology was used in the construction and maintenance of white male control in the colonies.

The legacies of racism and patriarchy continue on into our present political context. For example, certain male politicians in the United States continue to speak for women and on women's issues. They decide what is right for women and for women's bodies. They have tried to take away women's voices, rights, and decision-making, to the detriment of women everywhere. Instead of advocating for women and girls, especially the concerns of women of color, faith leaders are often silent.

Prophetic Christianity today must critically engage the problem of Euro-American racism and sexism. As Martin Luther King Jr. said at the Riverside Church of New York City on April 4, 1967: "A time comes when silence is betrayal."[4] The church needs to wake up from its slumber and prophetically confront the sins of racism and sexism in our society today. If we do not do anything about racism and sexism — even creating awareness in one's church is something proactive — then we are contributing to the problem. If we sit around and do nothing, we are permitting racism and sexism to exist and grow, because we do not insist that oppressing others because of their race or gender is contrary to Christian beliefs.

How do we eliminate this oppression and achieve justice and shalom for all humanity and all creation? How can we join in deep solidarity with the freedom struggles of women and people of color? How do we work towards healing, reconciliation, and justice among people, regardless of their race or gender? I suggest it is through the power of the Spirit.

The Power of the Spirit in Christian Theology

The Spirit is the heart and soul of Christian theology. While we are living in a period of great division and conflict, God's Spirit can bring healing and hope. While we often make people who are different from us the Other, the scriptural vision calls us not to ignore and neglect the Other, but rather to

---

4. Martin Luther King Jr., "A Time to Break Silence," *A Testament of Hope: The Essential Writings and Speeches of Martin Luther King, Jr.,* ed. James M. Washington (New York: HarperOne, 1986), p. 231.

embrace the Other. It is the power of the Spirit that opens our hearts to cross borders and embrace the Other.

Spirit is ubiquitous. Spirit of life energy is an idea that we see throughout the world. Chinese call it Chi or Qi, Japanese call it Ki, Hindus call it Prana, and Greeks called it Pneuma. In all languages, Spirit is associated with breath, wind, or life-giving energy. We need to recover the transformative power of life energy, the font of divine love and justice. Because Spirit is the underlying ethos of people around the globe, the concept of Spirit God can provide a more holistic understanding of God and humans that extends beyond skin tones, culture, religion, and power within society. This theology of Spirit is more inclusive and welcoming of outsiders, women, and people of different ethnicities — those who may be subjugated or Othered. Focusing on God as Spirit is more welcoming and inviting to all people within and outside of the church.

Recognizing that Spirit is what connects us all will open doors for further dialogue, understanding, and acceptance. This book contributes to the revitalization of North American churches and spirituality by providing a deeper theological perspective on God as Spirit by inviting all people into the discussion. The problem of the Other has become an important issue in theological discourse as the community of faith interacts with people of diverse faiths. The North American church needs to address this crucial problem of the Other if it is to survive and grow in this ever-expanding and globalizing world.

Overview

In order to develop a biblical understanding of the promise and the problems of embracing the Other, Chapter 1 explores foreign women in the Hebrew Bible. Using Ezra 9 as a historical and biblical backdrop, I examine how foreign women were treated back in Ezra's day and consider how women, especially immigrant women, are treated today. The phrase *foreign women* occurs ten times in the Hebrew Bible, always in the plural. The first usage of this phrase is significant because here Ezra's meaning is defined. In 1 Kings 11:1, the author states that Solomon loved many foreign women, identified as "Moabite, Ammonite, Edomite, Sidonian, and Hittite women." The only other non-Ezra occurrences of the phrase are in Nehemiah 13:26-27, which alludes to Solomon as well. When Nehemiah chastised the Jews who had married foreign women, he reminded them that Solomon's foreign wives turned his heart away from the Lord and caused him to sin despite the great favor he received from God. Foreign women are framed with foreign gods, and seen as seducing Solomon from complete covenantal loyalty to the God of Abraham, Isaac, and Jacob.

These scriptural narratives also depict foreign women and wives as pawns to be used in political negotiations, later to be marginalized. The story of Abraham sending away Hagar and her son can be viewed as a justification to dismiss the foreign wives and their children.[5]

Foreign women in the Bible are discriminated against both racially and religiously. In this chapter, I apply a postcolonial hermeneutic to illuminate these biblical texts that deal with foreign wives. While Israel came out of slavery in Egypt, sometimes it was difficult for them to overcome some of the oppressive ways of relating to others, especially foreign women. It is vital that we understand the historical and cultural contexts that have led to the oppression of women and what implications this legacy of oppression has for us. After all, how can one ask women to leave who have been fully immersed in the life of the family and community? This casting out has great consequences for the family, community, and the nation, not least that it perpetuates the false understanding that it is acceptable to dominate women in this way. For once the power elites in society label someone as different, inferior, or simply "the Other," it is a short step to terrible acts of violence, dominance, sexual objectification, and slavery.

Chapter 2 examines the particular history, social context, and life of Asian immigrant women in North America, thus illumining the existential plight of "foreign women" today. The history of the first wave of Asian immigration to North America stretches over nearly a century, much of which was plagued with hardship, turmoil, difficulties, and perseverance. Coming to North America is a difficult transition for all immigrants; Asian immigrants face a special set of challenges. A new culture, language, and religion often present a clashing of ideas and traditions that results in much confusion and chaos in the lives of immigrants. From the beginning of immigration, Asian North American women have been viewed both as the foreigner and as the exotic temptress.

White European immigrants were treated differently than Asians or

---

5. Danna Nolan Fewell, "Ezra and Nehemiah," in *Global Bible Commentary,* ed. Daniel Patte (Nashville: Abingdon, 2004), p. 130. For a thoughtful discussion of Hagar as a foreign woman see womanist theologian Delores S. Williams, "Hagar's Story: A Route to Black Women's Issues," *Sisters in the Wilderness: The Challenge of Womanist God-Talk* (Maryknoll, NY: Orbis, 1993), pp. 15-33.

people of color. Europeans entered the United States through Ellis Island in New York and had their identifications checked, and were registered to enter America. Asians, on the other hand, often came principally through Angel Island in San Francisco Bay, which immigrants recall as being more like a prison than a welcoming port of entry to America.[6] While European immigrants at Ellis Island waited a couple of hours or overnight before they were allowed to enter America, Asian immigrants at Angel Island had to wait sometimes weeks, months, or even years before they were allowed to enter the United States. Whereas only 2 percent of Europeans who applied for entry were sent back to their countries of origin, Asians were sent back at more than ten times that rate. The difference in treatment towards these two groups of people was racially driven.[7] It was not that European immigrants were any healthier or smarter than Asian immigrants; it was rather a difference of skin color and outward appearance signifying a racial difference that did not fit the white norm. The Japanese government actually did its best to send only the smartest, most educated, and healthiest people to America. Because white immigration officials already had preconceived negative and stereotypical views of Asians, they were blind to this racialized reality and participated in systemic racism.

While the white European immigrant women by and large were able to assimilate into the dominant Western culture, Asian immigrant women have struggled to find their way. It does not matter how many generations such women have lived in North America, their "yellow" skin continues to mark them as "foreigners." As foreign women were ostracized in the book of Ezra because of their cultural and religious differences, so too, Asian immigrant women are marginalized in the West because of their yellow skin tone, cultural difference, and religious diversity.

Chapter 3 focuses on women as the Other, from the perspective of postcolonial theology. In his magisterial book *Orientalism*, Edward Said argues that "the Orient" is an invention of the Western imagination and is part of a colonial strategy of cultural control and dominance. Orientalism is understood both as a tendency to dichotomize humanity into us-them con-

---

6. Regardless of their racial and ethnic backgrounds, all immigrants resented being confined like criminals behind barbed wire fences, locked doors, and wire-netted windows. "I had never seen such a prison-like place as Angel Island," recalled Kamechiyo Takahashi, a young Japanese bride in 1917. Many questioned as she did, "Why had I to be kept in a prison?" Erika Lee and Judy Yung, *Angel Island: Immigrant Gateway to America* (Oxford: Oxford University Press, Kindle Edition, 2010), locations 1362-64.

7. Paul Spickard, *Almost All Aliens* (New York: Routledge, 2007), pp. 421, 422.

trasts and to essentialize the resultant Other. Europeans and North Americans have used Orientalism as a way of dominating the East by exerting self-ascribed authority and power over people of "the Orient." European culture gained in strength and identity by positioning "the Orient" (which today is often referred to as the Middle East, East Asia, or the Far East) as a sort of surrogate and even underground self. In addition, Europeans have feminized the Orient as a further path to domination and subordination. By feminizing the Orient, it consequently considers the Orient as weak, helpless, and vulnerable. Orientalism is one strategy that white Euro-Americans use to subjugate people of Asian descent.

Asians are migratory people, always on the move. As a result they have complex cultural identities. In the second half of Chapter 3, I analyze Homi Bhabha's notion of hybridity. When Asians migrate to the West, they bring with them the legacies of Asian religious and cultural traditions, which they have to express in new ways. Postcolonial theory seeks to ensure that the needs and aspirations of the exploited are addressed and is concerned with the effects of unequal power relations between groups of people. Postcolonial theory provides a space for the once-colonized to decolonize and become creative agents in society. In our globalized world it is crucial to acknowledge the reality and sin of unequal power, and allow it to inform how we understand God, the gospel, and the Bible in our time.

Asian North American immigrant women come to accept that their identities and situations are hybrid given the complex, multi-circumstantial, and multifaceted contexts in which they live. I suggest that seeing Asian North American immigrant women as hybrid is a much better theological way to understand them, rather than as the Other who can so easily be discarded, dehumanized, and dominated. It challenges us to reexamine and reimagine the theological construction of the feminine and masculine subject and their relation to each other. It challenges us to ask how it is still possible to make and maintain women, in particular the foreign women, as the Other when society has worked so hard for gender equality.

Chapter 4 examines the historic trajectories of white feminist and Asian feminist theology. White feminist theologians like Elisabeth Schüssler Fiorenza set the groundwork for future feminist theological discourse by examining the biblical, historical, and theological liberation of women, and insisting on the inclusion of their experiences and voices within theological discourse.

As works of feminist theology reached out to many women and helped them to understand how their different experiences of God are played out in their lives and in the church, women of different ethnic backgrounds realized that white women couldn't speak to their specific experiences of cultural subordination, racism, and colonial subjugation. W. Anne Joh offers a theology of love that offers a promising trajectory for Asian North American feminist theology. She develops a dialectic between pain and love that is focused on the cross of Christ. Building on her work, I seek to deepen the pneumatology within Asian feminist theology.

Chapter 5 offers a theological reconstruction of Spirit as God. How we talk about God has deep implications for how we perceive and treat those who are different, in particular foreign women, and indeed our treatment of those who are different affects and reflects how we think of God. Within Western Christianity, our image of God has been one of a powerful, almighty, omnipresent, and dominating figure, and typically a figure who is, even if subconsciously, white and male. These images have contributed to a masochistic understanding of God, which in turn has glorified the image of men and the dominant white culture. As long as we perpetuate such understandings of God, we legitimize white dominant power and colonialism and the subjugation of all who are not white. Thus we need to move away from such images of God to ones that are more life-giving and that will speak across cultures and societies. Such life-giving images of God will more readily promote an equality of cultures and a movement away from the center, both within and outside of the church. In order to stop perpetuating this Othering of Asian North Americans, it is important to perceive the Divine in creative, nonhierarchical, non-Western, and hybrid ways. A de-centered theological perspective of God will in turn de-center the dominant culture and make room for the marginalized and the Othered in the circle of humanity.

A Trinitarian theology pervades this book, but its focus is away from Christology and toward the Spirit. The Spirit and Jesus are important parts of the Trinity, but the focus on Jesus has limited and restricted how we are to love one another and those of different faiths. Perhaps embracing the Spirit will also help us to move beyond Christianity and open the door for further dialogue with and acceptance of people of different faith traditions and those who are different from us. Perhaps embracing the Spirit will help us to engage in compassionate care of the Other. Perhaps by breathing the common Spirit-Chi[8] breath and by being more aware of our common humanity we will be empowered to do so.

8. Spirit-Chi is a term I use to indicate the hybrid life-giving Spirit of God that exists within the Asian tradition. More about this term will be discussed in chapters 5 and 6.

Connecting our very breath to the struggle for life unveils the erotic power that energizes the work of social justice for the vulnerable. Chapter 6 investigates Eros as the vital soul for transforming the world. God as Spirit-Chi ethos has the potential to treasure and champion the voice of the disparate spiritual Other and promote hybridity within the North American church. My approach will challenge the traditional patriarchal voice and understanding of biblical texts in order to develop a voice that can speak to the pluralistic makeup of today's church and society. This book will examine the concept of the Other using philosophers and social critics as well as the concept of God as Spirit, and the implications of this for the North American church.

Our understanding of God has been mainly a Eurocentric anthropomorphic understanding. To counteract this, I propose a Spirit God as a way of overcoming some of the traditional images that have contributed to the Othering of many groups of people, and in particular Asian North American women. This understanding of Spirit God will be built on my earlier work on hybrid Spirit-Chi pneumatology. For it is in such hybrid spaces that we find a theology of God that is liberating, empowering, and transformative. I suggest a focus on Spirit because as the undergirding ethos of people around the world, Spirit is beyond skin tones, culture, religion, and power within society. Spirit God works toward accepting, welcoming, and embracing those who are different and subjugated, and brings a more holistic understanding, which will change how women are perceived and are Othered. Understanding this Spirit God will help free us from some of our preconceived theologies and help us articulate a more inclusive Christian theology that speaks to the larger global community. A holistic understanding of Spirit God will aid the church in being a world leader in peace and reconciliation as the church embraces, welcomes, and accepts the Other. And in an increasingly multiethnic, post-Christian North America, Spirit God will help the church to understand and revitalize its role and purpose, and will strengthen its position in society for the good of all.

CHAPTER 1

Foreign Women in the Hebrew Bible

Many of us are familiar with the story of Giacomo Puccini's *Madama Butterfly*,[1] not only as an opera but also as a reality for many people of color in America. The story of *Madama Butterfly* begins with a U.S. Navy officer named B. F. Pinkerton, who wishes to marry a fifteen-year-old Japanese girl, Cio-Cio San (Butterfly) for convenience until he finds a proper American wife. Shortly after they get married, Pinkerton leaves. Butterfly waits for him faithfully, and gives birth to their son without him. After three years, Butterfly receives news that Pinkerton is coming back to see her. Her heart swoons, but little does she know that he has married a white American woman.[2]

The tragedy is not only that Butterfly was used as a temporary wife in a marriage of convenience, without her knowing it, but also that as a result of marrying an American, she was alienated by her own family. The tragedy is also that Pinkerton and his new wife are coming back because the American wife has agreed to raise the Japanese-American child. Once Butterfly realizes that the real reason for Pinkerton's visit is to take her child with him, she is devastated, agrees to the request, blindfolds the child, and commits suicide.

---

1. The Italian opera was based on an American novella of the same name by John Luther Long, published in 1897, and the French novel, *Madame Chrysanthème* by Pierre Loti, published in 1887.

2. Jean K. Kim uses this *Madama Butterfly* story in her analysis of Ezra-Nehemiah. Jean K. Kim, "Empowerment or Enslavement?: Reading John 4 Intertextually with Ezra-Nehemiah," in *Ways of Being, Ways of Reading*, ed. Mary F. Foskett and Jeffrey Kah-Jin Kuan (St. Louis: Chalice Press, 2006), pp. 99-111. I am indebted to her careful and insightful analysis of this story.

This is a tragic ending to a love story that Butterfly thought was hers, when in reality she was only used as a sexual partner while the naval officer was lonely and far from home. To him, Butterfly was a commodity, not a person in her own right. Pinkerton gave his young bride the name "Butterfly" because he did not even know her Japanese name! By relegating her to the world of nature, she became an object in the "background" of his own story and an object to be used and discarded. To use Rudolf Otto's[3] terminology, to him Butterfly was an "it" rather than a "thou."

We are all too familiar with this narrative. It is not necessarily the story of a white man marrying an Asian woman out of convenience, but more broadly the story of how a white person treats, or rather mistreats, a person of color as the Other and does as he or she wishes to them. The white person can throw away the Asian person, can exile her from both American and Asian cultures. Asian American women are caught between two cultures and never feel at home in either. They are exiled between cultures.

There are many variations on this story, such as in the 1954 James Michener novel *Sayonara,* and the subsequent film starring Marlon Brando, Red Buttons, and Miyoshi Umeki.[4] In this story, the American culture and Air Force refuses to recognize the union of a white American man (Kelly) with a Japanese woman (Katsumi). Kelly suffers further prejudice at the hands of a mean colonel. When he and many others who are married to Japanese are ordered back to the States, Kelly realizes he will not be able to take his wife, who is now pregnant. Finding no other way to be together, Kelly and Katsumi commit double suicide.

Still today, in all aspects of life Asian Americans encounter racism, prejudice, and stereotyping. That many consider them the "model minority" or "honorary whites" is no relief, but is only further evidence of that racism. This is discussed further in Chapter 2. Racism can take subtle forms. We tend to interpret the same actions by different people as being radically different. For example, when a person commits a mass murder, as Seung-Hui Cho did by murdering students at Virginia Tech on April 16, 2007, the person of color is often demonized, viewed as evil, and, as an immigrant, automatically put under suspicion. However, when James Holmes committed a similar crime by murdering twelve people and wounding another fifty-eight in an Aurora,

---

3. For more discussion see Rudolf Otto, *The Idea of the Holy* (Eastford, CT: Martino Fine Books, 2010).

4. In these roles, Red Buttons and Miyoshi Umeki both won Academy Awards for supporting actor and actress respectively. Umeki was the first, and only, Asian woman to win an Academy Award for acting.

Colorado, movie theater on July 20, 2012, rather than viewing him with suspicion we labeled him a "bad apple," a unique case.[5] We described his actions as a psychological breakdown or the consequences of a psychiatric problem for which he cannot be held responsible. We perceive him not really to be guilty of the crime. We see this again in the case of the Sandy Hook Elementary School killer, Adam Lanza, whom society labeled as "mentally ill" right after he was found responsible for the killings. Therefore the color of a person's skin determines one's character, one's place, role, and expectations in society — even if objectively one is a mass murderer.

Scripture: Foreign Women

Women are mistreated and oppressed by men in patriarchal societies. In many societies such oppression is masked by a difference in nongender-based status, such as cases in offices where all the "talent" and management are men and all the secretaries and clerks are women. This is dramatically shown in the first season of the TV show *Mad Men,* where all the women are in roles serving men. This television show is about the 1950s patriarchal business culture, which subordinated women. It is social injustice when half the population has been and continues to be denied equal rights and privileges based on their gender. That same patriarchy fuels the alarmingly high rates of domestic violence toward women. One in four women today is likely to experience domestic violence during her lifetime. Women may also experience assaults and rape committed at the hands of their partners.[6] And the darker one's skin color, the worse one is treated. There is a hierarchy of skin tones, even within one's own racial ethnic group; the lighter skin is more valued. In Asia, this perception is rooted in an agricultural context where the poor work outside all day long in the weather while the elite study and stay inside homes and buildings. Therefore the ones who work outside are darker and are often associated with the lower class and are more negatively treated. Racism is based on the color of one's skin and it has become an ongoing struggle for our society to overcome this problem.

The phrase "foreign women" occurs ten times in the New Revised Stan-

---

5. See footnotes about fan sites for Holmes in this Wikipedia article: http://en.wikipedia .org/wiki/James_Eagan_Holmes.

6. For more facts and information consult "Safe Horizon": http://www.safehorizon .org/index/what-we-do-2/domestic-violence-abuse-53/domestic-violence-the-facts-195.html.

dard translation of the Old Testament. There are many foreigners in the Bible. Moses' Midianite wife's story is about those who claimed that only *golah* (exiled) Jews and their offspring were part of Israel or the holy seed. All those who were not exiled were then viewed as foreign. In the book of Ezra, the writer argues that male *golah* Jews together with foreign women produced polluted offspring and therefore could be easily discarded from their community. However, the stories of Zipporah and other outsider wives or mothers such as Tamar, Asenath the Cushite, and Ruth indicate otherwise. These narratives show that foreign wives were important to the building of the people Israel and were intricately woven into Israel's historical narratives. It is intriguing to notice that the "insider" women, the sister/cousin-wives, were always barren until the Lord opened their wombs. (This includes Leah, Laban's older daughter, and her sister Rachel, the object of Jacob's affection; both became Jacob's wives.) The Lord intervened on Leah's behalf when he saw that "she was unloved" (Gen. 29:31-35). However, barrenness was not a problem for the outsiders: Hagar, Tamar (the wife of Judah's firstborn son), Asenath (the Egyptian given by Pharaoh to Joseph as a wife), and Zipporah (the daughter of a Midianite priest, given to Moses as a wife).[7] God uses those who are different to play a primary goal in redemption, and this is what God did with the foreign women. They became the mothers of important sons in the history of Israel. Sometimes God uses the foreigner to shame those who are of the dominant group who think so highly of themselves. They are brought down to illustrate that we are all equal in God's eyes. In this, as in so many instances throughout Israelite history, tradition itself constantly "subverts" attempts to ossify it.

The most common identification of the "foreign women" is as pagan, non-Jewish women from the nations surrounding Judah. The list of eight foreign nations in the context (Ezra 9:1) is usually the basis for this identification. Among those who agree that the foreign wives were pagan women, no agreement exists regarding why the marriages were a problem. One standard rationale is that the idolatrous practices of the heathen women drew the returnees back into the very sin that had precipitated the exile.[8] The Israelites also believed that the land ownership would pass to the hands of the pure-bred Judeans. However, this rationalizing would eliminate any responsibility of the Jewish community for their exile. This is scapegoating.

7. Karen Strand Winslow, "Ethnicity, Exogamy, and Zipporah," *Women in Judaism: A Multidisciplinary Journal* 4 (2006): 2, 3.

8. A. Philip Brown II, "The Problem of Mixed Marriages in Ezra 9–10," *Bibliotheca Sacra* 162 (2005): 439.

Foreign women are perceived in the Old Testament as the trouble-makers who have caused all the problems in the land and are never fully welcomed into the society. After the exile, the Israelites were worried about community and survival. They believed that God had exiled them as a pun-ishment for what they had done. They believed that in part it was the foreign women who had led them astray; therefore they gathered together and de-cided the fate of the foreign women.

They concluded that it was best to get rid of the women, whom they perceived to be the cause of their exile. So they gathered together to send the foreign women away. We are not sure whether these stories are historically reliable, but nonetheless the stories were remembered and passed along. This not only suggests that the authors of Ezra did not want the restored Judeans to forget this failing, but it tries to ensure that future generations will remember this lesson too. As twenty-first-century readers, we should be mindful of the patriarchal assumptions behind the text. Why were only the foreign women expelled when there were foreign men present as well? The answer then seems to be the same one many people give today: that the majority community desires to return to some previous, purer state and is looking for a scapegoat for its problems. Foreign women became easy targets; by blaming them, the people did not have to scrutinize themselves.

A key to this problem lies in the peculiarly gendered vocabulary that denotes, on the one hand, the community's holiness ("the holy seed"; Ezra 9:2); and on the other, the threatening contaminant (ΠΙ, "[menstrual] im-purity"; Ezra 9:11). The former is a male emblem of purity and the latter is a specifically female pollutant. This gendered language unavoidably positions women as signifiers of the stranger within. The female body represents, in Kristeva's terms, the abject (hopeless, miserable), which must be expelled.[9] The women are the problem and they are understood to be dirty and un-worthy. Women bring negativity to a community and pollute it with unde-sirables. Women need to recognize their abjection and understand that they are the element that needs to be expelled.

In Ezra 9, the defiling behaviors of foreigners are highlighted in the text's polemic against intermarriage. Such behaviors result in a particular type of pollution that adheres to the sinner and, according to several texts, threatens the holiness of the land and the sanctuary and can result in the expulsion of Israel from their land (e.g., Lev. 18:25, 28). Such "moral" impu-

9. Harold C. Washington, "Israel's Holy Seed and the Foreign Women of Ezra-Nehemiah: A Kristevan Reading," *Biblical Interpretation* 11, no. 3-4 (2003): 431.

rity cannot be removed by means of ablutions or other ritual actions, or the passage of a set period of time, as is the case with "ritual" impurities. It is only through the violator's punishment or atonement that "moral" impurity can be removed.

Nehemiah 13:28-30, a text from the Nehemiah memoir, bears witness to a second way in which Ezra-Nehemiah associates foreigners with defilement. In this passage, it is priestly intermarriage with aliens that pollutes and not necessarily what the foreigners actually do. Presumably, purification was secured through the divorce of the priests from their foreign wives and the expulsion of the wives and their children from the sanctuary and community. Such an action would result in the exclusion from the priesthood of all males in the priestly line with any alien ancestry.[10] This became a mode of separation and departure through a humanly designed notion of purity and defilement. It was not a heavenly ordained but a humanly conceived and executed way of erecting barriers and divisions that would keep the "insiders" in and the "outsiders" out, of a people keeping their land so that foreigners would not take it over. In a matter of economics, religious sentiments and ideas were executed so that a small community could survive after returning from their exile. But what seemed reasonable to them had grave consequences for the foreign women.

In some parts of Scripture, foreign women have been diminished and portrayed as the ones who cause problems for the Israelites. When Israel could not defend itself against invasion, and faced the virtual erasure of its identity by the foreign power of Assyria, prophets like Hosea described this as fitting punishment for "whoring" after foreign deities (Hosea 2). Thus foreign women are portrayed as sexually luring men's hearts away from their own women and from YHWH and causing them to become "whores."[11] Thus foreign women were negatively tied to sexual corruption and an ignorance of YHWH.

This negative feminine image of social actions occurring in their community gives rise to the gendering of language and ultimately of God. When a negative act is associated with women, the possibility of achieving gender equality diminishes drastically. Therefore as we continue to study imagery within Scripture and how foreign women are treated, we notice the gen-

---

10. Saul M. Olyan, "Purity Ideology in Ezra-Nehemiah as a Tool to Reconstitute the Community," *Journal for the Study of Judaism* 35 (2004): 5, 6.

11. Gail Corrington Street, *The Strange Woman: Power and Sex in the Bible* (Louisville: Westminster John Knox, 1997), p. 66.

dering of biblical language and its consequences. Foreign women are to be discarded and abandoned. This negative perception of foreign women has endured throughout history, not only in the biblical texts, but in lands where that text is read and held sacred.

Such is the case in the United States, and particularly so for women of color who, simply on the basis of their skin color, are often treated as foreigners. Asian American women have been living in the United States for many generations, as have other immigrants, but they are singled out because of their physical differences, such as the size and color of their eyes, the size of their nose, their skin color, etc., as being unlike the dominant (white) women. They are viewed as "perpetual foreigners"; it does not matter how many generations they have lived here, because they look different and will remain or be understood as foreigners. Asian American women who are viewed as "perpetual foreigners" are continually mistreated and subordinated by the dominant society, as we saw in *Madama Butterfly*, then discarded when they are no longer useful.

The trope we see in *Madama Butterfly* is familiar even from the Scriptures, with its many stories of the mistreatment and abandonment of foreign women. Some readers might think such mistreatment of foreign women is acceptable (to them and to God) because it is in a "Holy Book." Not so: women and men are created equal, not as an abuser and the abused, and surely God's heart breaks when human equality is ignored. In Scripture, the women of color or the foreign women are oftentimes treated as the Other, as disposable objects who find themselves at the mercy of the patriarchs and rulers. One such biblical woman was Hagar.

Hagar was a slave and was sent out to the desert with her son, Ishmael, by Abraham at his wife Sarah's request. The child, Ishmael, fathered by Abraham, may be viewed as disposable as he is born of a slave woman and not of Sarah. There has always been tension towards non-Israelites and they are discriminated against and viewed with suspicion. Hagar's life (Genesis 16) shows this pattern of mistreating the non-Israelite. In this story Hagar, because she is a foreign woman, and a slave to boot, like her son is considered to be disposable and is left to die in the wilderness. This pattern of biblical narrative resurfaces centuries later after Israel's rise to power as a kingdom and its subsequent defeat and exile in Babylon. Even when the Israelites themselves experienced being "cast out," they continued to cast out the foreign women who were deemed a hazard to their community (see Ezra 9).

In some ways, one cannot get to the Promised Land without the wilderness experience. Perhaps one needs to look at and study injustice to come to a deeper and more meaningful understanding of justice. There are many similar stories of injustices towards foreign women in the Old Testament that fit into this paradigm. This chapter focuses on the foreign women narrative in Ezra 9 as a backdrop for how foreigners are treated.

Exile and Identity

The book of Ezra covers an important moment in the history of the biblical community and gives a glimpse of how foreign women were treated during a difficult period upon Israel's return from exile. It was a crucial time in history as the people of Israel were trying to avoid extinction and were keen on rebuilding themselves. Ezra describes the reconstruction of the Jewish temple and state after the destruction by the Babylonians in 587/586 BCE and sets the theme of Early Judaism and the Torah. It describes the rebirth of the community of the people of God after the consequences of the fall of Jerusalem in 587 BCE. These events resulted in the loss of national independence, the destruction of the temple, and the deportation of their people.[12] These are tremendous losses for a people who believed that God had chosen them and was going to be with them always. For such a displaced and disillusioned people, it is crucial to quickly establish their racial, cultural, and religious identity so that they can restart and rebuild their lives as individuals and as a community. Necessary actions need to be done to begin the process of rebuilding and reestablishment as a people.

Once a lineage is defiled, this defilement is passed on from generation to generation, apparently disqualifying all males in the polluted line from priestly service (cf. Neh. 7:63-65 = Ezra 2:61-63). This transgenerational dimension of "moral" defilement resulting from intermarriage is rooted in the understanding that the communicable nature of the pollution of bloodlines resembles communicable impurities associated with "ritual" impurity. "Ritual" impurities are communicated through contact and are not long-lasting, whereas pollution of the lineage is understood to be permanent.[13] This contrast draws a sharp line between those who were exiled and those who remained; it affects how they understand themselves and the Other, and indicates the importance of marrying within bloodlines rather than marrying foreigners.

---

12. Nupanga Weanzana, "Ezra," *Africa Bible Commentary,* Tokunboh Adeyemo, general editor (Grand Rapids: Zondervan, 2006), p. 532.

13. Olyan, "Purity Ideology in Ezra-Nehemiah," p. 9.

The Jewish community itself was diverse, and diverse ethnic groups such as Ammonites and Moabites populated the land of Israel. In this diversity, there was strong tension between Jews whose families had gone into exile and those who had not[14] but remained in the land. As they were rebuilding their lives, they encountered a dilemma of what to do with foreign women who were in their community. One way to address the problem was to point a finger at and get rid of the most vulnerable members of the community — the "foreign" women.

So it is that in Ezra 9, the community decides to send away the foreign wives. Because these women are considered different from the others, they become the "Hagars" of Genesis. By regarding these women as unnecessary and expendable, the returned exiled community finds it easier to send them away. This undesirable action prompts us to examine and reexamine how we treat those we call foreigners in our own society. Do we welcome them, or do we also cast them away? The biblical story demands of us today that we consider how we will live in peace with those who have different cultural, religious, and social backgrounds and often speak a language we do not understand. Because people immigrate, move, and are forced into exile, there are many strangers and foreigners in our midst. Will we find new ways of living in peace with those who are different from us? For perhaps it is in the differences that we find meaningful life and richness in our own lives.

Ethnicity

The returning exiles saw themselves as constituting the only "true" Israel, and to reinforce this, they construed the foreign neighbor as the Other. As the children of the *golah* (Ezra 4:1; 6:19-20; 8:35; 10:7, 16), they believed they were the "holy seed" (Ezra 9:2; Ezek. 36:8-12).[15] The use of these controversial terms, *true* and *holy,* can be divisive and damaging to a community. These terms can be used to break ties, fragment families, and pit one group against the other. This is exactly what happens to the foreign women who are viewed as the Other and are not the true, holy Israelites. Controversial terms separate people rather than embrace and build communities.

---

14. Tamara Cohn Eskenazi, "Ezra-Nehemiah," in *The Women's Bible Commentary,* ed. Carol A. Newsom and Sharon H. Ringe (Louisville: Westminster John Knox, 1992), p. 117.

15. Gale A. Yee, *Poor Banished Children of Eve: Woman as Evil in the Hebrew Bible* (Minneapolis: Fortress Press, 2003), p. 145.

The *golah* community of Ezra thought ethnic pollution was a primary cause of the exilic experience and thus the community wrestled with the idea of ethnic purity.[16] They thought that ethnic purity was true, possible, and attainable. However, in reality nothing is pure and everything and everyone is a mixture and a hybrid. The people described in Ezra 9 were preoccupied with ethnic purity, which led to the unfathomable action against the foreign women. Even though hybridity exists, people do want to maintain a sense of purity; it seems to provide some sense of social cohesion, family stability, and cultural security. Yet such purity provides a false sense of security and as a result people are afraid to mix and live in hybrid identities or hybrid places.

Ezra regarded marriages to non-*golah* Jewish women as "foreign." Perhaps some of the concern about the foreign women was due to economics. The returning elites from the exile wanted to ensure that their land inheritance would remain in their family and not go to outsiders of the *golah* group. The elites who practiced exogamy to obtain the land and endogamy to keep it forgot that the land they now possessed had been obtained generations before through intermarriage with these "peoples of the land." This kind of socioeconomic contradiction they resolved through selective memory,[17] keeping whatever served their best interest or changing stories to fit their memories. People remember what is in their interest, especially if they have it written down in the Torah. In this case, selective memory becomes harmful to the foreign women, who are selectively forgotten, despised, and cast away as soon as the Israelites have, with the women's help, obtained the land.

Ethnic Purity

The exilic community came to view itself as the true ethnic Israel.[18] Those who stayed behind were not the true community, as there was a lot of intermarriage, which added to the hybridity of the people. The Jewish community did not want to think of themselves as a mixed people but a pure people, and so they constructed the patriarchal narratives themselves to camouflage the ethnic heterogeneity of Israel's origins. The patriarchs brought in wives from

---

16. Kenton L. Sparks, *Ethnicity and Identity in Ancient Israel* (Winona Lake, IN: Eisenbrauns, 1998), p. 295.

17. Yee, *Poor Banished Children of Eve*, p. 145.

18. Sparks, *Ethnicity and Identity in Ancient Israel*, p. 324.

other areas and also had children through multiple wives who were from different ethnic cultures. In the biblical tradition, according to Nehemiah 13:28-30, marriage to alien women pollutes the Judean priestly bloodline.[19] In such a patriarchal setting, men deem women to be the cause of evil, the ones who make things unclean. This long tradition of an unhealthy and distorted view of women needs to be rectified as Scripture has been used to go against women of color and present them in a distorted way.

The foreign women in Ezra were expelled even though many of them bore children with their Judean husbands (Ezra 10:3, 11-12, 19). This culture seems to be based on a repudiation of women's bodies (as is culture in general, according to Kristeva), and human subjectivity is based on the abjection of the maternal body. The Levitical purity and holiness system reinscribes this feminine role,[20] severely limiting it. This sheds light on some of the religious background and history of the rejection of the feminine. It has had long-lasting effects on our approach and understanding of the feminine.

Thus in Ezra, the fact that women are viewed as unclean makes the foreign women doubly expendable. The Ezra narrative is a tragic narrative of a fragile, emerging Judean subjectivity. The community is in friction and it must pull itself apart in order to constitute itself. In this struggle of rebuilding, the purity strictures fall disproportionately on the women,[21] a disproportionality made possible by society's ability to portray the women as the Other and subordinate and subjugate them. What happened so easily in the community Ezra describes can (and does) easily happen in our own communities today.

Women's bodies become commodities and can be easily disposed of when not needed or deemed unfit, as we see in Ezra. When women's bodies are sexualized, women are robbed of much of their authority and being as individuals with gifts and talents to offer the world. The women become the ones with the problem — rather than the men who are the actual problem for instigating such divisions — and especially women of color. "Foreign women" do well to recognize their lack of standing and understand that they are always at risk of being expelled.

The *golah* community opposed contact with all foreigners as such contact brought danger to the purity understanding of the "holy seed" (Ezra

---

19. Olyan, "Purity Ideology in Ezra-Nehemiah," p. 4.

20. Washington, "Israel's Holy Seed and the Foreign Women of Ezra-Nehemiah," pp. 427, 428.

21. Washington, "Israel's Holy Seed and the Foreign Women of Ezra-Nehemiah," pp. 428, 429.

2:62; 4:1; 6:21; Neh. 10:31; 13:23-28).[22] Hybridity is the notion of mixing; i.e., there is no pristine concept, idea, thing, or people, as all things are a mixing of things to produce a new idea. Hybridity tends to blur the rigid lines that exist between race and power. Even the clear distinction made between the groups of races is not as clear as it is made out to be, as all are hybrids. No one is pure and no one will ever be pure.

Intermarriage

The understanding and perception of marriage change over time according to how marriage is construed religiously, socially, and culturally. Certain societies will tolerate mixed marriages as democratic, or as an expression of equality. The notion of mixed marriage has also evolved over time, to the extent that in many societies it is now much more socially acceptable.[23] The notion of marriage as a civil contract between two persons or a contract between two families has also evolved as women's rights have evolved. Today some of us regard marriage as two people's "private business," while others are inclined to view marriage as "the foundation of the community," often in a very traditional sense. The huge divide between these two differing opinions draws attention to how difficult it is to have a consensus on the understanding of marriage. The entire question whether marriage is God-ordained or not also comes into the debate, specifically in our present-day discussions on marriage equality.

In our current debate about marriage equality, it is easy for those who are against marriage equality to label gay and lesbians as the Other. It is easy to state that there is something wrong with them, something that needs to be fixed. In this case it is not women but homosexuals who become "foreign" or the "Other," and thus the targets of accusations and blame. Just as in Scripture it was the foreign peoples who were blamed for "abominations,"[24] contemporary societies often do the same to gay and lesbian neighbors in our own communities, blaming them for the breakdown of marriages, society, social values, and religion. We easily make them our scapegoat of the day. We hope that by systematically classifying a group of people as the root

22. Kim, "Empowerment or Enslavement?" pp. 104, 105.

23. Daniel L. Smith-Christopher, *A Biblical Theology of Exile* (Minneapolis: Fortress Press, 2002), p. 155.

24. Smith-Christopher, *A Biblical Theology of Exile*, pp. 155-57.

cause of societal problems we have identified the solution to some deeper, internal problems. How we are to treat the foreigner or the Other is a crucial question for us to answer as we encounter immigration, globalization, and a shrinking world.

It is a difficult task to untangle the many strands that were woven together to create the label "foreign women." The basis for Ezra's objection is that the foreigners were simply Jews who were not in exile. The groups within which these "mixed" marriages were taking place were identified with stereotypically pejorative slurs against ethnic groups. The mixed marriages were condemned and believed to be unclean.[25] The migrants' hegemony over the Jerusalem temple enabled them to take possession of the land and channel its surpluses. They regained land and other resources through inter-marriage. Initially, it was in the interests of the returning exiles to establish good relations with the natives of Yehud, even though the former understood themselves to be superior. Many of the early returnees probably married into Yehud's landowning families. Some of these families were ethnic Jews who formed the upper class among those who had remained in the land. Others were landowning non-Jews, foreigners in and surrounding the regions of Yehud. By intermarriage, the immigrant elites exchanged their high status for access to the land as a means of production. For their part, the natives exchanged their land to "marry up" into the ranks of the returning elite.[26] Both groups of people benefited from these marriages.

Expulsion of Foreign Women

Four months after Ezra's arrival in Jerusalem, some princes reported to him that the returnees had been intermarrying with the peoples of the lands (Ezra 9:1-2). Ezra responded in horror, tearing his clothing and hair, and then sat in stunned silence. At the time of the evening sacrifice he rose and prayed. Shecaniah suggested that they make a covenant with God and send the foreign women away. Ezra made the elders of Israel swear to do as they had said, and he sent messengers to inform all the returnees that they must appear in Jerusalem within three days or face confiscation of all property and excommunication from the congregation. Three days later the whole congregation arrived, waiting for Ezra to address them. Rebuk-

---

25. Smith-Christopher, *A Biblical Theology of Exile*, p. 158.
26. Yee, *Poor Banished Children of Eve*, p. 144.

ing them for their unfaithfulness, he commanded them to separate from "the peoples of the land and from the foreign women." When the meeting concluded, a commission was established, and three months later 113 men sent away their wives.[27] This was a devastating conclusion to this meeting of the community.

Many of the Israelites felt that they were exiled as a punishment from the LORD because they had strayed from YHWH. They needed someone to blame for the exile and for causing the Israelites to stray from YHWH and worship false gods. The easiest target to which to direct one's anger is the most vulnerable person or class in a society, and in the post-diaspora Judean society this meant the foreign wives. Women had no attachment to the land except through their spouses. They were expendable. Men could do what they wanted with them. The foreign wives were similar to Hagar, except that Hagar was Sarah's slave, and not Abraham's wife, concubine, or slave.

Shecaniah's proposal is essentially one of repentance. The people must turn from their wrongdoing and renew their covenant in order to be wholly joined with Yahweh. When Ezra personally addressed the congregation of the *golah* three days later, he commanded the people to "do [Yahweh's] pleasure and separate [themselves] from the people of the land and from the foreign women" (v. 11). There can be no question that Ezra believed that sending the foreign wives away was in harmony with the Law.[28] It was solely for this reason that the women were asked to leave.

Ezra 9–10 narrates the story of the Persian-period community's mandating of a divorce and expulsion of all foreign women from its community. Some of the explanations for the divorces and expulsion were that: 1) the community was trying to prevent widespread apostasy caused by foreign women; 2) the community was hoping to define its ethnic identity more strongly; 3) there were economic and/or political factors that would benefit some or all of the community should these women be forced to leave.[29] The community believed that the benefits of sending away the foreign wives outweighed the negative consequences. In a rigidly traditional patriarchal society, women are expendable creatures who can be traded like cattle.

27. Brown II, "The Problem of Mixed Marriages in Ezra 9–10," pp. 437, 438. Please see Ezra 10:18-44.

28. Brown II, "The Problem of Mixed Marriages in Ezra 9–10," pp. 453, 454.

29. David Janzen, "Scholars, Witches, Ideologues and What the Text Said: Ezra 9-10 and Its Interpretation," in *Approaching Yehud: New Approaches to the Study of the Persian Period,* ed. Jon L. Berquist (Atlanta: Society of Biblical Literature, 2007), p. 49.

We do not hear the cries of these women, but that does not mean they approved of their own oppression. Just as we did not hear the cries of women who were forcibly divorced because religious law became the law, we will never hear these foreign women's cries or protests.[30]

The husbands were in a bind; apart from some of the personal feelings they may have had for their wives and children, they were also afraid of losing their land. It was the very land for which they or their ancestors had married their wives. These men understood that if they did not assemble in Jerusalem and consent to divorce their foreign wives (Ezra 10:7-8)[31] they could lose their land. So out of fear of losing their land, some were coerced into coming to the meeting and abandoning their wives.

This expulsion of foreign women is highly disturbing and it perpetuates the subordination and objectification of women. Women become objects of transaction in a patriarchal society, tokens in a relationship between the men, who are the agents of the exchange. Especially in a (de)colonizing and patriarchal context, women are diminished to objects of exchange between men, who may choose to discard them or trade them in.

This is the outcome of Ezra-Nehemiah's conjunction of the feminine with the unclean, a conjunction exceeding that of Leviticus, and this signifies an irreparable trauma at the core of Judean identity, a trauma that the text both records and tries unsuccessfully to repress. Ezra-Nehemiah is the tragic narrative of a fragile, emerging Judean subjectivity. The community is at odds with itself, and it must wrench itself apart in order to reconstitute itself. The question is, why could Ezra and Nehemiah not change the rules when they are in roles of leadership? Why was evicting foreign wives the only solution? Why didn't Ezra and Nehemiah get asked to leave? The purity strictures fall disproportionately on the women.[32] Women are scrutinized more and are under more pressure to conform. Due to their own desires for purity, and also for personal economic issues, the men decided to send the foreign women away. It is an unholy act of social injustice.

Scholars have tried to make sense of how women's bodies are viewed and the consequences that result. Kristeva's use of the word "abject" radicalizes the claim that the female body is the negative ground of the symbolic cultural realm. The "abject" becomes a term for everything that the subject

30. Elelwani Farisani, "The Use of Ezra-Nehemiah in a Quest for an African Theology of Reconstruction," *Journal of Theology for Southern Africa* (July 2003): 47.

31. Yee, *Poor Banished Children of Eve,* p. 146.

32. Washington, "Israel's Holy Seed and the Foreign Women of Ezra-Nehemiah," pp. 428, 429.

must renounce in order to *be* a subject. In biblical terms, this surely goes all the way back to the myths about Eve and her "shadow," Lilith. This is a story of abjection. The maternal and the feminine are represented as unclean and unwanted. Subjectivity is always provisional. An identity is generated through the negotiation of internal differences, but it never becomes finally accomplished or secured. Ezra 9–10 can be read as the vivid depiction of a communal "subject on trial." After the lament of chapter 9, the covenant and legal proceedings of chapter 10, the guilt offering and the pledge to send away the women, the text cannot bring itself to pronounce the expulsion.[33] A law prohibiting foreign marriages before they happen is bad enough, but a law that the wife should be returned to her family cuts much deeper, especially when no previous law had forbidden intermarriage.[34]

The divorce assembly scene of Ezra 10 therefore presents a communal subject on trial. The assembly contains not just those who are determined to expel foreigners, but the men who will have to dismiss their own wives and children. Among those assembled are some of the women threatened with expulsion. The rebuilding of the Judean identity comes at a very high cost, and the narrative of Ezra 9–10 is troubling for us. If abomination is the lining of our symbolic being, "we" are therefore heterogeneous, pure and impure, and as such always potentially condemnable.[35] Our identities are mixed, as are our cultures, languages, and religions. As such, we should all be expelled from the community.

Purity and Hybridity

The Ezra 9 passage is a discussion and action regarding what it means to have purity. Just as the foreign women in Ezra are cast away as a result of this discussion, so too are the foreign women today in our society. This is certainly true of Asian American women, although typically they are cast away in more subtle ways that include their silencing, marginalization, and discrimination.

Particularly for a people who feel victimized and disrespected, there

33. Washington, "Israel's Holy Seed and the Foreign Women of Ezra-Nehemiah," pp. 433, 436.

34. Mary Douglas, "Responding to Ezra: The Priests and the Foreign Wives," *Biblical Interpretation* 10 (2002): 13.

35. Washington, "Israel's Holy Seed and the Foreign Women of Ezra-Nehemiah," pp. 436, 437.

can be a great temptation to claim "ethnic purity." But as we have seen in our own time in the Balkans and Rwanda, this often has negative consequences such as genocide and so-called ethnic cleansing. But as I have already suggested, there is no such thing as purity. We are all hybrids. Can we recognize and embrace this hybridity rather than being afraid of it and seeking a nonexistent racial and ethnic purity? Part of the problem of a nostalgic return to ethnic purity is that it gives the "insiders" permission to do something bad to those of a different racial or ethnic background, based on the presumption that they have no kinship with or responsibility toward "them." This permission should not be allowed as an excuse for racism. Rather it should be named as such so that it will not keep occurring. Can we replace xenophobia with the gospel claim of all now being God's people (1 Pet. 2:10) through adoption in grace? All ethnic groups are part of the family of God and are equally accepted and loved. Our harmony can be by reason of having been claimed by the same Lord.

Within the postcolonial world, there is much acceptance of and rejoicing in hybridity. The quest for purity has created much dysfunction, harm, and breakup in our community and society. It is time to embrace hybridity as a route for building and strengthening our communities.

Prophetic Faithfulness

In contrast to the events of Ezra 9 and the expulsion of foreign women, we find a different way of treating women in the book of Hosea. Hosea is a man who loves his wife, Gomer, who is unfaithful to him. Small wonder that Hosea is credited as the originator of the famous depiction of God as faithful husband to Israel, his faithless wife. Very little is known about the northern prophet Hosea. The superscription to this book, which was added later by a redactor, identifies him as the son of Beeri and situates Hosea as living between 750 and 724 BCE, which is between the last years of Jeroboam II (786-746) and the fall of Israel to the Assyrians in 721.[36] The marriage metaphor becomes an effective vehicle to communicate the prophet's call to listen to the demands of God's covenant with Israel. It reveals that it is an intimate relationship and it is between unequal parties — a dominant and a subordinate. This relationship involves reciprocal commitments and responsibilities and any violation by the subordinate of these commitments

---

36. Yee, *Poor Banished Children of Eve*, p. 83.

and responsibilities will result in punishment. In this book, God is presented as an all-forgiving male and Israel is presented as an evil adulteress.[37]

The wife's/Israel's "lovers" in Hosea 1–2 are understood to be part of an idolatrous fertility cult. Hosea aims his accusations primarily at the king and his political and cultic elite. The marriage metaphor feminizes this male ruling hierarchy by connecting its members to a graphic image of a promiscuous wife. Hosea exploits the marriage metaphor to proclaim his covenantal fidelity. In a culture where wives owe sexual fidelity to one husband, Hosea depicts the exclusivity of Israel's relationship with its "spouse," YHWH. As wives are economically and socially dependent on their husbands, the marriage metaphor encodes similar relations of power. An adulterous wife and questionable paternity are threatening to a society in which male notions of descent, inheritance, and honor are intertwined with fathering legitimate sons.[38] In a patriarchal society, the lineage is important. This importance highlights the wife's role as a childbearer. This not only limits her role but reduces her role in humanity.

In Hosea 1:2, YHWH commands Hosea to take a "promiscuous wife" and bear "children of promiscuity." Hosea's true metaphor may be a familial rather than a marital one to criticize the deterioration of the larger social body. Although marginalized in androcentric Israelite society, a prostitute is still tolerated, while an adulterous, promiscuous wife is not. Hosea is ordered to marry this promiscuous woman, because "the land fornicates away from YHWH" (1:2). The "land" could represent the nation of Israel, the physical territory, and all of its inhabitants — the ruling elite, clergy, and populace. Hosea describes royal misuse of the land through a sexual trope: it "fornicates away from YHWH" (1:2). Hosea exploits various interconnections among land, ownership, marriage, female sexuality, and procreation to articulate his critique of the ruling elite and promote his notion of covenantal fidelity. His imagery is clear, poignant — and it subordinates women. As a wife belongs to her husband, so does the "land" belong not to the elite but to YHWH. As the wife belongs to her husband and becomes the field that her husband "plows," so does Israel belong solely to YHWH and become the land that "God impregnates." A faithful wife certifies the paternity of her husband's seed, providing legitimate sons who will eventually inherit the land. The adulterous wife/Israel, however, sabotages the legitimacy of her divine husband's seed by allowing herself to be "plowed" and "seeded" by

37. Yee, *Poor Banished Children of Eve*, p. 81.
38. Yee, *Poor Banished Children of Eve*, pp. 98, 99.

others (that is, the foreign nations). Even Jezreel's own legitimacy as Hosea's firstborn son becomes questionable due to Gomer's promiscuity.[39]

Punishment will not be the end. The drive of this speech from Hosea is toward reconciliation, pleading with Israel to quit her adultery (2:2) and to return to her true lover (2:7). Behind these words one senses a divine love that will not let even a faithless Israel go. The "marriage" between God and people will not end in divorce. This marriage will be saved. Here is a promise that one day there will be a second honeymoon (vv. 14-15). The Lord will show compassion to a people and once again they will say, "thou art my God" (2:16-23).[40] In Hosea 14:5-8, the prophet describes in images the blessed life of those who have experienced God's healing. He says they will be like a blossoming lily, a deep-rooted tree, a fragrant garden, a beautiful olive tree, a productive vineyard sustained by the Lord's dew and protected with the Lord's shade. The Lord will be to his people like an evergreen tree, which nourishes them with its fruit. He is their God who promises, I will "look after you."[41] On the one hand, this is a lovely image of faithfulness, reconciliation, and hope — the "romantic" view. On the other hand, Gomer is presented as a stereotype, a mere emblem of unfaithfulness with all the patriarchal machinery of the culture intact. Is there some way to "retrieve" the positive aspects of Hosea's vision without buying the whole package?

The prophet Hosea offers hope for us living in a broken world, hope for us so that we can act differently when it comes to women. We can love and embrace women regardless of their background or ethnicity. We can insist that expulsion is not the answer, that the fate of Madame Butterfly is not a model to follow. Yet such casual actions toward women of color are well reflected in the stories of the lives of military brides[42] today. We know women of color are used as commodities for the military. They are manipulated, used, and then easily discarded. We cannot allow foreign women to be expendable beings.

When women are treated as commodities, there is injustice. Women are unjustly treated because they become tokens to be traded. Unmarried women (or women whose marriages are dissolved) are "consumables." Korean women captured during World War II were used as "comfort women" to serve Japanese soldiers' sexual desires. Some of them were young teenagers

---

39. Yee, *Poor Banished Children of Eve*, p. 101.
40. James Limburg, *Hosea-Micah: Interpretation* (Atlanta: John Knox Press, 1988), p. 12.
41. Limburg, *Hosea-Micah: Interpretation*, p. 54.
42. Kim, "Empowerment or Enslavement?" p. 108.

when they were taken away from their families to sexually service an average of fifty men a night.[43] It was torture and nightmare for these young comfort women. Many of the women died of disease or were killed when they were of no more use to the men. The entire history of these comfort women is horrific and unacceptable. Such atrocities should not be allowed to continue.

Concluding Thoughts

The treatment of the foreign women in Ezra 9 shows how the foreign women lose their connectedness to the community when they are expelled from it and by it. Today, many Korean American women experience their lives as foreigners. They are not easily accepted into the dominant white culture and are socially marginalized. They experience hardship, difficulty, and pain as they try to live and survive in a new land. Much of their difficulty is due to being mistreated by white men simply for the color of their skin.

The prophet Hosea offers a new way of envisioning the world that finds all women important. This includes Asian American women who have been marginalized in many ways. Their marginalization should be challenged and reexamined rather than accepted. The next chapter introduces Asian American history and the hardships that Asian American women faced as immigrants as a way of helping us build a theology that will be liberating and empowering.

43. The data are from a testimony given by a Korean comfort woman survivor. She spoke at Bloor Street United Church in Toronto, Canada, in October 1994.

CHAPTER 2

The Lives of Asian American Immigrant Women

In this chapter I discuss the history, social context, and life of Asian North American immigrants, which spans over one hundred years. The advent of Asian immigration was neither easy nor pleasant; much of it was plagued by hardship and turmoil that was responded to with perseverance. Coming to North America was a difficult transition for many immigrants, who were met with prejudice and racism rather than a welcome. The juxtaposition of a new culture, language, and religion resulted in confusion and chaos in their lives. This was even more the case for Asian American women, who experienced much oppression from the dominant white culture as well as their own Asian culture. This chapter will unpack concepts of race, racialization, and perpetual foreigners to help us understand the difficulties that these women experienced. I begin with my own story.

My Own Immigration Story

My family immigrated to Canada in January 1975 when I was five. I had no say in this; it was my dad's decision. We left all that we had and took only a small bag of clothing each and started a new life in Canada. It was a life for which we were unprepared and which we did not anticipate.

I remember one of the first of many differences that I noticed: the people were very tall. They seemed to tower over my parents as we walked around this new land that we were calling home. They also appeared to have lighter skin and hair color than Koreans I knew.

I started kindergarten and became the Other; I looked different, and perhaps I smelled different as I ate different foods than my classmates. As a result, many people taunted me. When I told them I was Korean, they did not understand what that was. They repeatedly said that I was Chinese or Japanese. Some actually believed that when a Chinese married a Japanese, the result was a Korean.

My mother's silence about our experiences of racism has driven me to speak more loudly and more often about them. She was used to keeping one's family affairs and personal life private. She lived according to the honor/shame model; she expected to be shamed and segregated if she ever aired her "dirty laundry" in public.[1]

As a child attending school, I had a much more public existence than my mother. Wherever I went, people thought I was a foreigner. At first, with my limited English, it was difficult to argue with this. As my English improved, I came to understand how much that experience had hurt me. This rejection wounded me to the core because in Canada, an ostensibly bicultural country, immigrants from European backgrounds were accepted quite happily into the dominant cultures. As neither French nor English, I was considered a foreigner and therefore was not accepted.

This perception of being the perpetual foreigner[2] will rarely be part of the experience of European immigrants, but it is uncomfortably real for many Asian Americans. The fact that I am a woman made it doubly difficult for me as I tried to establish my identity and status between two cultures.

In the biblical record, we see that foreign women and wives became pawns — negotiated, traded, disposed of, and dismissed. Through the ages, the story of Abraham sending away Hagar and her son has been used as a justification to dismiss foreign wives and their children. Foreign women in the Bible are discriminated against both racially and religiously. Ezra 9 exposes some of the horror that foreign women faced. This image of casting away "undesirable" women has perpetuated the ongoing domination of women who are viewed as inferior and different. These women exemplify what we now understand as "the Other,"[3] a designation that describes those "not like us." The dominant culture always inflicts terrible acts of violence,

---

1. For more discussion see Grace Ji-Sun Kim, *The Holy Spirit, Chi, and the Other* (New York: Palgrave Macmillan, 2011), pp. 86-88.

2. Joseph Cheah, *Race and Religion in American Buddhism* (Oxford: Oxford University Press, 2011), p. 76.

3. For more discussion see Grace Ji-Sun Kim, *The Holy Spirit, Chi, and the Other*, p. 63.

dominance, sexual objectification, and slavery on "the Other," simply because they are "not like us."

One way to prevent the alienation of immigrant women is to remember the Divine in creative, nonhierarchical, non-Western ways. Words we use for the Holy One shape the image we have of the Divine. Within Western Christianity, our image of God has been one of power, domination, and omniscience. We have viewed God through the lens of white hegemony, which has contributed to an understanding of God as Great White Father, reflecting back to people the image of men and the dominant white culture.[4] We need a more life-giving description of the Divine, one that speaks across cultures and societies. Thus I propose the image of Spirit as a way of overcoming some of the traditional images of God that have contributed to the Othering of many groups of people.

Asian American History

Asian American history is an important part of America's history and has contributed to its economic, social, and religious growth. It began with Europe's search for an easy route to Asia in order to enrich the spice trades of Spain, the Netherlands, England, and the Italian cities of Venice and Genoa. Europeans named America's indigenous peoples "Indians," believing them to be natives of "the Indies," fabled lands of gold in the east.[5] Asians came to the Americas in the currents of commerce and conquest that began in the mid-sixteenth century with Spain's Manila galleon trade between the Philippines and Mexico. By the 1760s, Filipinos were coming to Louisiana and in the 1780s South Asians were settling in port cities along the eastern seaboard. Then in the 1790s the Chinese and Hawaiians came to California

---

4. The way of presenting authority to aliens in the American west was so thoroughly imbued with this idea that the well-known label of "Great White Father" for the American president appeared in the J. M. Barrie play *Peter Pan*: "They called Peter the **Great White Father**, prostrating themselves before him; and he liked this tremendously, so that it was not really good for him. 'The great white father,' he would say to them in a very lordly manner, as they grovelled at his feet, 'is glad to see the Piccaninny warriors protecting his wigwam from the pirates.'"

J. M. Barrie, *Peter Pan — Full Version (Illustrated and Annotated) (Literary Classics Collection)* (Amazon Digital Services: G Books, 12/5/2011, originally published in 1911), locations 2123-26.

5. Gary Y. Okihiro, *The Columbia Guide to Asian American History* (New York: Columbia University Press, 2001), p. xiii.

and the Pacific Northwest, principally as laborers for the fields and factories. Eventually, women and children followed their husbands, fathers, and brothers to these shores. Since the early days of Asian immigration to North America, the demographics have changed dramatically. Since 1980, the increase in proportion of the Asian American population has surpassed that of other groups, including whites, African Americans, and Latino/as.[6]

Over 300,000 Asians entered Hawaii between 1850 and 1920. The U.S. government and private companies ordered Asian labor as if it were a commodity and the Chinese were among the first to respond. This helped transform the sugar industry into a "King" industry,[7] while at the same time displacing native Hawaiian laborers. The annexation of California in 1848 opened the floodgates for Asian laborers. Aaron Palmer recommended the importation of Chinese labor for the construction of the Transcontinental Railroad,[8] and this increased the opportunity for more Chinese workers to enter the U.S. Other Asians also arrived: Japanese (1880s), Filipinos (1900), Koreans (1903), and South Asian Indians (1907).[9] In addition, Christian missionaries recruited Hawaiians and Asians to the United States to study theology and then return to their homelands to evangelize their own people. And California's gold rush attracted more than 20,000 Chinese. However, not all was pleasant for these arriving workers. Chinese migrants to California encountered restrictions and in 1850 California imposed a tax on all foreign miners, the majority of whom were Chinese. This tax became a burden to the workers. The Supreme Court in 1854 further ruled that Chinese could not testify for or against whites in the courts.[10] This heavy restriction meant that whatever wrong Chinese workers experienced at the hands of their white bosses could never be challenged in the legal system. Many of these restrictions and laws were put in place to control Asians and keep them subordinate to the white people.

6. Okihiro, *The Columbia Guide to Asian American History,* p. xiv.

7. The paradigm of a "King" industry is "King Cotton," so labeled before the American Civil War because the belief was that the need for American cotton would lead Great Britain and France to ally with the Confederacy. A "King" industry has such a great hold on the economics of a region that it controls political decisions. Examples are fruit in South America and oil in the Middle East.

8. Ronald Takaki, *Strangers from a Different Shore: A History of Asian Americans* (New York: Penguin, 1989), p. 22.

9. Grace Ji-Sun Kim, "Asian American Feminist Theology," in *Liberation Theologies in the United States: An Introduction,* ed. Stacey M. Floyd-Thomas and Anthony B. Pinn (New York: New York University Press, 2010), p. 132.

10. Okihiro, *The Columbia Guide to Asian American History,* pp. 11-13.

For Koreans, unlike the Chinese, emigration meant cutting off one's roots and blood ties to Korea. It was viewed as a kind of social or spiritual death. However, when the missionaries came to Korea, they encouraged emigration among the newly converted Christians, insisting that the new land would give them good fortune. Immigration of Koreans to the United States began in 1903, and nearly half of the 101 immigrants on the first ship to the United States were from the Rev. Jones's Yong Dong church in Inchon.[11] They left Korea with high hopes and aspirations for a better economic and political life. Korea had recently experienced several famines, which left many in hard economic situations. Furthermore, the sugar plantations in Hawaii were experiencing massive, well-organized protests by overworked Chinese and Japanese male workers and therefore another source of cheap labor was needed,[12] which was to be filled by Korean men. Many single Korean men left their poverty-stricken country and sailed to Hawaii with high hopes of earning lots of money.

In 1870, Congress passed a law that made Asian immigrants the only racial group barred from naturalization. To add to their woes, in 1882 the Chinese Exclusion Act was passed, suspending the immigration of Chinese laborers for ten years. This act also denied citizenship to Chinese Americans who were already in the U.S. as well as to their American-born children. The 1875 Page Law excluded most Chinese women from entry into the United States.[13] Many of these Asian single women who entered the U.S. became consorts or prostitutes. This act was later extended indefinitely, and was only lifted in 1943. The 1917 Immigration Act further limited Asian immigration, banning it from all countries in the Asia-Pacific Triangle except the Philippines, a U.S. territory. The 1924 Exclusionary Immigration Act was put in place to limit Japanese immigration.[14] The United States also passed the Gentleman's Agreement with Japan, legislation that informally persuaded Japan to limit emigration of its citizens to America. This period therefore witnessed the marginalization and legal constraint of Asian immigrants already in the United States by denying them citizenship, thereby also denying them the right to vote. The 1924 National Origins Act also specifically targeted Asians, denying immigration to anyone not eligible for citizenship

---

11. Ai Ra Kim, *Women's Struggle for a New Life* (Albany: State University of New York Press, 1996), p. 28.

12. Jung Ha Kim, *Bridge-Makers and Cross-Bearers: Korean-American Women and the Church* (Atlanta: Scholars Press, 1997), p. 3.

13. Okihiro, *The Columbia Guide to Asian American History*, p. 141.

14. Grace Ji-Sun Kim, "Asian American Feminist Theology," pp. 133, 134.

and setting quotas for immigrants. The act stood largely unchanged until it was abolished and subsequently replaced by the 1965 Immigration Act. The overwhelming majority of immigrants and refugees who entered the United States after this time were from Burma, during a period of more relaxed American immigration policies.[15] The legal difficulties that Asians faced during this period in America directly reinforced the prejudice and racism against Asian Americans.

In 1945, Congress repealed the Chinese exclusion laws, as well as the restrictions against Filipinos and Asian Indians. Chinese wives of American citizens were allowed into the United States on a non-quota basis in 1946. Furthermore, Congress amended the 1945 War Brides Act to allow Chinese American veterans to bring their wives to the United States. The "lifting" of exclusion laws against Chinese, Filipino, and Asian Indians was followed by a quota system that allowed about one hundred immigrants into the United States annually as a public relations effort in America's fight for democracy against fascism.[16] Thus certain acts were carried out solely to make white Americans "look good," not to make life for Asian Americans in America any better.

The anti-Chinese movement of the 1870s and 1880s came back to life in the new century as the anti-Japanese movement. Anti-immigrant sentiment broadened, as the openhearted impulses of the settlement house movement to teach immigrants life skills gave way to an increasingly militant Americanization movement during World War I. After the war, the anti-immigrant tide swelled, resulting in a drastic curtailment of further immigration from several parts of the world.[17] This trend was reversed in 1965.

The internment of Japanese Americans from a Pacific Exclusion Zone during World War II is a part of the history of special American suspicion of Asians. Americans did not intern Germans or any other nationalities during WWI or WWII, but they did intern the Japanese Americans simply for reasons of suspicion. Americans began to view Japanese Americans as more foreign than people who traced their ancestry to Europe.[18] In the first especially tense months after the destruction of the Pacific fleet (which had been seen as protecting the nation during WWII), when the West Coast seemed exposed to attack, those with Japanese American ancestry were forc-

---

15. Cheah, *Race and Religion in American Buddhism*, p. 82.

16. Okihiro, *The Columbia Guide to Asian American History*, pp. 24, 25.

17. Paul Spickard, *Almost All Aliens: Immigration, Race, and Colonialism in American History and Identity* (New York: Routledge, 2007), p. 273.

18. Okihiro, *The Columbia Guide to Asian American History*, p. 100.

ibly moved away from the West Coast until after the Battle of Midway, when the U.S. Navy defeated the Imperial Japanese navy. Remarkably, no such actions were taken against people of German descent on the East Coast, even though German U-Boats were operating a few hundred miles offshore.[19] Despite having lived in the U.S. for generations, Japanese Americans were still viewed as "the Other," and it was not until the Civil Rights legislation in 1965 that state-supported discrimination ended.[20]

Other patterns of racial exclusion or oppression towards Asian Americans include the development of the "yellow peril" and "model minority" myths.[21] Prior to the arrival of the first Chinese immigrants in the United States in 1849, most Americans already had unfavorable views of the Chinese. The characterization of Chinese and other Asians as the "yellow peril" not only sought to negatively portray Asians but also to justify and legitimate any mistreatment of them.[22] The "yellow peril" myth depicted Chinese Americans as unfair competitors and as a threat to white social, economic, and political stability in the United States. White laborers had the unfounded fear that Chinese migrant workers would force them out of work. Even if there was no competition for the work in which Chinese immigrants engaged (laundry, for instance), the very presence of the group was a source of hostility, suspicion, and violence. The dominant white Americans used the negative social functions of the "yellow peril" myth to encourage discrimination and violence against Chinese workers. As a result, these workers came to be viewed as foreigners, unable to assimilate, unfair competitors (as "cheap laborers"), and a threat to the white workers (as strikebreakers, for instance).

In addition, Asian Americans suffered humiliation and separation from the dominant culture. They were segregated in public facilities including schools; they endured heavy taxation, were prohibited from owning land,

19. President Carter's 1980 investigation of the incident ruled that there was no Japanese disloyalty among the Japanese living on the West Coast. Carter's commission ruled a $20,000 payment to all survivors and in 1988, Congress approved and President Reagan signed an apology on behalf of the U.S. Government. Payment to internees and heirs has reached 1.6 billion dollars.

20. Grace Ji-Sun Kim, "Asian American Feminist Theology," pp. 133, 134.

21. This term will be discussed further later in the chapter.

22. When "Oriental" is used pejoratively, usually before WWII, it may refer to all peoples from the Bosporus to the Philippines, and south to Ceylon (now Sri Lanka). In an early Sherlock Holmes story, "The Man with the Twisted Lip," Holmes's client encounters a miscreant Lascar, the Persian name of an Indian seaman who was employed on British ships. He is the guard/owner of a London opium den and beggars' lodging. See Sir Arthur Conan Doyle, *The Annotated Sherlock Holmes* (New York: Clarkson & Potter, 1967), pp. 368-88.

from marrying whites, and so forth. The difference in treatment toward these two groups was race.[23] Discrimination of Asian people based on color happened right at the immigration/border office. Angel Island was closed in 1940, and it was not reopened after WWII, but in 1952, the Walter-McCarran Act reintroduced quotas on "Asia Pacific Triangle" immigrants. This was a deliberate and systematic form of racism towards those from Asia who were not yet citizens, and who were attempting to enter the country. In 1965, Asians were given some parity with European immigrants through the Immigration and Nationality Act, in which national origin was removed as a criterion for immigration into this country.

Asian American Women

From the beginning of Asian immigration, Asian women have been viewed through the tropes of foreigner and exotic temptress. While white European immigrant women were able to assimilate into the dominant Western culture based on European language and culture, Asian North American women were not able to do so. No matter how many generations live in North America, an Asian's "yellow" skin still marks them as a "foreigner." Like the foreign women in Ezra, Asian American immigrant women are portrayed as perpetual foreigners, which has led to "racism," subordination, objectification, and discrimination. Since they are "foreign women," they are easily dismissed as unimportant members of society, experiencing alienation through an invisible boundary[24] often ignored or unnoticed by Euro-Americans.

Asian women's immigration to the United States was at times prompted by a desire for freedom, but many were misinformed about the reality of life in the United States. On the plantations of Hawaii and on the farms of California, these women cooked, washed, and cleaned not only for their own families but often, for a small fee, they also did these chores for bachelors and married men who had come without their wives. Such women had to get up at three or four a.m. to prepare breakfast for as many as forty men and pack their lunchboxes. Others who worked in the fields for wages spent a full day in the sun, sometimes with babies strapped to their backs, before returning home to cook dinner. Their day didn't end there, as in the evenings

23. Spickard, *Almost All Aliens*, pp. 421, 422.

24. Arun Mukherjee, Alok Mukherjee, and Barbara Godard, "Translating Minoritized Cultures: Issues of Caste, Class and Gender," *Postcolonial Text* 2 (2006): 1.

they washed, ironed, and mended. Those who bore children did this work even while pregnant.[25] It was a very difficult life, but with tenacity somehow these women endured. Because Asian women constituted a small percentage of immigrants in the nineteenth century, they were generally ignored. Nevertheless, in addition to physical hardships, Asian American women experienced psychological and legal hardships from the series of restrictive laws against Asians enacted in the 1850s.

Asian American Women and *Han*

Poverty, war, and oppression were key elements that drove women from Asia to America, some of whom came to America as brides of U.S. military men and as refugees. Asian women's labor was oppressive; many worked as prostitutes, sugar plantation workers, low-paid seamstresses, electronics assemblers, and South Asian fruit and vegetable cannery laborers. Asian American women struggled for their communities, families, and selves as they faced discrimination, racism, and sexism.[26]

Asian American women's lives intersected (then, as now) directly with racism, which is the *han* of our communities. *Han,* embodied and lived out in the lives of many Koreans today, translates roughly as "unjust suffering." People suffer to different degrees all the time. When the temperature is hot and I have no air conditioning at my house, I suffer due to the heat, but this is not *han.* This is not "unjust suffering." I am merely suffering from heat just as others in my area will also be suffering from the heat. *Han* is suffering when the social, political, and religious system is set up to oppress, dominate, and subjugate another or groups of people. *Han* becomes the opposite of grace. Grace is a free undeserved gift from God. *Han* is the undeserved pain, suffering, and turmoil that one endures due to systemic structures that oppress and harm individuals and communities.[27]

Han arises when institutions, communities, and nations create laws, policies, and institutions that cause subordination and subjugation of groups of people. Racism and racist policies cause tremendous pain and suffering

---

25. Grace Ji-Sun Kim, "Asian American Feminist Theology," p. 133.

26. Okihiro, *The Columbia Guide to Asian American History,* p. 145.

27. See my earlier discussions of *han* in *The Grace of Sophia: A Korean North American Women's Christology* (Cleveland: Pilgrim Press, 2002), pp. 56-61; and especially *Colonialism, Han and the Transformative Spirit* (New York: Palgrave Macmillan, 2013).

among large groups of people within a society. There is a deep sense of pain and piercing of the heart.

Korean North American women experience *han* due to the burdens of sexism and racism, which bring adversity and suffering. Asian American women must challenge and transform the structure of the *han* of racism and sexism in society.[28] Assimilation into the dominant culture was seen as a source both of alienation from Asian identity and of freedom from the constraints of the traditional "Oriental" culture.[29] However, there is an invisible boundary of racism and cultural exclusiveness that prevents some Asian American women from becoming part of the mainstream culture.

Despite the obstacles, women did contest gender relations during this time. Hawaiian women ended the "ai kapu" system in 1819. "The kapu was a system of laws of a religious nature that regulated the privileges and prohibitions of commoners and the alii [ruling classes] alike. The best-known of these affecting all classes was the ai kapu, the one forbidding men and women to eat together. This kapu was broken by the queens the day after the death of Kamehameha on May 12, 1819, although its abolishment was not announced officially until five months later."[30] The Chinese American women garment workers went on strike against the National Dollar Stores in 1938. Chinese American women achieved the vote in 1920, but lost their U.S. citizenship in 1922 if they married "aliens ineligible for citizenship."[31] Even today, Asian American women continue to face discrimination, stereotyping, racism, and sexism within North American communities.

Race and Ethnicity

There is a difference between ethnicity and race. Ethnicity refers to one's racial origin, cultural preference, and national characteristics. Ethnicity is

---

28. Andrew Sung Park, "Church and Theology: My Theological Journey," pp. 161-72 in *Journeys at the Margin: Toward an Autobiographical Theology in American-Asian Perspective,* ed. Peter C. Phan and Jung Young Lee (Collegeville, MN: Liturgical Press, 1999), p. 171.

29. Rita Nakashima Brock, "Interstitial Integrity: Reflections toward an Asian American Women's Theology," in *Introduction to Christian Theology: Contemporary North American Perspectives,* ed. Roger A. Badham (Louisville: Westminster John Knox Press, 1998), p. 189.

30. Moke Kupihea, *The Seven Dawns of the Aumakua: The Ancestral Spirit Tradition of Hawaii* (Manchester, VT: Inner Traditions Bear & Company, 2004), locations 602-5.

31. Gary Y. Okihiro, *The Columbia Guide to Asian American History* (New York: Columbia University Press, 2001), p. 39.

about a collective identity of peoplehood and belonging based on personal origins and cultural characteristics such as religion, language, and nation.[32] Ethnicity is considered a nonevaluative term and perceived by many as "safe" to use. Ethnicity is based on language, geography, education, cultural history, and traditions. The various ethnic groups within a race may have some similar physical characteristics. Their differences are based on cultural or national divisions, such as language, citizenship, religion, childrearing practices, food habits, clothing, and so forth. Ethnicity derives from an ancestral group, but it can be altered by changing one's behavior.[33] As behavior modifies, it modifies one's ethnicity.

Race, on the other hand, has its roots in the social structures of exploitation, power, and privilege. Manning Marable believes that "race is an artificial social construction that was deliberately imposed on various subordinated groups of people at the outset of the expansion of European capitalism into the Western Hemisphere five centuries ago."[34] While race is categorized in biological or social terms, it often serves a political function of stratifying different groups of people into a hierarchy of discrimination and prejudice. In the West, race is a cultural representation used powerfully to dominate another group of people through social structures.[35]

During the period of Western colonization, Europeans would racialize the indigenous inhabitants and enslaved Africans of the colonies in order to subjugate them. In the Americas, the indigenous people were racialized as "Indians," while enslaved Africans were racialized as "blacks." As J. Kameron Carter, Peter Goodwin Heltzel, and Willie Jennings have argued, Christian theology played an important role in providing a religious rationale for racism in the new world.[36]

"Whiteness" became the norm against which "race" was measured

32. One of the best examples of a strongly shared ethnicity is the German sense of *Volk*. "The Germans are a people *(Volk)* which, despite all wars and defeats, always manages to recover and to get on top of things again within the shortest possible time. . . . The Germans have always been a particularly orderly and clean people. . . . We Germans have certain good characteristics which other peoples do not have. . . ." Mary Fulbrook, *German National Identity after the Holocaust* (Oxford: Blackwell, 1999), p. 10.

33. Spickard, *Almost All Aliens,* p. 18.

34. Manning Marable, "The Rhetoric of Racial Harmony: Finding Substance in Culture and Ethnicity," *Sojourners,* August-September 1990, p. 16.

35. Cheah, *Race and Religion in American Buddhism,* pp. 12, 13.

36. See J. Kameron Carter, *Race: A Theological Account;* Peter Goodwin Heltzel, *Jesus and Justice: Evangelicals, Race and American Politics;* Willie Jennings, *Christian Imagination: Theology and Origins of Race.*

in the new world, unveiling the perpetual problem of white power and privilege. The differences the word "race" describes are used to create cultural barriers, while social institutions continue to support white power and privilege. The power that one race wants to hold over another has been problematic and has led to genocide, slavery, hate crimes, and diminished status in society. In order to prevent such acts and attitudes, it is important to understand the nature of racism, how it has developed, and how it functions today.

The ideology of race in America is based upon physical or biological traits, such as skin color, body structure, and facial features. These physical characteristics have been used to categorize people into inferior and superior groups. Ethnic minorities such as Asian Americans, African Americans, Native Americans, and Hispanic Americans live as subordinate and marginalized groups as a result of their biological and physical characteristics. For them, ethnicity and race have become inseparable. To be an Asian American means to be yellow, just as to be an African American means to be black. Ethnicity can include race. Both racial and cultural characteristics are included in the ethnicity of marginal people.[37] When ethnicity includes race, as with Jews, Gypsies, American Indians, and Arabs, it tends to marginalize people in society.

Furthermore, race and culture have become inseparable in many people's minds. The cultural determinant can be altered, while the racial determinant cannot and is immutable. Nonwhite immigrants can achieve cultural assimilation (adoption of American lifestyle), but structural assimilation (equal life-chances) is difficult to achieve as many see race as a permanently damaging factor. For example, second- or third-generation Asian Americans are often easily acculturated but it is difficult for them to be assimilated into American society on an equal basis because of their race; they will never be included as the dominant group of the "norm" in society. Race is a fundamental determinant of marginality for Asian Americans, for African Americans, Native Americans, and Hispanic Americans.[38] Race trumps culture, as race is written on people's faces and skin, while their history and culture are not.

---

37. Jung Young Lee, *Marginality: The Key to Multicultural Theology* (Minneapolis: Fortress Press, 1995), p. 34.

38. Jung Young Lee, *Marginality: The Key to Multicultural Theology,* p. 35.

Conceptualizing Race

Race functions as a category of human classification, identity, and differentiation for the benefit of some and the detriment of others. At times, it does not signify biological differences among groups of people but rather achievements or social constructions.[39] The traditional conception of race erases white people from being conceptualized as racial. To identify someone as "racial" is to say they are not white. Prior to the 1960s, the racial locations of whiteness, especially in the South, were overtly expressed within a white supremacist context. After the 1960s whiteness became the unspoken norm in American law and society.[40] The racial imbalance in power and opportunity has become so institutionalized that it is often very difficult to notice or identify. It has become the accepted norm of society where whiteness is good and whiteness is superior. These important factors need to be taken into consideration, itemized, examined, and critiqued as this important question of race is addressed.

Whiteness needs to be exposed, categorized, and become consciously racialized. Because whiteness is seen as nonracial, white privilege is upheld systemically through favorable rules and practices toward those racialized as white. Naming the locations and meanings of whiteness subverts the idea of a predetermined racial destiny and exposes the deep meanings attached to light or dark skin as the product of social forces rather than biology. The goal is to racialize whiteness, encouraging those racialized as white to see how it shapes their identity, experiences, opportunities, and future. This will shift the view of racism from individual acts and prejudices to include the less visible systems of privilege that maintain the status quo. White racial cognizance diminishes the authority of claims to racial neutrality[41] and challenges people out of their preconceived ideas and conceptions of themselves and the Other. It provokes white people to accept their position of undeserved privilege and motivates them to challenge this paradigm, working to shift the existing norms, concepts, and ideas.

Because whites often fail to recognize their power and privilege, it is

---

39. Jacqueline Battalora, "Whiteness: The Workings of an Ideology in American Society and Culture," in *Gender, Ethnicity, and Religion: Views from the Other Side,* ed. Rosemary Radford Ruether (Minneapolis: Fortress Press, 2002), p. 4.

40. Battalora, "Whiteness: The Workings of an Ideology in American Society and Culture," p. 5.

41. Battalora, "Whiteness: The Workings of an Ideology in American Society and Culture," pp. 6, 7.

sometimes necessary to prompt their awareness in order to work towards justice. In 1998 white parents in Riverside, California, fought against naming a new school for Martin Luther King Jr., arguing that the school would be "branded" black and this would hurt the students' chances of getting into college.[42] This prejudice perpetuates the unspoken racist narrative that whites have greater intelligence than African Americans. In order to address this kind of injustice, racialized whiteness must first be explicitly named.

Racism permeates all segments of society including culture, religion, and history. The European colonial idea that whites are superior is also theologically rooted in the problematic idea that the Christian is superior to the Jew. Racism is rooted in supersessionism, an interpretation of the New Testament that sees God's relationship with Christians as *replacing* God's covenant with the Jews.[43] Howard Thurman writes in *Jesus and the Disinherited*, "How different might have been the story of the last two thousand years on this planet grown old from suffering if the link between Jesus and Israel had never been severed. . . . [For] the Christian Church has tended to overlook its Judaic origins . . . the fact that Jesus of Nazareth was a Jew of Palestine."[44] Jesus' Jewish heritage may help to unravel the problem of white supremacy in the Americas. Christianity is rooted in the religion of Israel and emerged as a distinctive movement within Second Temple Judaism. The misunderstanding that Christianity replaces Judaism has led to anti-Semitism and has been the root of tragic consequences. Anti-Semitism and racism are intricately related,[45] and thus rebuilding the connection between Christianity and Judaism is vital to our livelihood, being, and common future.

Race is a term that seems static and essential, while racialization emphasizes agency and process. Racialization denotes an ongoing action taken to support hierarchy and to create an Other. Race is a story about asserting power vis-à-vis one another, and it is written on the body. Those with more power dictate and maintain the shape of the division between people. The racialization process creates the impression that cultural differences, like genetic and true racial differences, are permanent. Like sexism, the purpose of writing racial division onto the body is to naturalize it and to make it inevitable.[46] Race

---

42. "Some Parents Fear Stigma of King High," *Chicago Tribune*, 5 January 1998, as cited by Battalora, "Whiteness: The Workings of an Ideology in American Society and Culture," pp. 3-23.

43. Peter Goodwin Heltzel, *Resurrection City* (Grand Rapids: Eerdmans, 2012), p. 10.

44. Howard Thurman, *Jesus and the Disinherited* (Boston: Beacon Press, 1996), p. 16.

45. Heltzel, *Resurrection City*, p. 11.

46. Spickard, *Almost All Aliens*, pp. 19, 20.

is a category used to isolate, dominate, and subjugate groups of people; it is used by those in power to maintain their own position and to subjugate others.

Racialization of Asian Americans

As early as the fifth century BCE, Europeans, especially the Greeks, distinguished themselves from Asians, rather than just Persians, Scythians, Arabs, and Indians. In 472 BCE, in the play *The Persians,* Aeschylus referred to all non-Greeks against Greece as "Asians."[47] The ancient Greeks distanced themselves from the peoples to their north (whom they considered "barbarians") and those to their east (whom they termed Asians). This distinction between European and Asian differs somewhat from nineteenth-century U.S. representations but the concept of Asian appears persistently within the European imagination, and it typically appears as something pejorative.[48] The power and ability to name or define Asians as a group gave the "namer" undue power and privilege. Asians, unable to define themselves and their parameters, could not question or challenge the racist European imaginary.

Hippocrates held an environmental determinist view of human behavior. Asia, he speculated, with its mild and uniform climate, supported plentiful harvests, which engendered a lazy, monotonous, and pleasure-seeking people content to be ruled by others. Europeans were considered strong, courageous, and high-spirited people due to the colder climate. His representations can be seen as racialization of Europeans set in opposition to Asians. In addition, he gendered Europeans as masculine against the more feminine Asians.[49] This view highly misrepresents and misconstrues Asia. Asians are understood as feminine and therefore weaker and subordinate to Europe and Europeans.

Asian Americans include people whose ancestry lies in East Asia, Southeast Asia, South Asia, and West Asia. Europeans invented the category of Asian, delineating the Orient as spaces east of Europe and assigning the characteristic of Orientalism[50] to its peoples. From 1850 to World War II, U.S.

---

47. Aeschylus, *The Persians,* in *The Persians and Other Plays: The Persians / Prometheus Bound / Seven Against Thebes / The Suppliants* (London: Penguin Classics, Kindle Edition, 2009), locations 751-54.

48. Okihiro, *The Columbia Guide to Asian American History,* pp. 3, 4.

49. Okihiro, *The Columbia Guide to Asian American History,* p. 4.

50. Note that the interpretation of "Orientalism" as a derogatory term is relatively new. In many quarters, the Orient defines an area of study, as by the famous Chicago, London, Mos-

laws governing immigration, citizenship, civil and property rights lumped together Chinese, Japanese, Koreans, Asian Indians, and Filipinos as an un-differentiated group.[51] Over time, Asians adopted the label assigned to them by outsiders. The differences they perceived as fundamental were laid on their bodies and essential character, thus creating a racial moment.

Racialized identities are not simply imposed; they are often the out-come of resistance and political struggle. Thus it may be advantageous and more accurate to speak of a racialized rather than a racial group, since race is a product of racism rather than the source.[52] Racism promotes domination of the vulnerable by a privileged group in the economic, social, cultural, and intellectual spheres.[53] We live in a society in which racism has been inter-nalized and institutionalized and is woven deeply into a culture from whose inception racial discrimination has been a regulative force for maintaining stability and growth and for maximizing other cultural values. Racism is the manifestation of the deeply entrenched determination to maintain the status quo. Only a full awareness of this reality leads to a new insight into what is possible and how racism can be eliminated. "The nation cannot redeem what has not been established."[54] Neither can the church redeem what has not been established.

The Racial Moment for Immigrants

Racism is a result of Westerners' act of racializing immigrants, which is a Western construct to further separate and dominate the "races." Racism has become institutionalized and internalized by those who believe there is a center, and see themselves in it, and as a result see others on the margins. It is intrinsic to the structures of society[55] and is seen overtly in the form of

---

cow, and Indian Oriental Institutes. For many centuries it was an area of interest, especially in Romantic movements, and in art, most famously by Mozart, Handel, Mahler, Vivaldi, Verdi, Flaubert, Hesse, Tolstoy, Goethe, Byron, Marlowe, and Victor Hugo, among others.

51. Okihiro, *The Columbia Guide to Asian American History,* pp. xiv-xv.

52. J. Solomos, "Beyond Racism and Multiculturalism," *Patterns of Prejudice* 32 (1998): 49.

53. Fumitaka Matsuoka, *The Color of Faith: Building Community in a Multiracial Society* (Cleveland: United Church Press, 1998), p. 3.

54. Matsuoka, *The Color of Faith,* p. 95.

55. Stanley R. Barrett, *Is God a Racist? The Right Wing in Canada* (Toronto: University of Toronto Press, 1987), p. 307.

violent physical attacks and covertly in the form of variations in wages and employment opportunities based on "racial" criteria. Racism exists in corporate and government boards and among manual laborers. Covert racism can be subconscious, nondeliberate racism that is often not recognized by the perpetrators themselves.[56]

The term "minoritized" also helps us grapple with racialization. Immigrants become minoritized by "racist" systems.[57] "Majoritization," the complementary term to "minoritization," is used to indicate the positions of those who are culturally dominant as an outcome of historical, cultural, and economic processes whose legacies remain powerful, precisely because they are part of the culture of the dominant society.[58] Dominant cultures manipulate the minoritized for their own personal gain and benefit, while minoritized cultures live in a fragile space of uncertainty, domination, and relative powerlessness.[59] This power struggle often results in feelings of *ressentiment* in those who feel themselves under the thumb of the ruling "race." Immigrants living in this space seek out sources of agency and empowerment to resist the barriers set in place by the Western world instead of embracing their alienation and their ghetto status. Their fragility entails existing in a hyphenated reality, belonging in two worlds, yet at the same time not belonging in either.

Whiteness

Critical race theory evolved out of opposition to dominant conceptions of race, "racism," equality, and law in the post–civil rights period in the United States.[60] White Supremacy is the ideology of calling people "white," even those with different ethnicities (such as Danish, Irish, Polish, and Russian), as long as they have fair skin. The purpose is not to find a common ethnic name for these people, although it is used as if it were an ethnic term. Rather,

---

56. Barrett, *Is God a Racist?* pp. 308, 309.

57. Mukherjee, Mukherjee, and Godard, "Translating Minoritized Cultures," p. 1.

58. For a graphic depiction of this difference, see F. Scott Fitzgerald's novel *The Great Gatsby.*

59. Grace Ji-Sun Kim, "What Forms Us: Multiculturalism, the Other, and Theology," in *Feminist Theology with a Canadian Accent: Canadian Perspectives on Contextual Theology,* ed. Mary Ann Beavis et al. (Ottawa: Novalis, 2008), p. 82.

60. Battalora, "Whiteness: The Workings of an Ideology in American Society and Culture," p. 3.

white is used as a term of "ethnic erasure." The distinct histories and ethnicities of people who are Irish, English, French, German, Italian, Jewish, Arab, etc., are erased by being made "white."[61] *Whiteness* erases the differences, specifically the different ethnicities, of an entire group of people into one monolithic group as if differences do not exist. People who are different from the white group are considered ethnic while the white group is not considered ethnic. Ethnic people belong to the "different," less dominant group who are not white and thus are made to appear foreign, impure, and other. Similar to the Hindu caste system and the English class system, these categories are used by the powerful to keep others in place and should be viewed with suspicion.

Nationalism and patriotism combine with white supremacy to entrench "whiteness" as normative in North America, so much so that it appears normative not only to whites but also to Asian Americans. This is the cultural power of "whiteness": it does not need to name itself explicitly to make its presence felt. Even newly arrived Asian immigrants internalize the image of what "real" Americans ought to look like (that is, white), thereby manifesting an internalized form of white supremacy. It is not insignificant that the Statue of Liberty is on our eastern coast, facing Europe, and that it was presented by a European nation. Americanism is associated with "whiteness" which is associated with a pan-ethnic conglomeration of European immigrants, further cementing the stereotype of Asian Americans as "perpetual foreigners."[62] Since the age of colonialism and imperialism, race has often been a significant factor in the rearticulation of Western ideas about the beliefs and practices of Eastern religious traditions.

U.S. law has played a strong role in the social construction of white racial identity.[63] Whites in the U.S. have had access to a range of resources and opportunities that have been restricted or denied to people of color. In 1790, the U.S. Congress limited those who could become naturalized citizens to "white persons" and this remained a part of U.S. naturalization law until 1952. The federal courts, in determining who was white and who was not, revealed disturbing contours of the social architecture of race. Throughout much of U.S. history, state laws codified the definition of black, Indian, mulatto, mongrel, etc., but the laws did not define whiteness. Federal and state

61. Rosemary Radford Ruether, ed., *Gender, Ethnicity, and Religion: Views from the Other Side* (Minneapolis: Fortress Press, 2002), pp. x, xi.

62. Cheah, *Race and Religion in American Buddhism*, p. 76.

63. Battalora, "Whiteness: The Workings of an Ideology in American Society and Culture," p. 3.

laws regarding whiteness varied; a person could be white one moment and upon crossing a state line become not white.[64]

Whiteness as a social construct that shapes and constitutes mainstream U.S. culture and society[65] must be dismantled and replaced with a paradigm of plurality, equality, and mutuality. "White power" and privilege result from the presumption of the racial superiority of whiteness. To dismantle the injustice of white privilege, we must first recognize it. As race provides unearned advantages to those racialized as white, those institutions that maintain white privilege need to be identified and viewed with suspicion. The "colorblind" approach in the U.S. legal system is one example of failed attempts to avoid explicitly naming racism and whiteness as sources of oppression and division.[66]

Within Christianity, Jesus was racialized as white in twentieth-century German and Anglo-American iconography. His Mediterranean Jewish olive-skinned identity was erased in favor of whiteness as the primary matrix for understanding Jesus. As America rose out of Europe's colonial expansionism, and white became the normative ethnic identity, Jesus and Christianity were also racialized as white.[67]

Racializing Jesus as white is heretical. During the Third Reich, German Protestant theologians redefined Jesus as an Aryan. These strongly supersessionist theologians argued that the New Testament replaced the Old Testament, seeking to dejudaize Christianity and advocate a white Christ as a savior of the Aryans. Whiteness became a strategy for maintaining political power.[68]

In order to dismantle the myth of whiteness in white Christianized America, prophetic Christians must exorcize the demon of white supremacy and actively work to recover Jesus the Jewish prophet from Nazareth, recov-

---

64. Cheryl I. Harris, "Whiteness as Property," *Harvard Law Review* 91 (1994): 1707; Barbara Flagg, " 'Was Blind, but Now I See': White Race Consciousness and the Requirement of Discriminatory Intent," *Michigan Law Review* 91 (1994): 953.

65. Battalora, "Whiteness: The Workings of an Ideology in American Society and Culture," p. 3.

66. Battalora, "Whiteness: The Workings of an Ideology in American Society and Culture," p. 10, pp. 11-13.

67. In the Roman world, the olive-skinned Mediterranean was the ideal, and northern barbarians were too light (and too tall and too heavy-boned) while the southern "Ethiopians" were too dark (and too thin and too small-boned).

68. For a thoughtful analysis of Christian anti-Semitism during the Third Reich that includes an analysis of Christology see Susannah Heschel, *The Aryan Jesus: Christian Theologians and the Bible in Nazi Germany* (Princeton: Princeton University Press, 2008).

ering the Jewish origins of prophetic Christian faith.[69] Jesus the Liberator, as understood in Latin American liberation theology, black theology, womanist theology, and *minjung* theology, offers an important Christological horizon for an anti-racist, intercultural theology today.

Model Minority

Instead of actively challenging white supremacy, many Asian American immigrants decided to assimilate into whiteness, being called a "model minority" by the white dominate society. The notion of "model minority" was originally a social science construct. It was coined by William Peterson and first used by conservative political commentators to compare the educational and cultural achievements of Asian Americans with programs such as "affirmative action" and "governmental entitlements." The model minority image depicts Asian Americans as self-reliant, hard-working, successful, and assimilating. This image of Asian Americans proliferated in the media beginning in the mid-1960s and continued throughout the 1970s and 1980s, altering society's view of Asian Americans. They were seen as "no longer occupying a minority status, but fully participating in American society with its economic and political benefits. The educational and cultural achievements of Asian Americans were considered proof that independent assimilation of a minority group was possible without special programs and other forms of assistance from the government."[70] Therefore they were viewed as a model that other minority groups could imitate to attain the same results and achievements.

This model minority trope, which on the surface appears to be aiding Asian Americans, is not necessarily doing so. Racial oppression and exclusion foster assimilation as an ideal, which legitimizes the continued oppression of African Americans and Latino/as while denying the existence of present-day racism and discrimination against Asian Americans. During the civil rights movement, Asian Americans were perceived as largely politically silent, and neoconservatives opportunistically represented them as the "model minority" worthy of emulation by other minorities. The neoconservatives utilized the "model minority" myth to seek to persuade African Americans and Latino/as that institutionalized racism did not exist. The

---

69. Heltzel, *Resurrection City,* p. 12.
70. Cheah, *Race and Religion in American Buddhism,* p. 84.

implication of this model is that if you remain silent and work hard, you can overcome all barriers and achieve upward mobility, moving economically closer to the normative white upper-middle-class ideal. The "model minority" myth is a clever tool that pits people of Asian heritage against African Americans and Latino/as, effectively becoming a minority politicizing game between Asian Americans and other minority groups. It also renders invisible the enormous difficulties and hardships that Asians face as they fight against racial discrimination within their own communities.[71]

Asian Americans have not always received the same types of civil rights protection as have other racial minorities. A clear example is in the 1982 killing of Vincent Chin in Detroit. He was a Chinese American severely beaten, which led to his death. The killers were a Chrysler plant superintendent and his stepson, who were upset with the many layoffs in Detroit's auto industry due to the increasing success of Japanese automakers. These two men were charged with second-degree murder but were convicted of manslaughter and sentenced to three years of probation. Many do not think that Asians, perceived as honorary whites, need civil rights protections.[72] As a result, the killing of Vincent Chin was not decried as racial discrimination or a hate crime. Chin's killers were not charged with second-degree murder, and justice was neither attempted nor achieved.

The image of the yellow peril was thus replaced by the model minority myth, motivated by many whites' fear of losing their social, economic, and political dominance and to justify discriminatory actions against Asian Americans. Yellow peril exemplifies overt racism while the model minority myth functions as covert "racism."[73] Covert racism escapes criticism as it hides and refuses to be named. Nevertheless, Asian Americans remain oppressed and trapped by the aggressive racism of the model minority myth.

Perpetual Foreigners

Asian Americans, depicted as perpetual foreigners and unassimilable, consistently face the question, "Where are you *really* from?" The assumption behind the question is that Asian Americans cannot be "real" Americans as they look different and are thus unassimilable. Even Asian Americans whose

---

71. Cheah, *Race and Religion in American Buddhism,* p. 86.
72. Cheah, *Race and Religion in American Buddhism,* p. 86.
73. Cheah, *Race and Religion in American Buddhism,* pp. 86, 87.

families have made their home in North America for many generations are assumed to be foreigners. The questioners who pose this question embody white privilege,[74] legitimize white "normativeness" within American society, and feed into the racism and prejudice that exist in our society.

The fluidity of color is important to remember as we critically reflect upon Asian Americans understood as the foreigner. While the category of white constantly changes its constituency, Asians — unlike the Irish, the Italians, the Poles, the Russians, and the (Christian) Slavs — never become accepted as white. At most, Asians are viewed as "honorary whites," implying a clear hierarchy of people, race, and ethnicity: whites are the best and those others perceived as almost like the "whites" are second best. Asians were never given a "pass" to be part of what it means to be American. While there are many ways of being an American, being Asian American is still not commonly counted as one of them. After five generations of living in the United States, and even after naturalization, we are still considered, and mistaken for, foreigners.

No matter how many years or generations they have lived in the United States, those who "look" Asian are perceived as foreigners. This is not because Asians have different foods, different cultural practices, various religious heritages, or because they can speak multiple languages. Certainly, Irish, Italian, Russian, and Swedish immigrants also possessed different foods, cultural and religious practices, and languages when they arrived in the Americas, and yet their descendants have been absorbed into the narratives and identities of North America without much of a ripple. Despite the fact that Asian immigrants have been an important part of building both the U.S. and Canada, the fact that Asians "look" different from members of what is considered to be the dominant culture prevents many people from ever recognizing that we belong here just as much as any other immigrant community (which is all of us except the original First Nations/Native American communities). For instance, Japanese Americans, many of whom have been in the United States for four or five generations, are continually lumped with the recent Asian immigrants and understood by members of the dominant society to be foreigners.

If interracial marriage does not occur, Asians will continue to look like Asians no matter how many hundreds of years they live in North America. This appearance of "Asianness" will override the facts of their citizenship, their country of birth, and their country of allegiance; in other words, they

74. Cheah, *Race and Religion in American Buddhism*, p. 132.

will always be seen as the foreigner. For the white dominant culture, Asianness cannot be accepted as part of the North American racial norm.

Asian American Women's Identity

Foreign women, and in particular Asian American women, have long been cast out of dominant cultures (as discussed in chapter 1). In many ways, Asian American women are not physically cast away, but are metaphorically made invisible within our society. We are not seen as leaders, contributors, or partners within society. Rather, Asian American women are marginalized and "silenced"; our voices of pain, subordination, and marginality are not heard. Asian Americans represent only 6 percent of the U.S. population, but even within this small percentage, Asian American women are further marginalized by Asian American men who are dominant and patriarchal.

This discrimination occurs both in the home and in religious communities. Many Asian American women, particularly those of East Asian heritage, may continue to live within households where Confucianism still structures behavioral norms. What this means is that women are expected to be obedient to the male leadership of the household, and these subservient roles are played out strongly even among second, third, and fourth generations of Asian women living in North America. In a sense, Asian American women become cast out even within their own Asian communities due to Asian traditions, heritage, and culture.

Outside the home, Asian American women's achievements and works are diminished, marginalized, and disregarded. There is an underlying understanding that Asian American women's contributions are unworthy and unrecognizable. Their visible minority status ironically makes their presence in society invisible.

This continues to play out in my own life. I am the daughter-in-law, so my power is diminished within the household. My worth is dependent on whether I bear a son so that the son can carry on the family name. This cultural dynamic plays out very strongly in many households. In the wider faith community, Asian American women's leadership within the church and faith community is not highly regarded or is often met with resistance, and it is difficult for ordained women ministers to serve within Asian congregations. When women are ordained, they are often relegated to children's ministry, work that is seen as a better maternal fit for women clergy. They are often regarded as an accompaniment to the male senior pastor, lacking in authority.

Even outside of the church and the home, it is rare to see Asian American women in positions of power. Constraints placed on women by patriarchal household and church structures leave women without the energy to fight against discrimination set in place within society. Faced with discrimination both within and without their marginalized communities, Asian American women feel cast out in many ways. They are perpetual foreigners who will not be given a chance to fit in or become part of the dominant culture or society. For women it is even more complex than for men: they must endure both the patriarchal attitudes of their Asian ethnicity and those of their U.S. context.[75] This is an ongoing problem that needs to be addressed as we engage in life with people from all parts of the world here in North America.

It does not sit well with me that my children, who were born in Canada, continue to be viewed as foreigners. I know that even if my three children intermarry with non-Asians, their children will continue to be seen, and thus treated, as foreigners so long as they look "physically different" from the American norm.

Plastic Surgery

Asian women's obsession with Western norms of beauty is driving many Asian women and young girls (in their teens) to go under the knife. The two most popular surgeries are rhinoplasty, or a "nose job," to produce a more defined nose bridge, and blepharoplasty or eyelid surgery to get bigger and more "Western"-looking eyes. Among Asian immigrants in North America, the desire to change their Asian face to a more Western face is a move away from being understood as the perpetual foreigner. The less Asian one looks, the less chance that one will be understood as the perpetual foreigner. The dyeing of dark brown/black hair to a lighter shade is another step away from looking Asian.

Asian American women experience the perpetual foreigner syndrome primarily because of racist attitudes toward their physical appearance (hair, eyes, nose, etc.). Plastic surgery has become a popular way to overcome this, but there are many dangers to the surgery and becoming "Western" does not solve the problem. The problem can only be solved by a change in how white

---

75. Gale A. Yee, "Where Are You Really From? An Asian American Feminist Biblical Scholar Reflects on Her Guild," in *New Feminist Christianity: Many Voices, Many Views,* ed. Mary E. Hunt and Diann L. Neu (Woodstock, VT: Skylight Paths, 2010), p. 79.

people perceive Asian immigrants and their descendants. The problem will not be solved until the dominant group decides to change their perspective and celebrate the differences.

Marginality

Asian Americans live in a perplexing world, cut off from their cultural roots, estranged from Anglo-Americans for being "too Asian," and cast out by Asians for being too Americanized.[76] There are certainly different cultural norms and values between Asian and American contexts. There is also a loss of language as second-generation Asian Americans are often unable to speak their respective Asian languages. With the loss of language comes a loss of heritage, which further increases the gap and alienation. This cultural exile has left Asian Americans on the margins of society, not knowing where they belong exactly. Famous ghettos such as the Chinatowns of New York City, Los Angeles, and San Francisco sprang directly from this sense of exile and alienation. Some ethnic European groups have been able to assimilate better and more quickly into the dominant white American culture, but it has been much more difficult for Asians.

Asian immigrants experience a betwixt-and-between predicament, which serves as a resource for a creative rethinking of cultural traditions — both native and foreign. Being in-between is being neither this nor that but also being both this and that. Immigrants belong fully to neither their native culture nor to the host culture; they belong to both, though not fully.[77] Socially to be in-between is to be part of a minority. Culturally, it means not being fully integrated into and accepted by either cultural system, being a mestizo, a member of a marginalized group. Psychologically and spiritually, the person does not possess a well-defined and secure self-identity and is often marked with excessive impressionableness, rootlessness, and an inordinate desire for belonging,[78] which comes with limitations. However, it is

---

76. Peter Phan, *Journey at the Margins: Toward an Autobiographical Theology in American-Asian Perspective*, ed. Peter C. Phan and Jung Young Lee (Collegeville, MN: Liturgical Press, 1999), p. xix.

77. Peter C. Phan, *Christianity with an Asian Face: Asian American Theology in the Making* (Maryknoll, NY: Orbis, 2003), p. 9.

78. Peter C. Phan, "The Dragon and the Eagle: Toward a Vietnamese American Theology," in *Realizing the America of Our Hearts: Theological Voices of Asian Americans*, ed. Fumitaka Matsuoka and Eleazar S. Fernandez (St. Louis: Chalice Press, 2003), p. 165.

also in these limitations that there is energy, creativity, and liveliness that brings forth new life. The margin cannot be easily discarded as fruitless, as it is simultaneously a place of wonder that helps us all become renewed.

Ongoing issues of gender regarding being the Other, such as racism and marginality, stand as crucial issues that need to be addressed daily and seriously as they affect the means of survival. These pressing issues encompass the very being of Asian American women, affecting how they perceive themselves and the Divine. As Asian American women work to liberate themselves from sexism, Orientalism, racism, and marginality, they will continue to work towards building a theology that is truly authentic and liberating to their souls.

The marginalized and the downtrodden receive special insights. They are the ones who can see the pain and injustice that are killing the world. It is to these voices that we must turn. The church rarely listens to the prophetic voices of the marginalized. Within American history, it is the black people who have been the most oppressed, marginalized, beaten up, killed, and hung on a cross. Through their suffering they have developed special insight into God's love as greater than many people have shown it to be.

Asian American scholars construct space even as they naturalize and universalize their social geographies. As Michel Foucault reminds us, space is treated as fixed, unchanging, and monotonous whereas time appears as moving, transforming, and various.[79] Urban Asian America is assumed to be typical of the Asian American experience. Japantowns, Chinatowns, and Koreatowns are often built on the foundation of East Asian culture and its supposed dependence on collectivity and hierarchy. Those urban spaces have been classed as self-contained isolated communities, ethnic enclaves that are both insular and connected. They are transnational ports for the flow of goods, capital, and labor. Chinatown is a constructed space initiated by whites and abetted by certain classes of Chinese, a place of racialization for whites and Chinese alike. Asian suburbia and new urban aggregations cast a different light on the nature of Asian American communities, and the contrasts point to the static and situational character of the urban model. Space is both social and historical.[80]

The term "Third World" can also be used metaphorically to convey

---

79. Michel Foucault, "Questions of Geography," in *Power/Knowledge: Selected Interviews and Other Writings,* ed. Colin Gordon (New York: Pantheon, 1980), as cited by Okihiro, *The Columbia Guide to Asian American History,* p. 135.

80. Okihiro, *The Columbia Guide to Asian American History,* p. 135.

a "Third Space," a space that is not bound by a binary mindset or dualistic and hierarchal constructions. Homi Bhabha calls the "Third Space" the in-between space, which questions established categorizations of culture and identity and opens up the possibilities of renegotiating power and creating new cultural means. The voices of women have been least heard in theological discourse, and including their critical insights with the voices of Christian women struggling for justice, liberation, and peace is long overdue.[81]

Concluding Thoughts

As immigrants try to assimilate into the dominant culture, they experience alienation because of invisible boundaries that they cannot seem to permeate. Since they are relegated to the margins, they remain in the margins of society and maintain a bicultural identity mixed from their own ethnic culture as well as the newfound Western culture. Thus many find themselves inhabiting and constantly negotiating this hybrid location, which is not stable. In this location, they are often racialized as the Other, who is inferior, weak, and less intelligent. The Other is dominated with no risk of reprisal. In the past, this was reinforced by law in parts of the U.S., but now these distinctions are not only not reinforced, they are illegal. Yet those who have been Othered need a theology that is empowering to work towards eliminating their marginalization. It is here in this hybrid location that creativity and innovation of new ideas can take place. This is where one can think outside of the mainstream theological perspective and get a closer glimpse of theological truth. In some ways, the margins become a sacred place, and it is in this sacred hybrid location that people can begin to understand themselves and God. It is in this location that they encounter a God who exists with them. It is here that they recognize their worthiness, love, and full humanity.

Asian Americans are a silenced minority group. Due to the model minority myth, many Asian Americans suffer prejudice, discrimination, and racism in silence. This is even truer of Asian American women who are cast out from our society as the biblical foreign women were cast out by the Israelites. Asian American women are doubly bound as they are dominated by both the Western culture and the patriarchy in their native culture. Due to this they suffer deeply and experience tremendous *han*. This is not a just

---

81. Kwok Pui-lan, *Hope Abundant: Third World and Indigenous Women's Theology* (Maryknoll, NY: Orbis, 2010), p. 2.

society, and white privilege reinforces Asian American women's suffering. New ways of thinking and building a society must be imagined, particularly within Christian theology. The next chapter will explore in greater depth the subordination of women and the part that colonialism had in furthering women's marginalization.

CHAPTER 3

Women as the Other: A Postcolonial Perspective

Religions are famous for making distinctions between "us" and "them." They intentionally or unintentionally build these walls to separate individuals into two or more groups of people. We see this throughout religious histories, and indeed we continue the practice by dividing and separating people according to religious heritage, background, and belief. One of the most famous divisions is the now-illegal caste system of four Varnas and untouchables in India. Not only is there division in India between Hindus, Muslims, Buddhists, and Sikhs, there are also different groups and separations within the Hindu religion itself. Throughout history we see the emergence of social hierarchies as a strategy for organizing the life of the community within a given culture, while religion would often offer the theoretical justification for hierarchy.

During the period of European colonization, we see a new set of hierarchies develop in the European colonies. Christopher Columbus led the first wave of Spanish colonialism of the Americas (1492-1504). Searching for a new route to the "Indies," Columbus ended up "discovering" a "new world" in the Americas. The dark-skinned natives of this new land were named "Indians," and we witness the beginning of the production of race in the new world. While indigenous people were racialized as "Indians," when enslaved Africans began to be shipped into the Americas, they were racialized as "black." Within this racial hierarchy, Native Americans and African Americans were seen as subhuman, compared to the Christian white man who was seen to be the ideal for all humanity.[1]

---

1. For recent accounts of race as a theological problem in the Americas see J. Kameron

In this new-world hierarchy, women, especially women of color, were on the bottom of the hierarchy. The Roman Catholic Church would reinforce this racist and sexist patriarchy through an entrenched male system of leadership, where the men were priests of European descent. The Western binaries of white and black, male and female would dominate the world of European colonies in the Americas, Africa, and Asia.

Edward Said (1935-2003) unveils the strategy of Othering with the Western imaginary through constructing dualism in his book *Orientalism*. A Palestinian American literary theorist, Edward Said is an architect of postcolonial studies. Postcolonial studies grew out of the field of literary study, interpreting fiction through the lens of the function of imperialism. Is it possible to imagine a colonized people and land after colonization? The aftermath of the arrival of and occupation by an imperial power, the struggle against it, independence, and post-independence movements for freedom and justice are the context of postcolonial studies. Engaging themes such as conquest, displacement, exile, forced migration, and cultural assimilation, which intersect with issues such as ethnicity, gender, class, and political power, postcolonial studies offers an interdisciplinary approach to the study of Christian theology and ethics today.[2]

Said was interested in the interactions between colonizer and colonized in the lands that the West had conceived of as "the East" or "the Orient." *Orientalism* unveils the way the West invented the "Orient" as a way to assert its cultural superiority over the East. Orientalism is a form of Western hegemony, a strategy of subjugation.

Said understands Orientalism as a tendency to dichotomize humanity into us-them contrasts and to essentialize the resultant Other. Europeans and North Americans have used Orientalism as a way of dominating the East by exerting self-ascribed authority over people of the "Orient." European culture gained in strength and identity by positioning the "Orient" (which today is often referred to as the Middle East, East Asia, or Far East)

Carter, *Race: A Theological Account* (Oxford: Oxford University Press, 2008); Peter Goodwin Heltzel, *Jesus and Justice: Evangelicals, Race and American Politics* (New Haven: Yale University Press, 2009); Willie Jennings, *Christian Imagination: Theology and Origins of Race* (New Haven: Yale University Press, 2011); Reggie L. Williams, *Bonhoeffer's Black Jesus: Harlem Renaissance Theology and an Ethic of Resistance* (Waco, TX: Baylor University Press, 2014).

2. For two recent anthologies of postcolonial theology see Catherine Keller, Michael Nausner, and Mayra Rivera, eds., *Postcolonial Theologies: Divinity and Empire* (St. Louis: Chalice Press, 2004), and Kay Higuera Smith, Jayachitra Lalitha, and L. Daniel Hawk, *Evangelical Postcolonial Conversations* (Downers Grove, IL: InterVarsity Press, 2014).

as a sort of surrogate and even underground self. Europeans have feminized the Orient and by extension consider it to be weak, helpless, and vulnerable. Orientalism is one strategy that white Euro-Americans use to subjugate people of Asian descent.

Born a Palestinian American in Jerusalem, Said had a unique subject position through which to understand Western cultural representations of the East. Said was an American citizen through his father, Wadie Said, who was granted citizenship by fighting as a U.S. soldier in World War II. Wadie and his wife Hilda raised Edward in the Greek Orthodox Church, where he was exposed to the theology and liturgies of holy Byzantium. Being Palestinian in Jerusalem, shaped by Eastern Orthodox theology, Said forged his own agnostic intellectual identity through an American Ivy League education. Studying at Harvard and Princeton, Said would teach English and Comparative Literature at Columbia University until his untimely death in September 2003.

Said was angry about the way that the people of the Middle East, North Africa, and East Asia were marginalized and misunderstood within the Western academy. In *Orientalism,* Said unveiled the romantic projection of "the Orient," exposing how it distorted reality. This distortion came in the form of the West's attempt to define the East's history, culture, and politics through the lens of the West. This insidious intellectual construct manipulated how the East was perceived and presented to the world.

While the East was seen as exotic, the West's romance with the East was short-lived. The East was romanticized in order to advance Western domination and power. Said writes, "The relationship between Occident and Orient is a relationship of power, of domination, of varying degrees of a complex hegemony, and is quite accurately indicated in the title of K. M. Panikkar's classic *Asia and Western Dominance.* The Orient was Orientalized not only because it was discovered to be 'Oriental' in all those ways considered commonplace by an average nineteenth-century European, but also because it *could be* — that is, submitted to being — *made* Oriental."[3] Submission unveils the domination in this social imaginary. Said clearly unfolds the relationship of Orientalism as a cultural project and the political project of Euro-American dominance.

Said traces the roots of Orientalism to a time when Europe had dominated most of the Middle and Near East. From the West's position of power, influence, and imperialism, they unwittingly defined who the East was. The

3. Edward W. Said, *Orientalism* (New York: Random House, 1978), p. 4.

West inadvertently named "the Orient" as "the Other," which has had severe consequences on the East and how the East is viewed by the West. This perspective of being "the Other" has lasted centuries and continues to pervade much of Western thought, ideas, and perceptions of the East. Said writes,

> Consider how the Orient, and in particular the Near Orient, became known in the West as its great complementary opposite since antiquity. There were the bible and the rise of Christianity; there were travelers like Marco Polo who charted the trade routes and patterned a regulated system of commercial exchange, and after him Lodovico di Varthema and Pietro della Valle; there were fabulists like Mandeville; there were the redoubtable conquering Eastern movements, principally Islam, of course; there were the militant pilgrims, chiefly the Crusaders, although an internally structured archive is built up from the literature that belongs to these experiences. Out of this comes a restricted number of typical encapsulations: the journey, the history, the fable, the stereotype, the polemical confrontation. These are the lenses through which the Orient is experienced, and they shape the language, perception, and form of the encounter between East and West.[4]

These archetypes, symbols, and cultural encapsulations were woven together to create the "Orient" in the Western imagination.

A deep consequence of the East being viewed as "the Other" is the failure to give the East its own permission to define itself, its history, culture, religion, and spirituality. Rather the West stoops down into stereotyping and racially discriminating against the people of East.

> Many terms were used to express the relation: Balfour and Cromer, typically, used several. The Oriental is irrational, depraved (fallen), childlike, "different"; thus the European is rational, virtuous, mature, "normal." . . . Yet what gave the Oriental's world its intelligibility and identity was not the result of his own efforts but rather the whole complex series of knowledgeable manipulations by which the Orient was identified by the West.[5]

Noetic manipulations lead to relational manipulations. As Westerners imagine the Orient, so, too, will they live out a fantastic relationship to the Orient.

4. Said, *Orientalism*, p. 58.
5. Said, *Orientalism*, p. 40.

Positional Superiority

Edward Said unveils that Orientalism is ultimately a fiction that is used to hold up the "positional superiority" of white, wealthy men. Said believes that "it is hegemony, or rather the result of cultural hegemony at work, that gives Orientalism the durability and the strength I have been speaking about so far."[6] The West is contrasted to the East by way of negation. For example, if the West claims to be the center of learning, then those in the West believe the East is a place of ignorance. The study of how the Western colonial powers represented the Middle East, East Asia, and North Africa is what Said refers to as Orientalism. Orientalism in broad terms is "a Western style of dominating, restructuring, and having authority over the Orient."[7] This observation is still played out today as the West continues to exercise some power over the East.

Westerners could not imagine that indigenous people or others could contribute anything of value and they therefore perceived the East as inferior to the West. This sense of supremacy was based on a kind of "flexible positional superiority, which puts the Westerner in a whole series of possible relationships with the Orient without ever losing the relative upper hand. The belief . . . that European identity is superior in comparison with the non-European peoples and cultures" is a result of cultural hegemony at work.[8] For many of the last centuries, Europe also thought itself culturally superior to the cultures of the Americas.

The superiority of the West over the East was the result of the larger "racial projects" of imperialism. White people were presumed to be at the apex of all these hierarchies. The ideology of positional superiority was influenced by the racial categorizations of social Darwinism. These racial discourses disclose how a construct was put into place in which Euro-Americans exercised cultural and political power over Asians, Africans, Latinos, and other people who did not fit the norm of whiteness. This construct was codified in U.S. immigration laws such as the Chinese Exclusion Act of 1882 and the National Origins System launched with the passage of the Immigration Act of 1924.[9] All this was accomplished without resistance as it was constituted organically into the social and political system of the West.

6. Said, *Orientalism,* p. 7.

7. Joseph Cheah, *Race and Religion in American Buddhism* (Oxford: Oxford University Press, 2011), p. 19.

8. Cheah, *Race and Religion in American Buddhism,* p. 20.

9. Cheah, *Race and Religion in American Buddhism,* p. 21.

The dominance of the Euro-American culture or the ideology of this framework as normative is understood as white privilege. This "positional superiority" was powerfully reinforced by European and American imperialism, which conceived the world as divided along racial lines, with "Europeans and Americans" as superior and "others" as negative. This established a Euro-American dominance in which the exploitation and enslavement of others could be rationalized. Such categorizations racialized nonwhite people as the Other,[10] and a new world order arose based on the white assumption of special privileges for white people.

Western imperialism runs rampant in the romantic imaginary of the West. The West's romantic strategy can be illustrated in the construction of the oriental woman as an exotic Other. This brings us back to the story of Madame Butterfly discussed earlier, where the West reimagines her and redefines her. Madame Butterfly becomes romanticized and is viewed as the ideal "oriental woman." She is beautiful and subservient, small and fragile, like a butterfly. Her name, Cio-Cio San, means "butterfly." Lieutenant B. F. Pinkerton of the U.S. Navy is drawn to the beauty of this exotic young Japanese maiden. The exotic becomes erotic, as Pinkerton longs for a sexual union with *his* little butterfly. Capitulating to cultural convention, he works through a matchmaker, *Goro*, and marries the fifteen-year-old oriental princess. She surrenders not only herself to his love, but also her ancestral religion, secretly converting to Christianity. Madame Butterfly enters into this music-drama of the "Orient," metamorphosing into an "oriental woman," while gradually losing the rootedness and inner strength of her ancestral gods.

When Lieutenant Pinkerton ships out to return to America, Butterfly waits patiently for him with her trusted maid, Suzuki. Three years later, she is told by Sharpless, the U.S. Ambassador in Nagasaki, that Pinkerton is back in Japan. She waits up all night for him, only to learn in the morning that he has married an American woman named Kate, breaking his marital vows to her and betraying her love. Pinkerton and his new wife demand to have Dolore, the son that Butterfly bore for Pinkerton. It is in that moment of tragic heartbreak and maternal relinquishment that Madame Butterfly enters the endless abyss of *melancholia*. She has lost her love and now must sacrifice her son, Dolore, meaning "sorrow."

When Butterfly realizes that she has been used, not loved faithfully, and that her son is (in essence) stolen, she takes up her father's knife, which

---

10. Cheah, *Race and Religion in American Buddhism*, p. 32.

bears the inscription "who cannot live without honor must die with honor." In the tradition of *hara-kiri,* she commits suicide to save face and restore her honor. The tradition of women of the "Orient" being used, dominated, and left powerless by the white men of the West continues today.

Asian Women as the Other

The story of Madame Butterfly continues to occur in the lives of Asian women today. Asian women's sexuality continues to be exploited by the white men of the West. During the Vietnam War, a sex industry was created for the "rest and recreation" of American service personnel. Prostitution outside military installations in Asia has been widespread.

The U.S. military has been integral to the building and supporting of the Asian sex trade.[11] After the Korean War, many American G.I.s were stationed in South Korea. With the tradition of being "comfort women" to Japanese soldiers during Japanese occupation in Korea, Korean women have often been exploited again by U.S. servicemen. Young Korean women are often used for sexual pleasure and then easily discarded later. So many young Korean women's lives are taken advantage of and viewed as servants to be obedient to the whims of men.

In the context of military prostitution, Korean women become "Orientalized" and continue to become the Other in a way that damages their subjectivity. As Said states, "Orientalism is a Western style for dominating, restructuring, and having authority over the Orient."[12] Sexuality becomes a theater through which Westerners can project their power and wealth through buying sex, but in the process they are deeply disrespecting the image of God within every person.

Today, sex tourism is highly institutionalized and globalized, with the cooperation of local law enforcement agencies, national governments, travel agencies, and the international business community. Many women and girls are illegally trafficked to Europe, North America, Southeast Asia, Japan, and Australia.[13] This has become an unspeakable danger for young girls, and so the unimaginable pain and suffering of Asian American women continues.

11. See Saundra Pollock Sturdevant et al., *Let the Good Times Roll: Prostitution and the U.S. Military in Asia* (New York: New Press, 1992).

12. Said, *Orientalism,* p. 3.

13. Kwok Pui-lan, ed., *Hope Abundant: Third World and Indigenous Women's Theology* (Maryknoll, NY: Orbis, 2010), p. 4.

In this postcolonial world, immigrant women are understood to be the foreigner and thus the ones who can be easily neglected, dehumanized, and discarded. As a result, they have consistently been viewed as the subordinate, the weak, the unclean, the fragile, and the Other. Asian North American immigrant women already oppressed by their own cultures are now further subjugated by the dominant Western culture. They become racialized as "foreign women" in the Western imaginary, reinforcing their own subjugation in traditional Asian cultures. This double oppression requires them to reexamine their social, cultural, and religious place in society.

Empire and Migration

Migration has followed colonialism in many parts of the world. People migrate in search of better jobs and better opportunities, often in the land of the colonizers, such as Algerians in France, Indians in England, and Koreans in America. (Many argue that the U.S. occupied South Korea from 1945 to 1948.) Both colonialism and migration affect how people are welcomed and treated at home and in the land of the landlord.

Traveling is central to colonial narratives. The traveler's self-proclaimed authority is grounded in race, religion, technology, and knowledge, and along with that, the traveler's recognition of "deficiency" in the lands they visit, forcing and then teaching the colonized people to depend on them. What we see throughout history, for example in the aftermath of the British Empire, is that the subjugated may travel to the lands of their masters, but that they do so as strangers, as exiles, slaves, servants, students, or refugees who depend on the benevolence of their masters, benevolence that can take the form of educational scholarships, visas, or employment. Colonizing texts present a gendered perspective of their subject and use language such as "entered," "penetrated," and "subjugated."[14] The colonized, and particularly the women, become symbols of certain qualities, such as backwardness, evil, and helplessness. Thus imperialism is a male game with women subordinates. Postcolonial texts are born or interpreted in settings of intense power struggle. Their exegesis articulates that struggle. Some colonizing texts are

---

14. This is not to deny the fact that sometimes the colonizing or "imperial" power liberalizes local gender doctrines, such as with the American incursions into Iraq and Afghanistan. This has the quixotic effect of reducing separation of roles between genders while increasing alienation between liberal America and orthodox and conservative Islam.

driven by expansionist aims and disguise their economic interests[15] under the pretense of providing aid. Under this guise it is difficult to detect the wrong or the evil that is occurring.

Modern life for many of us has become a life of transit, a search for identity in the presence of other identities in various locations and places. This creates what R. S. Sugirtharajah calls the "ambivalences and contradictions of being at home in many places, and among many peoples and many experiences."[16] The search is for an answer to the basic question: "Who am I?"[17]

International migration is a product of the logic[18] and development of capitalism, which leads to economic imperialism.[19] As imperialism takes hold there is a development and need for more labor, especially cheap labor, which is difficult to find unless you find workers who are willing to give up their own personal identities and to work for less for the sake of their children's future. As migrant workers enrich the imperial power, the colony loses its productive members and natural resources.[20] Employers in the receiving country benefit from and hence welcome migrant workers, but local laborers see them undercutting their wages and thus as threatening their employment.

Those competing interests result in anti-immigrant sentiments towards migrant workers, sentiments that with time become movements that stress ethnic and racial differences. At the same time employers deploy racism to keep the migrants dependent, exploitable, and lacking class-consciousness. As a consequence, migrant laborers are excluded from the mainstream of

15. Musa W. Dube, "Toward a Post-Colonial Feminist Interpretation of the Bible," in *Hope Abundant: Third World and Indigenous Women's Theology,* ed. Kwok Pui-lan, p. 94.

16. R. S. Sugirtharajah, *Postcolonial Criticism and Biblical Interpretation* (Oxford: Oxford University Press, 2002), p. 184.

17. Some of the best literary examples of this come from French existentialist drama and fiction, such as Albert Camus's novel *The Stranger.*

18. "The frequency of emigration from Scotland, and the rarity of it from England, sufficiently prove that the demand for labour is very different in the two countries. The proportion between the real recompence of labour in different countries, it must be remembered, is naturally regulated, not by their actual wealth or poverty, but by their advancing, stationary, or declining condition." Adam Smith, *The Wealth of Nations* (Illustrated) (Amazon Digital Services, 2011), p. 143.

19. We recognize that classic imperialism, invented by the early Mesopotamian civilizations and perfected by Rome, worked to secure wealth and trade for the nation, the army, and the oligarchs, which is different from economic imperialism, which worked to secure wealth driven by corporations, and which was therefore not only driven by national interests.

20. Gary Y. Okihiro, *The Columbia Guide to Asian American History* (New York: Columbia University Press, 2001), p. 71.

the working class and forced into enclaves that resemble "internal colonies." Racism against immigrant workers, therefore, is a product of the world capitalist system. This is not a scenario of all worker immigration. After WWII, Germany was so short of men to work in light industries that small German companies paid Greek and Turkish men to come there to work.[21]

Modern imperialism is a capitalist ideology of maximizing profits, but it also involves various forms of imposition such as one group's language, trade, religion, economic system, and political rules on other nations, people, and lands.[22] Imperialism comes out of some of the crises of capitalism, such as declining profits, reduced investments, and rising unemployment. It is an attempt to resolve some of these crises. The cost of labor rises with capitalism's development. Modern imperialism is sustained not only by economic motivation but also by colonization. In the eighteenth and nineteenth centuries, the state enabled political annexation and provided the military force required for conquest. This is the model for English and French colonization. Imperialism is also advanced by ideology, as in the West's "civilizing" mission, which assumes the burden of the social uplift of benighted races. Imperialism is racialized. English, French, Dutch, Portuguese, Belgian, and German imperialism carved out new territories for Europe's surplus population and its poor, reducing unemployment at home and transforming those migrants into cheap labor in the colonies.[23] Imperialism provides space to invest in land and create income for the already wealthy. This is the link between classical and modern imperialism. The rich will continue to get richer by divesting the poor of new opportunities. Imperialism is always devastating to the poor.

Our unjust world order benefits the elites but leaves 2.7 billion people to survive on two American dollars or less per day.[24] To maintain its global hegemony, the United States has resorted to threat and use of military force.[25]

---

21. The Greeks and Turks were paid the same rate as the German workers. I know a person who filled their pay envelopes.

22. Grace Ji-Sun Kim, *The Holy Spirit, Chi, and the Other* (New York: Palgrave Macmillan, 2011), p. 65.

23. Okihiro, *The Columbia Guide to Asian American History*, p. 72.

24. "Wherever white men of 'superior races' have found able-bodied savages or lower races in possession of lands containing rich mineral or agricultural resources, they have, whenever strong enough, compelled the lower race to work for their benefit, either organizing their labour on their own land, or inducing them to work for an unequal barter, or else conveying them as slaves or servants to another country where their labour-power could be more profitably utilised." In John Hobson, *Imperialism, A Study* (Amazon Digital Services, Kindle Edition, 2011), pp. 354-57.

25. Kwok Pui-lan, *Hope Abundant*, p. 5.

This has led to the death of many innocent people. Therefore, we need to seek alternative ways of spending resources and money, and providing security for all involved and not just for the rich.

As we begin to reimagine theology and how theology functions to help the most marginalized, we need to make an effort to understand the systems that hold us or restrain us from taking steps to help the poor and subordinated. In certain ways, globalization has questioned the future of liberation theology (theology placed at the service of political aims), especially the inadequacy of analyzing social and economic status to make important changes and improvements in our society. Enrique Dussel insists that liberation theology, which has a strong commitment to the poor who are excluded from the wealth created by the globalization and modernization process, is still relevant because it aims "toward an alternative of greater justice for the people at the periphery."[26] Liberation theology still asks us to see how globalization has devastating effects on those who live on the underside of world capitalism. Asian women are on the underside of modernity. As men progress, women become sexualized, commoditized, and destroyed. They are viewed only as commodities that are expendable as nonessentials. Asian women are at times considered worthless as people and pushed to the margins of society.

Globalization is a massive force today. It restructures economics, alters the roles of the state, and affects people's worldviews, behavior, and religious identities. Mass media and social websites have created global mass cultures, which affect culture and world perspectives. One such consequence of globalization has been the emergence of religious fundamentalisms, often in the name of protecting "traditional" values and identities. The tensions between tradition and modernization are not new, since modernization usually means Westernization, as in eighteenth- and nineteenth-century Japan and India and twentieth-century China. This has exacerbated some of these tensions as Western ideas get exported to other areas of the world.

It is disproportionately women who are caught in and suffer as a result of the "culture wars," whether in the West or in so-called traditional societies such as Muslim and Hindu worlds. Because women are often seen as the guardians of tradition, once their influence is minimized, it is much

---

26. Enrique Dussel, "The Sociohistorical Meaning of Liberation Theology (Reflections about Its Origin and World Context)," in *Religions/Globalizations: Theories and Cases,* ed. Dwight N. Hopkins, Lois Ann Lorentzen, Eduardo Mendieta, and David Batstone (Durham, NC: Duke University Press, 2001), pp. 33-45.

easier to alter culture and substitute new values, such as the values of technology and finance. Along with social and cultural propaganda, Christian religious fundamentalism in general treats women as subordinate to men and prescribes codes of female conduct and behavior that perpetuate that subordination and inferiority.[27]

How can the cycle be broken so that women can be liberated from their subordinate position? One Christian response has been liberation theology, but even that has its limitations.

Limitations of Liberation Theology

Christianity has contributed much to society in affecting, modifying, and adapting cultural norms, behaviors, and understandings. Despite some positive contributions, it has also done its share of negative things to society and culture. This can be clearly seen in how Christians have damaged and harmed Native Americans. Christians have taken over Native American land and have imposed White Western European culture and religion upon the Native Americans. This has displaced and disenfranchised them and the damage is felt today. Over time, Christianity has been able to achieve conquest in such an unsuspecting way that it has gone unnoticed. For example, Christianity is a temporally rather than a spatially based tradition and not tied to a particular land. Because it is "detached" from the land, Christianity seeks converts from anywhere and anyplace. Missionaries have gone all throughout the world to convert the heathen. On the other hand, adherents of spatially based religions will not try to convince other peoples of their religious truth claims. Hence, all Christian theology, even liberation theology to a certain degree, remains complicit in the conversion or genocide of all subordinate peoples. This can be seen in poorer nations around the world where genocide occurs in the name of Christianity and liberation theology remains quiet or silent.

Robert Allen Warrior argues that the Bible is in no way a liberating text for native peoples. When we examine the liberation motif commonly adopted by liberation theologians, the Exodus story, it ends with the genocide of the Canaanites and others, and the occupying of the Promised Land by the Israelites. This is not a liberation story but a massive genocide and conquest story. The early Deuteronomic history operates as a narrative of

---

27. Kwok Pui-lan, *Hope Abundant*, p. 6.

conquest, a narrative that appears to have been foundational to the European conquest of the Americas, enhanced by the narrative of colonists escaping religious persecution in England. Furthermore, there is a problem to liberation theology's conceptualization of a God of deliverance. This concept understands that God delivers one people but ignores those being dominated, killed, or evicted. Warrior contends that "as long as people believe in the Yahweh of deliverance, the world will not be safe from Yahweh the conqueror."[28]

Those who conquer and colonize continue to perpetuate a conquering God. It is a form of liberation theology that has survived over the past thirty years. Conquering and repossessing land at all cost is the message that survived when the Israelites were liberated from Egypt. It is a powerful image but also a damaging and hurtful one for those who are on the dominated side. For this reason it is imperative to remove this concept from our religious and personal consciousness. We must forgo our religious inheritance of deliverance and replace it with another more welcoming and loving image of God. This concept of a delivering God has had negative effects on women, for it views women as objects of conquest accomplished physically, mentally, psychologically, and sexually. The damaging portrayals cannot go uncontested and unchallenged but must be reexamined, reevaluated, and most urgently replaced. These negative concepts have already caused grave damage and must not continue. It is important to find alternative ways of looking, thinking about, and reimagining God that are good for all of humanity and not only for a select few rich and powerful groups of people.

William R. Hutchison writes that "Christianity as it existed in the West had a right not only to conquer the world but to define reality for other peoples of the world."[29] This is a huge undertaking that Christianity was able to master without being readily questioned by the masses. Some of this was accomplished under the name of Christianity and some under the pretense of Christianity. Much of the white European ideology was transported to all parts of the world under the movement and guise of "Christianity." However, in reality much of it wasn't Christianity at all. Rather, it was the ideology of the colonizers. This has happened all too frequently throughout history, so

28. Robert Warrior, "Canaanites, Cowboys, and Indians," in *Native and Christian: Indigenous Voices on Religious Identity in the United States and Canada,* ed. James Treat (New York: Routledge, 1996), p. 99.

29. William R. Hutchison, "A Moral Equivalent for Imperialism: Americans and the Promotion of Christian Civilization, 1880-1910," in *Missionary Ideologies in the Imperialist Era: 1880-1920,* ed. Torben Christensen and William R. Hutchison (Copenhagen: Aros, 1982), p. 172.

much so that it is often difficult to differentiate Christianity from the colonizer's ideology. As religion and culture mix, it is at times hard to see the difference.

This uncontested privilege of whiteness and imperialism has dominated much of Western thought. In light of colonialism, globalization, and postcolonialism, it is not only necessary but essential to reexamine this historical practice. We cannot continue to dominate and subjugate people due to their ethnicity, gender, race, and sexual orientation. But how can we reexamine our practices and convince ourselves of the merit of allowing all people to flourish each in their own ways?

When a group of people understand themselves as oppressed people who are to be delivered at all costs, they necessarily become complicit in oppressing those who stand in the way of their deliverance. Warrior argues that we need to reconceptualize ourselves as "a society of people delivered from oppression who are not so afraid of becoming victims again that they become oppressors themselves."[30] This may be a key to survival, not just for one group but for all.

Though we often fail to acknowledge it, religious studies is a colonizing discourse, particularly within native communities.[31] Christianity, for example, disguises itself; by calling its task of evangelism the spreading of good news, it gives itself permission to dominate people and conquer the land and shape them according to its own philosophies. It cleverly presents itself as doing the work of God, often to the extent of pressuring the church into sanctifying its will. "The academic study of religion has often failed to acknowledge what it is. It is academic; it is Western; it is intellectual."[32] Without this acknowledgment, theology cannot move forward as a way to work towards eliminating the dominant Eurocentric Christianity. Liberation cannot occur until Christianity dismantles its strong Euro-American intellectual influence upon the people around the globe. Only if and when it is able to achieve this can steps be taken to work towards liberation, equality, and freedom of people. One step toward this is doing a critical analysis of colonialism. Influenced by Christianity, colonialism has subjugated many

---

30. Warrior, "Canaanites, Cowboys, and Indians," p. 99.

31. Emile Durkheim, *The Elementary Forms of Religion,* trans. Karen E. Fields (New York: Free Press, 1995), p. 420.

32. Sam Gill, "The Academic Study of Religion," *Journal of the American Academy of Religion* 62 (Winter 1994): 967.

people and in particular women. Until we stop subjugating others,[33] it is not possible to treat others equally and fairly.

Center and Margins

The boundary between the colonizer and the colonized separates the dominant from the dominated. There is a center and a margin. The center marginalizes further those who are at the margins, and this action escalates the domination of the powerless. In other words, no group functions in isolation. bell hooks[34] states that the center cannot speak from its powerful position to the margins. The center needs to move to the margins in order to (re)position its location to speak and be heard. This will make them heard, as they will then be with those who are outside the center. This avoids defining the margins and enables those on the margins to define themselves. In hooks's words, "I want to know your story. And then I will tell it back to you in a new way. Tell it back to you in such a way that it has become mine, my own. Re-writing you, I write myself anew. I am still author, authority. I am still the colonizer, the speaking subject, and you are now at the center of my talk."[35]

To break such patterns of domination, resistance must occur. Counter-language is a form of resistance. Likewise, resistance and change require space. In the space of "Otherness" the distinction between being silenced and withholding speech is learned and the ability to say no to the colonizer is rehearsed. "Homeplace" becomes the social context within the interstices of power. It is a space protected and created for survival and resistance. The colonized develop a counter-language, which serves as a language of resistance,[36] of refusal, and from the margins. The deliberate choice of mar-

---

33. It is folly to believe that any matriarchal or even any gender-balanced cultures were turned into patriarchies by Anglo-European colonization. The history and fragmentation of female theologies shows that women in precolonial times were no better off than their European counterparts. However, there are periods in history before contemporary times when women were somewhat better off than at other times. One such time might have been the era of the Roman Principate and Pax Romana, from 31 BCE to 64 CE.

34. "bell hooks" is the pen name of Gloria Jean Watkins.

35. bell hooks, in Steed Vernyl Davidson, *Empire and Exile: Postcolonial Readings of the Book of Jeremiah* (New York: T. & T. Clark International, 2011), p. 103.

36. The example of Ho Chi Minh shows that these languages of resistance are not made from whole cloth, especially not purely native cloth. Ho Chi Minh lived for a time in the United States, in England, in France, and in the Soviet Union and China, where he learned his Communism. His nationalistic anti-colonialism was fueled by what he considered the

ginality exists as a critical response to being dominated. Marginality enables the re-creation and maintenance of the subjectivity of the colonized. The binary opposition of center and margins surfaces in hooks's representation of power, and her mapping separates the two into distinct and oppositional categories. Power still derives from a central source and remains correspondingly undiminished.[37]

Rather than having such distinctions, it may be more helpful to talk about mixing or hybridity. For Homi Bhabha, hybridity may or may not be a permanent marker of diasporic identity, but rather a strategic choice made to adapt to and survive in the context of colonialism.[38] Hybridity may be a way to overcome the unjust dichotomy that exists, such as the preference of white over black, rich over poor, men over women.

Postcolonial Biblical Readings

A written book belongs to its author and to its readers. The history of the biblical story is not limited to the first three centuries of the Jewish tradition, and so the selection of one particular historical period as the prime reference for determining textual meaning in biblical studies is intentionally done. It is quite plain that the Bible includes events of imperialism.[39] Though used to understand God and bring humanity towards God, the Bible has been misused in every possible way: to legitimize sexism, racism, classism, colonialism, slavery, homophobia, and other evils. Yet it is not the cleric or theologian who is constructing these understandings and roles, but a political agenda that misappropriates isolated biblical statements for its own ends.

The New Testament reflects the imperial power of the Roman Empire as Judea itself was divided into three territories with local rulers under Roman power and rule. Christianity embraces the command to spread its word independent of the empire's wishes. When Christianity became the official religion of the empire, it (and several of its heresies) spread to the north and the east, to Armenia, India, Teutonic lands, and Slavic lands. In ancient and modern times, it is commanded to evangelize over different people and places. The Bible has often been used as a colonizing influence. Sometimes

---

most powerful doctrines of resistance whose theory originated in Imperial Germany in the nineteenth century.

37. Davidson, *Empire and Exile*, p. 104.

38. Homi Bhabha, *The Location of Culture* (New York: Routledge, 2004), p. 120.

39. Dube, "Toward a Post-Colonial Feminist Interpretation of the Bible," p. 91.

that influence has been benign and sometimes it has been appropriated by political forces and used to subvert local customs. The Bible has been used repeatedly as a colonizing text to authorize the subjugation of foreign nations and lands. Furthermore, the content of the Bible has emerged from domination and colonialism of different people. The New Testament emerged from imperialist settings and themes and has become a postcolonial book.[40] The colonized are depicted as helpless, evil, inarticulate, backward, lazy, exotic, and as babies in need of instruction. This gives the perception that it is perfectly right to dominate others; indeed, it imagines colonialism as a tool by which to help them. The colonizers are then portrayed as civilized, Christian, articulate, and literate, which legitimizes their domination of the people. In the Bible, and by extension in every time and place, we depict some lands as empty and waiting to be discovered, and others as being the symbol of light and holiness. The narratives construct a normative fact that someone (usually a white man) owns plantations, mines, or farms in other places that are run by native servants.[41] The deep and unforgiving contrast is clearly laid out to distinguish the colonizers from the colonized.

The biblical narratives contain the various cycles of land getting, land losing, and land reclamation. This search for a place to reside is a concern of contemporary communities as well as those described in the ancient text. Space is often seen as divinely granted and thus one can fight for it. The new space of (dis)placement is in tension and place defines subject identities.[42]

To move towards decolonization, we need to resist the exploitative hermeneutics of imperialism. We should seek liberating ways of interdependence in our multicultural and postcolonial world.[43] Careful analysis and reading of the self-serving interpretations of the text should be done. Nothing can be taken at face value, as the colonial hidden agenda that lies behind the exegesis needs to be unearthed and exposed to what remains of

---

40. If one considers the Old Testament as well, one may interpret the Israelite conquest of Canaan as an imperialist action. But, the Old Testament is far more dedicated to the suffering of the Israelites at the hands of other far more powerful imperial powers — Egypt, Assyria, Babylon, Persia, and Greece. In a sense, for centuries, the Old and New Testaments have been seen as part of a colonizing struggle between the covenant of Moses and the covenant of Jesus. The bottom line is that there are so many different themes in the Christian Bible that one can craft just about any position one wishes from its texts. This works to the colonizer's favor.

41. Dube, "Toward a Post-Colonial Feminist Interpretation of the Bible," pp. 92, 93.

42. Davidson, *Empire and Exile,* pp. 7, 8.

43. Dube, "Toward a Post-Colonial Feminist Interpretation of the Bible," p. 98.

the "First World" world, which still insists that it is good to colonize and to dominate others. The powerful believe they are doing it for their own good, to prevent a hypothetical threat, or as punishment for a wrong where the conquered are primarily guilty by association.

Being/Becoming Woman

A discussion of women's identity and being will help us move forward towards equality and reconciliation between men and women. In a postcolonial context, identity is often contested. For in the midst of travel it is easy to lose one's identity, change one's identity, and reform one's identity, either intentionally and by choice or under external pressure. Colonial disruptions radically alter one's identity.[44] For example, in 1911 when my grandmother was a child during the Japanese occupation of Korea (1910-1945), an order came for people to change their given names from Korean to Japanese and to speak Japanese instead of Korean. This name change had a deep impact on my grandmother's identity as a young Korean girl living under Japanese occupation. The demand to speak only in Japanese was distressing and difficult to live with for my grandmother and the Korean people.

One's identity formation living along borders involves the struggle to be one or the other.[45] On the borders of life, people are aware of multiple ethnicities, multiple languages, and multiple ideologies out of which they construct their identities and allegiances.[46] This mixing of multiple entities produces hybrid identities.

By raising questions about assumed binaries and recognizing the hybrid nature of all cultures and identities, contrapuntal themes blur the lines

---

44. This case is actually a mixture of different identity themes, at the time of the Constitutional Convention in 1787. All thirteen colonies were decidedly in the camp of English liberalism, but with a desire to avoid the pitfalls of English Parliamentarianism. On the other hand, religious sentiment was all over the map, from Catholic Maryland to Anglican Georgia to Puritan New England, to Quaker Pennsylvania. So, the Constitution united what was in common, while the Bill of Rights left that which was different to *adiaphora*.

45. It may be instructive to follow culinary trends as a way to map elements of culture that few people would contest. In other words, there are cultural elements that are contentious, such as language, and cultural elements that are not, such as how to make sauerkraut. The Vietnamese will adopt recipes for braising but they will reject French language and legal systems.

46. Jon L. Berquist, "Psalms, Postcolonialism, and the Construction of the Self," in *Approaching Yehud: New Approaches to the Study of the Persian Period*, ed. Jon L. Berquist (Atlanta: Society of Biblical Literature, 2007), p. 199.

of center/periphery, male/female, straight/queer, East/West, and citizen/ noncitizen. Through this interplay of imperialism, colonization, gender, and sexuality the ideal "heteropatriarchal American" is formed, one who does not transgress clear boundaries. By the same token, the notion that feminist theology is universal is not correct, for women's experiences are hybrid, not universal. Women's issues vary from one group to another, and one individual to another due to their different experiences and context. A great variety of cultural, religious, social, and historical aspects influence the dynamics of women's experience around the world. This variety influences the type and degree to which women may experience a particular event or action. By building coalitions and solidarities among various women's groups, we can generate a worldview that embraces differences among and within us,[47] rather than one that insists on homogeneity and sameness. By seeking difference and embracing and welcoming difference with dignity and grace, we can begin to live holistically with others who are far removed from us culturally, religiously, and socially.

Alienation

Women have different experiences and thus it is impossible to say women's experiences are universal. There are some key experiences that women experience in common but at various levels and depths. One such experience is alienation. Women who work may feel alienated from their work. Their work is not valued, and they feel a disconnect between their work and their identity. Women who raise children can feel alienated in their own homes. This alienation creates a feeling of strangeness and hostility. The experience of being a stranger is, like abjection, the sign of separation from our first home, our mother's body.[48] We cannot find a comfortable place when we feel alienation, isolation, destruction, or pain, as there is no welcoming place for the dispossessed. Exile deprives people of a sense of possessing an interior space from which to reflect, to love themselves. Exile creates an instability in one's heart, which leads to difficulty in embracing oneself. Furthermore, it is difficult to project oneself out towards an exterior through loving oth-

47. W. Anne Joh, "Race, Class, Gender, Sexuality," in *New Feminist Christianity: Many Voices, Many Views*, ed. Mary E. Hunt and Diann L. Neu (Woodstock, VT: Skylight Paths, 2010), p. 63.

48. Anna Smith, *Julia Kristeva: Readings of Exile and Estrangement* (New York: St. Martin's Press, 1996), pp. 23, 24.

ers. Without the inner peace to love oneself, it is difficult to have the outer peace in order to love others. The exile's sense of space is dislocated in that no place offers itself as home.[49] One continues to live in a sense of constant flux and instability. Similar to the foreigner, one's alien status makes one abject, an asocial creature stuck with a mutated identity and understanding. So the space of reflection in the abject person or foreigner is foreshortened and thus, Kristeva believes, the shock of displacement into a new language foreign to one's mother tongue condemns one to partial silence. It prohibits one from fully sharing one's perspectives and makes one incomprehensible to the rest of the world. The foreigner can get involved in projects, but cannot seem to reflect on one's own status as a marginalized person. It leads to further frustration and difficulties, as one feels silenced and ignored.[50] One may also be more willing to do morally and culturally questionable acts to restore one's place in one's culture.[51]

Abjection is "a composite of judgment and affect, of condemnation and yearning, of signs and drives."[52] That is why the abject person is the supreme example of the voyager, one who is always on the move, never home. This situation has become part of female existence in a world that is patriarchal, colonial, and dominating.

A borderline patient who suffers from abjection will be unable to differentiate between personal subjective space and another's will. A paradigm for this might be the Norman Bates character in the 1959 story "Psycho" by Robert Bloch, made into a film of the same name by Alfred Hitchcock in 1960. Norman views himself as an ideal for an Other (originally his mother), and thus as having a false self or selves. The subject of abjection is an exile preoccupied not with name but place. When abjection occurs in the infant at the stage when he or she is heavily in need of good mirroring from the parent figure, serious problems of identity can ensue. Abjection is a disorder

---

49. The condition of exile is a remarkably common one in speculative fiction, usually following the template of Moses, who is not removed from his homeland, but is forbidden to enter it. One classic example is Robert A. Heinlein's short story "Requiem," where the architect of travel to the moon cannot himself travel there. The Steven Spielberg film *E.T.* is about an exile. It is a theme in Evelyn Waugh's novel *A Handful of Dust*. One may even consider it the major theme in Shakespeare's *The Merchant of Venice*.

50. Smith, *Julia Kristeva: Readings of Exile and Estrangement*, p. 24.

51. This is one theme in the film *Avatar*, where the hero agrees to spy on the Na'vi, the Other, until he discovers a new and better "home" among the Na'vi themselves.

52. Julia Kristeva, *Powers of Horror: An Essay on Abjection*, trans. Leon S. Roudiez (New York: Columbia University Press, 1982), p. 10.

associated with the mirror stage;[53] its subject demonstrates serious problems with living and conceptualizing space.[54]

Abjection occurs relatively frequently in Asian American women's subjectivity. Asian American women's experience of sexism and racism has often led to a wretched understanding of self. Typically it is white supremacy and the ensuing everyday experiences of racism that create Asian American women's feeling of alienation. Racism like a disease will seep into one's existence and can be undetected as it presents itself as a guise for how society exists in the Western world. It poses as a cultural aspect that one needs to accept if one wants to be a true American. Racism poses great problems for Asian American women. Due to difficulties of racism and sexism, Asian American women become separated from themselves.

Asian American women deal with both the sexism of the dominant (white) culture and the embedded Confucian culture that benefits men. In this culture, women are to obey men at all times whether the male be a father, uncle, husband, or son. To survive, Asian American women either follow those cultural conventions, live under the radar, or suffer the cultural consequences. These consequences may appear as hatred from the mother-in-law or the entire in-law family who will make it their priority to make the life of a disobedient daughter-in-law as miserable as humanly possible.

Thus a long historical, cultural, and religious heritage of sexism is woven into the lives of Asian American women and often creates in them a sense of powerlessness, hopelessness, wretchedness, and shame.

History of Subordination

Women experience subordination to varying degrees. Women's subordination has a long history and is reinforced through various social and cultural aspects in many cultures and communities around the world. One way to maintain women's subordination is through denying them the right to own land. Indeed, men who owned land were able to claim ownership of women in some way attached to that land because women typically could not own

---

53. The "mirror stage" was a term and concept invented by Jacques Lacan. To see his treatment of it, see Jacques Lacan, "1. The Mirror Stage as Formative of the Function of the *I* as Revealed in Psychoanalytic Experience," in *Écrits,* trans. Alan Sheridan (London: Routledge, Kindle Edition, 2007), pp. 3-9. One of the most evocative artistic depictions of a pathology of "The Mirror Phase" is in the story of Pete Townshend's opera *Tommy.*

54. Smith, *Julia Kristeva: Readings of Exile and Estrangement,* p. 151.

land. This claim of ownership would subsequently subordinate women to men. Likewise, the work of the family means that the workers belong to the men including his wife and children. They are under the power and domain of the male leader of the house. Furthermore, when men needed heirs, in whom their earthly life would be prolonged, men would lay claim to another man's children.[55] Because men have held power for so long, they feel entitled to possess everything, including women and children, much as the animals bought or sold in the marketplace. This further reinforces women's subordinate status and institutionalizes women's role as the weaker sex. This perception of women as the weaker sex has continually kept women in their place as subordinate others in the family, culture, and wider society.

As we examine some different historical eras, we find various negative attitudes towards women. Aristotle stated that woman is only matter, whereas man is "better and more divine."[56] Aristotle elevates men into heavenly beings. They are thought of as being above women in the physical, mental, and spiritual realms. In this world, the father is the active *dominus* (master) or lord[57] and the mother's role is passive, her status as subordinate to men even further reinforced. She will only act when acted upon. She does not initiate but rather reacts to her husband.

This understanding raises questions about the ancient myths and Greek drama. Were they intended to reinforce the conception that men are really stronger than women? How did the men gain all that power or did women just give up their power? Like many feminists, I believe the subordination of women to be a created role, not one supported by biology or moral thought,[58] so its creation needs to be examined and questioned.

At the time of patriarchal power, man took control from woman of her right to possess and bequeath property.[59] Women lost much of their power through the advent of private property, for the concept of private property allowed an owner to transfer his identity into his property;[60] of course the owners were always men. This allowed a man to pass on his property to

55. Simone de Beauvoir, *The Second Sex* trans. and ed. H. M. Parshley (New York: Vintage, 1989), pp. 78, 79.

56. De Beauvoir, *The Second Sex*, p. 79.

57. The Latin word for "master" was also adopted as a title for the emperor. But, there is a widely used feminine form *domina*, which applied to widows in charge of wealthy houses, especially in the later empire.

58. Judith Butler, *Undoing Gender* (New York: Routledge, Kindle Edition, 2004), p. 89.

59. De Beauvoir, *The Second Sex*, p. 82.

60. For example, a titled person, a person "of name," was a person who owned land.

his sons and thus to keep it in the family since by patriarchal convention a son carries on the family name and assumes title to the property. A man's property continues to exist beyond death only if it belongs to individuals in his family or those whom he adopted, as Julius Caesar adopted Octavian. To reverse patriarchy, we need to undo the effects of private property ownership. This is a large and harrowing (stressful) task but a necessary one. The cycle of oppression causes an enormous amount of pain.

Ecofeminist theories of the lost paradise often include the idea of an original matriarchy, when women ruled over men. It is a story found in many cultures, and is often associated with male puberty rites. In the late nineteenth century, some anthropologists popularized a theory of human development in which society progressed from an initial stage of promiscuity to matriarchal rule and then to patriarchy.[61] This contrasts with histories that teach that patriarchy has always existed and always will exist.

Matriarchy should not be viewed as a primitive time, but as a time of high culture in early Egyptian and Near Eastern civilization. It was a prosperous time when women were in charge of family, religion, and society. The worship of the Mother Goddess was important in matriarchal cultures, but this matriarchal society was overthrown by the regressive influence of patriarchal religions and social organization, mainly Jewish and Christian traditions built on Roman models.[62] Patriarchal religions have damaged what matriarchal societies had accomplished. They eliminated women's power and made them subordinate to men. To free ourselves from patriarchy's damaging hierarchy, we seek to redress the balance between men and women.

Much of the balance or imbalance between the sexes is tied to religion. Some faiths believe the subordinate position of women in this life is willed in heaven and advantageous on earth. The religions invented and perpetrated by men reflect this wish for domination. In the legends of Eve and Pandora, men have accused women of being responsible for the woes of this life. They have made use of philosophy and theology to reinforce the subordination of women.

Since ancient times satirists and moralists have delighted in showing the weakness of women. As Montaigne said, "It is easier to accuse one sex than to excuse the other."[63] This is what has happened throughout much

---

61. Rosemary Radford Ruether, *Gaia & God: An Ecofeminist Theology of Earth Healing* (New York: HarperCollins, 1992), p. 145.

62. Ruether, *Gaia & God*, p. 146.

63. De Beauvoir, *The Second Sex*, p. xxviii.

of our history. Society became used to blaming women for all the mistakes that men have made and are continuing to make. Women are easy targets. They have been ordered back into the home more harshly as emancipation became a real possibility. Within Scripture, males have interpreted the Adam and Eve story to blame women for all the troubles of hard labor and physical illness. Men imagine the idyllic time as one prior to hunting, agriculture, and technology, a gatherer paradise in which humans could simply pluck the fruits of an abundant earth. Woman being blamed for the lost paradise may have roots that go back to primal human social patterns.[64] When problems lead to a need for a scapegoat, a weaker class of people often gets blamed or is believed to be the cause of the problems.

Even within contemporary working and business classes, men endeavor to restrain women's liberation, because they see women as dangerous competitors, the more so because women have been accustomed to work for lower wages.[65] This also is what happens among people of different races. When immigration occurs, people who are working low-paying jobs feel they will lose their jobs to immigrants willing to work for even lower wages. This begins the process of Othering and making people subordinate or lesser beings. To overcome this reality, we need to strive for equality between sexes and between races.

Marriage

The history of marriage reveals how it has been used to subordinate and oppress women. It binds a woman in a contract that makes the woman part of the man's family living under patriarchal systems and values. Simone de Beauvoir understands marriage to be a process of trade. Through marriage, a woman is now no longer only lent from one clan to another; she is torn up by the roots from the group into which she was born, and is annexed by her husband's group; he buys her as one buys a farm animal or a slave; he imposes his domestic divinities upon her; and the children born to her belong to the husband's family.[66] In Confucian cultures, a woman had to be obedient to her father, husband, or son. This patriarchy stabilized society by putting women in their place and preventing them

---

64. Ruether, *Gaia & God*, pp. 144-45.
65. De Beauvoir, *The Second Sex*, p. xxix.
66. De Beauvoir, *The Second Sex*, p. 82.

from rioting or challenging the status quo. Marriage became viewed as almost a divinely instituted action that placed women in a subordinate position to men. Asian tradition has been used to further men's lineage and to further men's status through the addition of male children born to their subordinated wives.

There are other ways to suppress women's power. One way to keep a woman subordinate is to exclude her from the succession,[67] by prohibiting her from moving wealth to her father's family. Thus a woman does not enjoy the dignity of being a person but rather forms a part of the patrimony of a man: first of her father, then of her husband. Under the strictly patriarchal regime a father can, from their birth on, condemn to death both male and female children, but in practice it is only female infants who are killed. When she becomes a young girl, the father has all power over her; and this power is transferred to her husband when she gets married. A man can naturally have as many wives as he pleases. A woman is subjected to a strict practice of chastity because when she marries, the man wants her to be a virgin and he requires complete fidelity.[68] Such virginity and fidelity is not required of men. It is used simply to subordinate women to men.

The patriarchs of biblical times were polygamous, and they could put away their wives almost at will. We see this in the marriage of Jacob to Leah. He wants Leah's sister Rachel and in a figurative way gives Leah a lesser status than Rachel by favoring Rachel's two sons, Joseph and Benjamin, over Leah's six older sons. The story of Abraham and Sarah is another story in which a woman is cast away. Sarah, who is unable to give birth, offers her slave woman Hagar to Abraham. Hagar bears a son, Ishmael, and this makes Sarah upset and jealous. Sarah then tells her husband Abraham to send Hagar into the desert with her son, Ishmael (Genesis 16).

Furthermore, in Old Testament times, it was required under severe penalties that the young wife be delivered to her husband a virgin. Men could take a widow for a wife, or perhaps a divorced woman as a wife, but if the woman were "advertised" as a virgin and was not, she could be stoned. To prevent adultery from occurring, she was kept in the confinement of domestic duties.[69] This was an inequality towards women, for men committed infidelities without any consequences.

---

67. This was not true of all societies. Even in ancient Rome, there were types of marriage separations where the wife retrieved her dowry.

68. De Beauvoir, *The Second Sex*, p. 83.

69. De Beauvoir, *The Second Sex*, p. 85.

In Asian cultures, women are called *"an-ae"* (in Korean), which literally means "inside person." Korean and other Asian women were expected to stay within the house or the house complex and perform traditional chores like cooking, cleaning, bearing and rearing children while the men were free to be outside of the home. This ensured that they were loyal to their husbands. It kept the women indoors where they could not learn from or interact with the local community and wider world and allowed the men to do what they wished within the larger society.

Such expectations still exist in households today, particularly in the life of immigrant Asian women and other immigrant cultures in North America, who are expected to take care of the children, cook, clean, and do most of the household chores. This is irrelevant to whether or not she holds a paying job outside the home as well.

Women as the Other

Imperialism involves women both wealthy and impoverished, women of color and white women, and women in developed and underdeveloped countries, because imperialism is a global phenomenon. It has made a huge impact and it informs our perception of the Other.[70] As imperialism makes its impact, women may find themselves living in cultures where men compel them to assume the status of the Other. Men profit in many ways from maintaining this otherness and subordination of women,[71] chief among them, men's power and control.

Women's otherness takes shape in different forms and in different spheres. Beauvoir writes that woman is a man's sexual partner, a reproducer, an erotic object and an Other through whom he seeks himself.[72] In some ways, women become viewed as an extension of the male selves. Women become the Other within the sexual realm, where they are viewed as objects to be conquered. Patriarchy exists to benefit and protect the men. We demonize sexuality and perceive women as sexualized beings who bring fulfillment to men. They are not co-partners but are those who are dominated and used for pleasure. Patriarchy thrives within this dualistic worldview that portrays men as good and women as evil. If we constantly think and the world un-

---

70. Musa W. Dube, "Toward a Post-Colonial Feminist Interpretation of the Bible," p. 97.
71. De Beauvoir, *The Second Sex*, pp. xxxi, xxxv.
72. De Beauvoir, *The Second Sex*, p. 59.

derstands itself in dualistic terms, it limits how we perceive the world and in particular women. To free ourselves of dualistic thinking will be a step away from making women the Other.

To claim that woman is the Other is to say that a reciprocal or equal relationship does not exist between the sexes. Women as the Other constitute a part of the property possessed by men. A woman is always under the guardianship of a male[73] and appears to be no one if she is not associated with a man in society. Within many societies it is only an illusion that women seem to have power and authority in a marriage or family.

Condemned to play the part of the Other, woman was also condemned to hold only uncertain power: slave or idol, it was never she who chose her lot. "Men make the gods; women worship them," Frazer has said. In many cultures men decide that the divine shall be female or male. Men have so much power over women that women's place in society is always that which men assign to them;[74] at no time have they ever imposed their own law.[75] This is true even in historic Christianity, a predominantly patriarchal religion where even God is male. What a unique way to keep women in their place and make them the Other! Religion is a powerful force in our society and it can have devastating effects on women if this hierarchy of genders goes unchecked. It is important for all parties involved that this is recognized and steps are taken to fix this misperception. For the liberation of women is the liberation of all.

The patriarchal notions within Christianity need to be challenged. Without this, it will continue to perpetuate negative images of women. This can also apply to women of different races. Christianity has become so westernized that anything non-Western sounds foreign or untrue or even evil. Reshaping the understanding of faith as culturally bound will work towards eliminating racism, prejudice, and subordination of nonwhite to white people. A new paradigm must exist to create a notion of equality between different women of color as well as between men and women.

There are various factors that come into play in building one's identity. For Kristeva, subjectivity is always provisional, contested, and in process. Identity is precariously generated through the negotiation of internal differences, but it is never finally accomplished or secured. As we recall, Ezra 9–10 can be read as the vivid depiction of a communal "subject on trial."

73. De Beauvoir, *The Second Sex*, pp. 70, 71.
74. De Beauvoir, *The Second Sex*, p. 77.
75. De Beauvoir, *The Second Sex*, p. 77.

The women are sent away and the text does not pronounce the expulsion.[76] Perhaps there is guilt on the part of the people who have done an undesirable act. Perhaps there is anger about the crowd's decision to do such horrific acts against innocent women. The text does not make it clear, but rather leaves it up to us to decide what are the ramifications of this wrongful decision.

For women, mixed marriages have been problematic. Opposition to mixed marriages is not simply a matter of ethnic or religious purity, but is tied to the impact of marriage on communal land ownership. Marriage with outsiders spells loss of land to the Jewish province. Therefore there is a dynamic of gender, economics, and race taking place. For women, the problem is not simply a matter of being foreign but also a matter of the social, economic, racial, and religious implications that will impact their lives in this context. Marriage would secure partners and families for the women of the new Judahite community in the face of competing possibilities. It is a matter of maintaining communal cohesiveness and continuity. When women can inherit land from their husbands or fathers, foreign women pose an economic threat of loss of land to the community.[77]

In Ezra 9, the defiling behaviors of foreigners, referred to as "abominations," are brought into the text's polemic against intermarriage. These behaviors result in a pollution that adheres to the sinner and threatens the holiness of the land and can result in expulsion from their land (e.g., Lev. 18:25, 28). Such "moral" impurity cannot be communicated by the sinner to others, cannot be removed by means of ritual actions. It is only through punishment or atonement that "moral" impurity can be removed. Nehemiah 13:28-30, a text from the Nehemiah memoir, bears witness to a second way in which Ezra-Nehemiah associates foreigners with defilement. Here it is priestly intermarriage with aliens that pollutes rather than alien actions. Purification was secured through the divorce of the priests from their foreign wives and the expulsion of the wives and their children from the sanctuary and community. Such an action would result in the exclusion from the priesthood of all males with any alien ancestry.[78]

Feminists should seek to recognize, honor, and carefully listen to the

---

76. Harold C. Washington, "Israel's Holy Seed and the Foreign Women of Ezra-Nehemiah: A Kristevan Reading," *Biblical Interpretation* 11, no. 3-4 (2003): 436.

77. Tamara Cohn Eskenazi, "Ezra-Nehemiah," in *The Women's Bible Commentary*, ed. Carol A. Newsom and Sharon H. Ringe (Louisville: Westminster John Knox, 1992), p. 121.

78. Saul M. Olyan, "Purity Ideology in Ezra-Nehemiah as a Tool to Reconstitute the Community," *Journal for the Study of Judaism* 35 (2004): 5, 6.

voices of those who have been silenced.[79] We need to seek out these voices and decolonize them. Many of the silenced voices are Asian American women. Their perception of being the perpetual foreigner has been damaging to their personal, social, cultural, and religious selves. This negative understanding of themselves has stunted their personal and spiritual growth. As a result, many of their perceptions and beliefs have been silenced or relegated to the sidelines. It is essential for the women to regain their own voices and contribute to the discussion of feminism so that all women will be liberated.

But we must do so circumspectly. For, as bell hooks relates, she experienced feminist scholars who "now fully participated in the construction of a discourse about the 'Other,'" and she "was made 'Other' there in that space with them."[80] This scenario happens too often and in all places. We relinquish our stories as our own and give them to the oppressors and colonizers so they can retell them and make themselves look a lot better than they really are. They mask themselves as the liberator of the colonized and portray themselves as giving up their authority so that the voices of the marginalized women are heard. However, this is only an act and should be stopped so that the truly marginalized voices and stories can be heard. In turn, those voices and stories can begin the process of resistance against the oppressors.

Women live in a fragile space where their livelihood can be drastically altered by the decisions of the powerful — in most cases, powerful men. In particular within the Asian American community, women frequently experience verbal, physical, and mental abuse. One small misstep can set off abusive behavior. Women live in fear and within fragile and delicate spaces that they must learn to maneuver so they can survive.

Asian American women's lives can be torn and turned upside down as they are easily understood as the Other. Women somehow become the problem — sometimes, as bell hooks says, even for other women. I know this from personal experience. There have been instances where I have been publicly viewed as the problem. This occurred within society as well as within the cultural community to which I belong. When difficulties arose within our extended family in relation to my marriage, I became a scapegoat and an easy target of blame for all the problems. Within my social experiences, I

79. Debra Dean Murphy, "Power, Politics and Difference: A Feminist Response to John Milbank," *Modern Theology* 10 (1994): 140.

80. bell hooks, "Marginality as Site of Resistance," in *Out There: Marginalization and Contemporary Cultures,* ed. Russell Ferguson, Martha Gever, Trinh T. Minh-ha, and Cornel West (New York: The New Museum of Contemporary Art, 1990), p. 342.

have also been viewed as the problem. I have heard people make statements such as "the 'colored people' (meaning myself) bring all the problems." These types of experiences are difficult to endure.

In the midst of such discrimination and subordination, women must recognize their abjection. Women become the signifiers of the Other and the one that we are too afraid to welcome. To work toward removing these injustices, we must recognize the stranger within us all. Women and men need to be able to embrace one another amidst all the problems and difficulties created by patriarchy and oppression and to empower each other so that we can all live abundantly.

It is clear that Asian women have been displaced in a Western cultural setting. We live in locations where multiple strands of race, gender, and cultural difference come together.[81] The developing world crosses multiple boundaries of difference and Otherness. The developing world exists within as well as outside the boundaries of the so-called First World. These very categories depend on Western dualisms and protect the hegemony of Western cultural forms of knowledge. As developing-world women cross boundaries of gender as well as culture, they disrupt expected notions of authenticity in cultural difference. Trinh Minh-Ha "re-write[s] the ethnic female subject as site of differences,"[82] refusing to remain within the bounds of the "i," the Other as a subject of knowledge. She seeks suppressed knowledge in "crack and interstice," making visible the "failures operating in every system"[83] or master discourse. Feminists should seek to recognize, honor, and carefully listen to the voices of those who have for so long been silenced. The danger is to assume that what those voices have to say will always speak to some common core of experience, to our own questions and desires. To make such an assumption is to once again "colonize" the Other — to make the Other a projection of our own image.[84] As discussed earlier, men see women in their own image and make them mere extensions of themselves.

Condemned to play the part of the Other, woman holds only uncertain power. She cannot choose her lot. Religion remains a force in our society and it can have devastating effects on women if this hierarchy of genders goes unchecked. Christian denominations have made major strides in bringing women not only into the clergy and other leadership roles, but also into posi-

---

81. Trinh Minh-Ha, *Woman, Native, Other: Writing Postcoloniality and Feminism* (Bloomington: Indiana University Press, 2009), p. 113.

82. Minh-Ha, *Woman, Native, Other,* p. 44.

83. Minh-Ha, *Woman, Native, Other,* p. 44.

84. Murphy, "Power, Politics and Difference," p. 140.

tions managing entire denominations. It is important for all parties involved that this be recognized and that steps be taken to continue this progress.

To reduce women to "Other" as a means to account for injustice is to erase women once more from history. Toril Moi maintains, "Simply to equate women with otherness deprives the feminist struggle of any kind of specificity. What is repressed is not otherness, but specific, historically constructed agents."[85] Therefore, women need to regain their own agency and become agents of change. Women need to regain their ability to change society, influence culture, and redefine religion in ways that work for the liberation of all people and not only a select few.

When it comes to Asian American men, the oriental male was feminized, portrayed as homosexual, or else depicted as a lusty villain from whom the European could rescue the native (or the European) woman. After the middle of the eighteenth century, Asia is often personified as a turbaned potentate. If women were Native American or African, they were usually represented as savage. However, the images of "the Orient" cluster around riches, splendor, and plenty. The veiled Asian women become a recurrent colonial fantasy to the European self. The ancient Ethiopian story/myth of the Queen of Sheba arriving in Solomon's court and willingly surrendering her enormous wealth in return for sexual gratification initiated a long tradition of stories in which the desire of the native woman for the European man illustrated the submission of the colonized people.[86]

A dualistic understanding of and separation between men and women is dangerous. There is much overlap between men and women, and there needs to be a clear understanding that this dichotomy should no longer exist. It leads to essentialization and this leads to rigid dogma. Women must speak up and stop saying that they have nothing to say. Women must study and learn and gain knowledge. If knowledge is power, then women have a long

85. Toril Moi, "Feminism, Postmodernism and Style: Recent Feminist Criticism in the United States," *Cultural Critique* 2 (1988): 12. Cited by Marsha Aileen Hewitt, "The Eclipse of Subjectivity and Idealizations of the 'Other,'" *Journal of Dharma* 22, no. 3 (1997): 342.

86. Not all "brown" or "black" women are represented as victims, or as desirable or passive. The non-European woman also appears in an intractable version, as "Amazonian" or deviant femininity. The Amazons are located by early colonial writings in virtually every part of the non-European world, and provide images of insatiable sexuality and brutality. Thus female volition, desire, and agency are literally pushed to the margins of the civilized world. But not all margins are equally removed from the center: skin color and female behavior come together in establishing a cultural hierarchy with white Europe at the apex and black Africa at the bottom. See Ania Loomba, *Colonialism/Postcolonialism: The New Critical Idiom* (New York: Routledge, 2005), pp. 130, 131.

way to go to gain the knowledge to overturn the tables of power. This begins when women who simply thought that they had no voice and to that extent were "nobody" are enabled to discover and use their voices.

Closing Thoughts

Colonialism has had devastating effects on the poor, the disenfranchised, and women in annexed lands. Women throughout the world have experienced subordination, abjection, alienation, and diminution to different degrees. As colonialism continues to hold a grip on our world, it is important to recognize the problems women face and then to dismantle the system that gives rise to them. It is necessary to fight against the adverse effects of colonialism, empire, and imperialism. For example, women's fragile identity pushes women to become helpless beings in need of a white male savior who will rescue them. We need to eliminate this damaging construct and mentality. This damage is even harsher on women of color, and in particular Asian North American women.

If theology is to address the concerns of the marginalized, theology should be critical. It is perhaps only recently that theology has taken this to heart and said, "Cease this hypocrisy," to those who practice all sorts of alienations on the variety of cultures we can find among our sisters and brothers, fellow *homo sapiens*. We need to identify how our comrades in faith have made aliens of our brothers and sisters of other lands and cultures, thereby "doing harm."

How can our faith traditions become wellsprings for social change? How can we build each other up rather than tear each other down? How can we strengthen relationships rather than divide and conquer? How can we love one another rather than discriminate? This is an important mandate and we must all be involved as participants in a wonderful march for justice and equality. An important part of this journey to justice is healing the wounds between women and men. In order for this to happen we need to reimagine women as liberating leaders who embody a hidden wholeness.

CHAPTER 4

Overcoming the Gendered Division of Humanity

Introduction

Reconciling the gendered division of humanity begins by an affirmation of the lived experience of women. Throughout history women have struggled for existential and physical survival in a patriarchal world. The women's movement affirmed the inherent dignity of women, advocating for issues that nurture their well-being and support their leadership in all sectors of society.

Women of faith have a crucial role to play in the healing work between women and men. In addition to feminism's commitment to a society in which all people can be socially and economically empowered, feminist theologians have argued that women need to be spiritually empowered. Since the 1960s, white feminist theologians have foregrounded the importance of women's experiences in theological discourse and understanding. Mary Daly (1928-2010), Letty Russell (1929-2007), Rosemary Radford Ruether (1936-), and Elisabeth Schüssler Fiorenza (1938-) laid much of the groundwork for future feminist theological discourse by examining the biblical, historical, and theological liberation of women and reimagining them for the next generation of women.

Feminist theological writing reached out to women and helped women understand how their different experiences of God are played out in their lives, communities, and churches. As feminist theology arose and developed, women of different ethnic backgrounds realized that white women could not speak for them or address fully their experiences of cultural subordination, racism, and colonial subjugation. Therefore, in the 1990s the voices of women of color emerged in theological discourse, voices of women such as Rita Nakashima Brock, Ada María Isai-Díaz, Chung Hyun Kyung, Emilie Townes, and Mercy Amba Oduyoye began to critique and build upon white feminist theology.

Presently, with the impact of globalization and postcolonial literature, feminist postcolonial theologians such as Kwok Pui-lan, Namsoon Kang, Monica Coleman, Musa Dube, Choi Hee An, W. Anne Joh, and Catherine Keller have begun to define, explore, and expand this field of theological discourse. While this body of literature is still in a nascent stage, it is a crucial component of contemporary constructive theology. This chapter analyzes postcolonial feminist biblical interpretation and theology, setting the stage for chapter 5, which examines new ways of thinking about God, ways that have a positive effect on how we view women and empower their leadership in society.

In this chapter, we consider some historic and contemporary examples of faith-fueled feminism. While women's options were limited within the covenantal theology and patriarchal customs of the Ancient Near East, feminist and womanist theologians draw on stories of women in the Bible to forge a theological vision of healing and hope. Strong women leaders in Scripture like Ruth and Orpah offer alternative forms of prophetic female subjectivity. We need to reimagine God and women's leadership in ways that are liberative for all God's children. Intercultural feminist theology provides an important theological trajectory for constructive theology today.

Some Gender Issues Today

Misinterpretation of Scripture has had grave consequences for women. Most women's scholarship globally recognizes the webs of oppression that can even lead women to oppress other women. The cycle of women's oppression needs to stop, whether it be men oppressing women or women oppressing other women. Gender analysis needs to identify cases of gender injustice, developing faith-rooted organizing and advocacy strategies to end gender injustice.[1] By using gender analysis for our theological explorations, we seek to

---

1. Musimbi R. A. Kanyoro, "Engendered Communal Theology," in *Hope Abundant: Third World and Indigenous Women's Theology,* ed. Kwok Pui-lan (Maryknoll, NY: Orbis, 2010), p. 22.

learn about and understand how our societies are organized and how power is used by different groups of people. Feminist theology needs to examine the discrimination as determined by social, economic, religious, and cultural factors.[2] Systematic examination of the subordination of women can give a clearer picture of the history of subordination within culture and religion.

A deeper historical understanding will help in taking steps of removing subordination of women. The term "engendering cultural hermeneutics" reflects the challenges with which African, Asian, and Latina women approach the theology of inculturation from the subject position of being a woman.[3]

Within Asian feminism, Kwok Pui-lan has called for a new interpretive paradigm, which she calls feminist intercultural hermeneutics. She writes that "feminist theology in the past has challenged the tendency to universalize the self and highlighted the difference of the other women because of class, race, age, and sexual orientation. But the notions of the multiple-subject positions of women and the hybridized self would open new possibilities for the overlapping of identities and for mutual engagement. It is important for women working across differences to challenge the binary and exclusionary construct of the self and other, to begin to see the self in the other."[4] Within the trajectory of the European Enlightenment the white self, especially the white male, was forwarded as the universal self. As the civil rights movement and black power movement interrogated the problem of race, the feminist movement interrogated the issue of gender. While Asian women have often been romanticized in the Western imagination, we have argued that this exotic essentialism was a strategy of colonial subjugation. Shaped by postcolonial studies, the feminist intercultural hermeneutic honestly acknowledges the violent shadow-side of Western colonialism and seeks to decolonize Christian theology from the subject position of women of color. Breaking the binary of modernity opens up the possibility of a

---

2. Kanyoro, "Engendered Communal Theology," p. 23.

3. Kanyoro, "Engendered Communal Theology," p. 27.

4. Kwok Pui-lan, "Feminist Theology as Intercultural Discourse," in *The Cambridge Companion to Feminist Theology* (Cambridge: Cambridge University Press, 2002), pp. 23-39. Shaped by her Korean cultural context, biblical scholar Seong Hee Kim in *Mark, Women and Empire: A Korean Postcolonial Perspective* (London: Sheffield Phoenix Press, 2010) offers one important recent example of intercultural feminist hermeneutics applied to the Gospel of Mark. Kim interprets Jesus' redemptive interaction with women in Mark's Gospel, highlighting their subversive moral agency as these prophetic women seek to bring life and flourishing to their communities. From the persistent widow to the women who witnessed the resurrection of Jesus Christ, women in Mark's Gospel embody life-giving leadership.

construction of identity that acknowledges the real difference that race and gender make. Prophetic intercultural hermeneutics offers a set of concepts — the hybridized self, collective trauma, and intercultural solidarity — that can help us better understand the biblical narratives and apply them to the work of healing between men and women today.

Ruth and Naomi: A Feminist Intercultural Analysis

We turn now to examine the relational dynamics between Naomi and her two daughters-in-law, Ruth and Orpah, to illustrate the promise of feminist intercultural hermeneutics. In many ways, Ruth the Moabite is a positive portrait of a woman from a foreign country known for its enmity to Israel and for its "deviant" origins and sexual behavior (Gen. 19:37; Num. 25:1-5). Despite her apparently wanton behavior at the threshing floor, Ruth is never called or referred to as a prostitute (Hebrew: *zonah*). This may be in part because she does not cause Israelite men to "prostitute" themselves before alien deities (Ruth 1:15-16). Ruth, although a foreign woman, is not sexually "loose." She flirts with the upright Boaz but only after being directed to do so by her mother-in-law Naomi (Ruth 3) so that she can continue the line of her husband's "house" in Israel. The risk Ruth poses as a Moabite woman is nullified, as she herself is absorbed into the community of Bethlehem. She is praised by the male authorities who might otherwise have shut out the dangerous foreigner. She marries Boaz and gives him a son, and eventually takes her place as an Israelite ancestor comparable to Tamar (4:12).[5] Foreign women like Ruth are acceptable, "if and when they [are] prepared to forsake their previous ethnic, cultural and religious ties, and to adopt the values and beliefs prevalent in their new environment."[6] To give up one's self-identity in order to be accepted into the other group is a huge sacrifice. As long as the group perceives the foreign women not to be a threat to its own cultural, religious, and societal beliefs, foreign women are either ignored or accepted. As long as the foreign women remain invisible, then there is social harmony in the homogenized culture. However, as soon as the foreign women challenge the dominant cultural and religious norms, they are understood as the deviant one and a threat to the power structure.

---

5. Tamar was Judah's daughter-in-law, the wife of Judah's son Er. See Genesis 38:6-24.

6. Gail Corrington Street, *The Strange Woman: Power and Sex in the Bible* (Louisville: Westminster John Knox, 1997), pp. 71, 72.

Ruth's identity is not one of ethnic conversion, but rather, of "inter-ethnic bonding." "Ruth the Moabite" acts as an antidote to the xenophobia of the postexilic Jewish community.[7] Rather than rejection of the Moabites and acceptance of the Israelites, Ruth's story conjures a vision of ethnic and cultural harmony through the house of David, which claims her as a direct ancestor.[8] Soon after Ruth marries Boaz, the text states that she conceives and bears a son, Obed (Ruth 4:13-17). Ruth's assimilation becomes complete through Obed's transfer to Naomi, the proper Jewish woman, and to Boaz, the Israelite husband.[9] The subsequent birth of the one who will become King David occurs through the lineage of this foreign woman, Ruth.

Foreign women are valuable and their importance should not be ignored or neglected. They are woven into the historical narrative and lineage of the Israelite people. The important role that foreign women and their biracial offspring play in redemptive history unveils the importance of hybridity, that nothing is really pure or "untouched." Purity is a myth perpetuated by those in power to subordinate and subjugate certain groups of people. It has been used in history and in our present time to maintain the status quo. Therefore a deeper analysis and understanding of the foreigners within the biblical stories will add depth to our understanding of how we are to treat foreigners today with dignity and respect.

That Rahab, according to Matthean tradition, is Ruth's other mother-in-law and that she is the Canaanite prostitute who gave birth to Boaz (see Matt. 1:5) further reinforces that the lives of foreign women are intricately woven into Israelite history. During the battle over Jericho, Jericho does fall, "But Rahab the prostitute, with her family and all who belonged to her, Joshua spared. Her family has lived in Israel ever since" (Josh. 6:25). Like her daughter-in-law Ruth, Rahab embodies a foreign woman who crosses over from paganism to monotheism and is rewarded for her theological border crossing. She becomes absorbed into the genealogy of her husband and son and ultimately into the house of King David and Jesus of Nazareth. Like Ruth, Rahab represents those people who occupied the Promised Land before the invasion of the Israelites. This story of Ruth has been taught within the Christian church as a harmless, beautiful story of how a foreign woman's obedience led to the lineage of King David. It is portrayed as a story of love for her mother-in-law,

---

7. William E. Phipps, *Assertive Biblical Women*, Contributions in Women's Studies, vol. 128 (Westport, CT: Greenwood Press, 1992), p. 67.

8. Laura E. Donaldson, "The Sign of Orpah: Reading Ruth through Native Eyes," in *Hope Abundant: Third World and Indigenous Women's Theology*, ed. Kwok Pui-lan, p. 142.

9. Donaldson, "The Sign of Orpah," p. 144.

Naomi, and the extent to which a woman will go to listen to and obey her mother-in-law. In a patriarchal society, it contains all the necessary elements of a woman's redemption: she follows a man who will ultimately provide for her and save her. However, if we view this narrative from a feminist intercultural view we recognize that this biblical story of Ruth is full of oppression and colonial desire. Rayna Green, a Cherokee writer, identifies this story as exemplifying "the Pocahontas Perplex,"[10] the dynamic and often-difficult relationship between the foreigner and the oppressor that also outlines one of Euro-America's most important narratives about Native women.[11]

The stories of Rahab and Ruth can be understood as the Israelite version of the Pocahontas Perplex. In this biblical scenario, Salmon[12] and Boaz stand in for John Smith, and indigenous women Rahab and Ruth stand in for Pocahontas, who forsakes her people. For example, Ruth aligns herself with the men to whom Yahweh had referred when he directed the Israelites to "break down their altars, smash their pillars, burn their Asherah poles with fires, and hew down the idols of their gods, and thus blot out their name from their places" (Deut. 12:3). But Ruth chooses Israel rather than go back to her own people after her husband's death. Orpah is Ruth's sister-in-law and is from Moab. By contrast, Orpah decides to go back home and as a result she is charged with abandonment. Some writers even suggest that she later becomes the mother of Goliath,[13] though this is clearly an example of vilify-

10. Rayna D. Green, "The Pocahontas Perplex," *Massachusetts Review* 16 (1975).

11. The "Pocahontas Perplex" is named for Pocahontas, the daughter of Powhatan, who experienced a significant encounter between Indians and whites. Powhatan Indians capture Captain John Smith and his men while they are exploring the territory around what is now called Jamestown, Virginia. After marching the captured Smith to their town, the Indians lay his head on a large stone and prepare to publicly kill him with their clubs. At that moment, Pocahontas, the favorite daughter of the chief, uses her body as a human shield to prevent Smith's execution. She also intercedes on behalf of the English colonists, who were starving after a long winter, and consequently saves the future of English colonization. Pocahontas decides to go against her own native people and family and help the white colonizers who have come to take over the land. Her actions save the colonialists from starvation and death. Despite the hardships that the Powhatan Indians experience at the hands of the English colonists, they are unable to defeat them but rather enhance the colonizers' mission and task of continuing to oppress the Indians. Cf. Jayachitra Lalitha, "Postcolonial Feminism, the Bible, and the Native Indian Women," in *Evangelical Postcolonial Conversations: Global Awakenings in Theology and Praxis*, ed. Kay Higuera Smith, Jayachitra Lalitha, and L. Daniel Hawk (Downers Grove, IL: InterVarsity Press, 2014), pp. 75-87.

12. Salmon is the son of Nahshon who married Rahab. Salmon is the great-great-grandfather of King David. See 1 Chronicles 2:10-11, Ruth 4:20, 21, Matthew 1:4-5, and Luke 3:32.

13. Donaldson, "The Sign of Orpah," pp. 146, 147.

ing a foreign woman. Therefore, foreign women who do not comply with the dominant culture are vilified and are viewed as dishonorable and unworthy. However, those who, at the expense of forsaking their own people, comply and ally themselves with the dominant culture, are honored, respected, and given a place in society.

A tension and dichotomy exist between various groups of women in the biblical traditions. One group is viewed as "good" and the other is not. This tension works to the advantage of patriarchy, where women are compelled to be against one another rather than work together, as we see in the examples of Eve and Mary, Orpah and Ruth, Mary and Martha, Leah and Rachel, where one woman is juxtaposed with another woman. This paradigm needs to be rectified, as it precludes the ability to be in the continuum or in the middle or in places of interstitial hybridity. A woman should not be demonized by men based on her repressed desire, or seen as a threat that should be expelled from the community. Women are subversive moral agents who are free to cross boundaries and not bound by the circumscriptions imposed on them by patriarchal customs and colonial desire. Dealing with the collective trauma of leaving her people, Ruth courageously confronts the pain in her heart, while being open to a transformative friendship with Naomi and embodying intercultural solidarity.

As one reads Scripture against colonialism, it becomes essential not to dismiss Orpah and impose negativity on her, but to view her in a new light, as claiming her power by leaving a culture that has viewed her as inferior. Assuming that the women are inferior infantilizes them, portraying them as helpless, vulnerable, and unpredictable. This type of projection upon women needs to be eliminated for women to gain true equality within this society. Women need to be understood as courageous, complex persons who can define themselves, create their own futures, and be understood on their own terms. By courageously refusing to go to the culture of her deceased husband, Orpah becomes a model of hope for foreign women, not a selfish and disobedient woman who does not care for her mother-in-law. Orpah is a moral exemplar for Asian women immigrants, who need to fully experience their agency of freedom in hope as they adjust to the challenges of a new future in a new land. Orpah symbolizes hope rather than perversity because she is the one who does not reject her traditions or her sacred ancestors and family. Like Cherokee women who stayed true to their tribe for centuries, Orpah chooses the house of her clan and her spiritual mother over the perceived desire of freedom in joining another culture and family. Cherokee women not only chose the mother's house, they also owned it. Husbands customarily went to live with their wives, and their wives' families,[14] unlike cultures where women give up their birth family to be part of their husbands' families and households. Matriarchy within indigenous cultures sheds new light on how women's subversive moral agency can be embodied in communal life, whether in traditional indigenous cultures or feminist microcultures and intentional communities within the West.

What interpretive pathways open up when we understand women in a different way in light of this biblical narrative of Ruth and Orpah? The text underlines that when a woman chooses her destiny, whatever decision she makes, it needs to be respected. A woman can choose to ignore the patriarchal norms that she has immersed herself in and decide to be bold, pursuing her own destiny. Instead of being criticized, her boldness should be seen as acceptable and honorable. Just as Orpah chose to return to her family and land and Ruth forged intercultural solidarity, we women today can choose to do what is beneficial for us and our community, regardless of the personal cost.

It is time to embrace all aspects of women and to welcome them into positions of leadership in all sectors of society. It is time to resist patriarchy and colonialism in our biblical interpretation, constructive theology, and political economy. Instead, we need to push the patriarchal boundaries that constrain women and work towards the empowerment of people everywhere. Holy Scripture should not be used to subordinate or dominate people, as the good news is for everyone, especially the least and the lost. It is time for us to love and embrace each other as people of Spirit God, so that the all-embracing love of God can be experienced by all people, regardless of their race, gender, and class. Building on feminist intercultural studies of Scripture, feminist theory is an important resource for developing a constructive theology of gender justice.

The Transformative Power of Feminism

The feminist movement offered important theoretical resources to Christian theology to help it become more inclusive, affirming, and transformative. Feminism grew in the 1970s and it became apparent that there was a commonality of women's experience, namely that what was touted as human experience was not in fact inclusive of women's specific experience. Women's

---

14. Donaldson, "The Sign of Orpah," p. 148.

lives were different from men's, and it was precisely this difference that required a rigorous analysis.[15] Faith-rooted feminism requires reimagining
and remaneuvering traditional paradigms and ways of thinking, so that we
can achieve equality between women and men through restoring relationships and dismantling patriarchal structures, building a more just and sustainable world.

Feminist studies are as complex as women are diverse (married/un-
married; virginal/mother; celibate/prostitute; young/old; healthy/dying;
prosperous/destitute; widow/matron, etc.). Therefore, what is good or bad
for one group of women may not be good or bad for another. Many feminist
issues have to do with questions of economic justice and with some variety
of bias. To end subordination of all women, feminists cannot afford unques-
tioned assumptions, orthodoxies, or commitments to positions whose only
virtue is that they are "politically correct."

Starting with our embodied existence and the human soul's insatiable
desire, feminists desire in excess. Feminists desire to create a world in which
women never feel compelled to choose between our gender, family, political,
ethnic, or class identity.[16] Feminists desire women of all backgrounds and
aptitudes to be understood not merely in the roles that they perform, but
as full and whole persons, equal to all men.[17] Women's desire for justice,
equality, and love is based in a deeper desire for God, who is the source of
their life and love.

Within the Christian theological vision, God desires a loving relationship with humanity, calling us to surrender ourselves to divine desire and
to embody an all-embracing love with our fellow humans and the whole
community of creation. Reformed theology is based on the idea of constantly
reforming and refining Christian doctrine so that God's word of grace can
be heard clearly in a particular context. Feminist theologians are aware that
there is no such thing as "timeless truth" when talking about theology or
God. Theological construction is deeply affected by our cultural context(s).

---

15. Hester Eisenstein and Alice Jardine, eds., *The Future of Difference* (New Brunswick,
NJ: Rutgers University Press, 1980), p. xvii.

16. Alison Jagger, ed., *Living with Contradictions: Controversies in Feminist Ethics* (Boul-
der, CO: Westview, 1994), pp. 10-12.

17. Judith Butler, *Undoing Gender* (New York: Routledge, 2004). Butler unveils the social
construction of gender: "Terms such as 'masculine' and 'feminine' are notoriously changeable;
there are social histories for each term; their meanings change radically depending upon
geopolitical boundaries and cultural constraints on who is imagining whom, and for what
purpose" (p. 9).

As cultures change, so do our thoughts, ideas, and perceptions about the faith.

We all read Scripture and interpret Christian tradition from our own cultural perspective, including the long dark shadow of patriarchy that shapes many cultures in both East and West. Kristine A. Culp argues that our Christian witness must be "always reforming, always resisting."[18] Feminist theologians seek to reform Christian doctrine and resist patriarchal practice, in the church, academy, and society. Feminism inspires Christianity to be a faith-rooted movement for racial, gender, economic, and ecological justice.

White Feminist Theology

Feminist theology emerges boldly in the biblical scholarship of Elisabeth Schüssler Fiorenza, who examines the early context of Jesus and his apostles from the experience of women. A German Bible scholar, Schüssler Fiorenza is emblematic of the first wave of white feminist theology. She argues that the central symbol of the movement named after Jesus is the *basileia*[19] or the kingdom of God. The term may express a Jewish religious political vision but it is a very hard term to translate. *Basileia* can mean "kingdom," "kingly realm," or "domain" or it can be rendered as "empire," "monarchy," "kingly rule," or "sovereignty." The word has monarchical and patriarchal notions that were prevalent in that culture. A term that is entrenched in patriarchy requires a new term to help imagine a more egalitarian world.[20] God emancipates women from socioeconomic and biological constraints that force women to remain or stay in prescribed roles in patriarchal culture. Schüssler Fiorenza writes, "As a feminist vision, the *basileia* vision of Jesus calls all women without exception to wholeness and selfhood, as well as to solidarity with those women who are the impoverished, the maimed, and outcasts of our society and church."[21] *Basileia* can be a site for emancipation.

18. Kristine A. Culp, "Always Reforming, Always Resisting," in *Feminist and Womanist Essays in Reformed Dogmatics* (Louisville: Westminster John Knox, 2006), pp. 152-66.

19. Βασιλεια in Roman times was specifically used to refer to the empire and its royal ruler.

20. Elisabeth Schüssler Fiorenza, "Critical Feminist Biblical Studies: Remembering the Struggles, Envisioning the Future," in *New Feminist Christianity: Many Voices, Many Views*, ed. Mary E. Hunt and Diann L. Neu (Woodstock, VT: Skylight Paths, 2012), pp. 86-99, esp. 96ff.

21. Elisabeth Schüssler Fiorenza, *In Memory of Her: A Feminist Theological Reconstruction of Christian Origins* (New York: Crossroad, 1990), p. 153.

It becomes a transitional space where people can experience freedom and liberation away from the bondage of socially, biologically, historically, and religious oppression.

Jesus' teaching of the Kingdom inspires us to search for a more egalitarian embodiment of Christianity that is actively working to overcome the gendered division. Ushering in a more gender-just future demands that we improvise, creating fresh theological language to name the future we desire. It is important to move away from masculine overtones and move towards a feminine tone. For example, theologian Ada María Isasi-Díaz (1943-2012) proposes the language of "kin-dom" as a replacement for Kingdom, which has a patriarchal and militaristic connotation.[22] A more inclusive term will help us conceive and build a more equal world. To begin to create an egalitarian society, one needs to create a new social imaginary.

The heart and soul of the message of the gospel is liberating the oppressed (Isaiah 61; Luke 4). Biblical scholars have raised questions about the paucity of women's presence and leadership in Holy Scriptures.[23] Schüssler Fiorenza understands that women played an active role as leaders in the early Christian movement and became targets within the Greco-Roman cultural context. The androcentrism of the biblical text is a grammatical feature which is common to the culture and must be read against the grain of patriarchy. We must keep in mind the workings of the *ekklesia*. When viewed in light of Greek democracy, including the collective decision-making of the democractic assembly, the *ekklesia* was a regular gathering of early Christians that sought to be inclusive of all people. The inclusive character of the church inspires us to work towards an emancipation and liberation of all people that allows women to become what Schüssler Fiorenza called a "discipleship of equals."

Fiorenza's "discipleship of equals" is helpful in working toward women's liberation. Through the power of the Spirit, women need to reach their full personhood and overcome the barriers that have traditionally limited their roles. In his letter to the Galatians, St. Paul writes, "There is neither Jew nor Greek, there is neither slave nor free, there is neither male nor female; for you are all one in Christ Jesus" (Gal. 3:28), arguing that the mediation of Christ provides the conditions for a society where the full equality of all

22. This is Ada María Isasi-Díaz's replacement for the Bible's "kingdom of God" with the more egalitarian construction "kin-dom" in her article "Solidarity: Love of Neighbor in the 1980s," in *Lift Every Voice: Constructing Christian Theologies from the Underside,* ed. Susan Brooks Thistlethwaite and Mary Potter Engel (San Francisco: Harper, 1990), pp. 31-40, 303-5.

23. Schüssler Fiorenza, *In Memory of Her,* p. 153.

people is affirmed. It is a Christian self-definition that makes no distinction between religion, race, class, or nationality.[24] The embodiment of the egalitarian ideal of the early Christian movement is a goal that we should all be working towards achieving.

This egalitarian movement had many barriers that prevented society from fully realizing this ideal during Second Temple Judaism. The early Christian community lived in tension with the pagan community. Because of the difference in values and cultural codes, the Apostle Paul encouraged Christians not to marry pagans. According to the "household" rules of the time, in a marriage between a Christian and a pagan, the pagan partner had the final decision about divorce.[25] Therefore, Christian women married to pagan men risked whatever economic status their marriage afforded them. Poor women were the most disadvantaged as they were fully dependent on their husbands for economic sustenance. Within this context it is very difficult to fight against a system that already has economic injustices towards women built into its architecture.

Paul's understanding of women in leadership roles was both positive and negative. Paul welcomed Christian equality and freedom as he allowed for an independent lifestyle for women by saying they do not necessarily need to get married. He even encouraged them to live lives of celibate singlehood so they could devote themselves fully to Christ's ministry as he was able to as a single man. However, Paul also restricted women's behaviors in marriage and worship, while men received no such explicit restrictions.[26] These gender inequalities were as much cultural as they were religious.

Thus, it became increasingly difficult for women in the church as restrictions were placed on them. The early Christian vision of "discipleship of equals" attracted many slaves and women, but at the same time caused problems between the church and the dominant Greco-Roman culture. The Household Code was in place, creating the conditions for domination and exploitation. Seeking to embody the egalitarian ideal, early Christians were accused of political subversion through destabilizing the social order.[27] Affirming that in Christ Jesus women and men were one community of equals stood as a direct threat to the patriarchal mores of the time. A woman's identity was based on more than being a faithful wife and nurturing mother.

24. Schüssler Fiorenza, *In Memory of Her*, p. 213.

25. See the Apostle Paul's discussion of the "Household Code" in Ephesians 5:21–6:9 and Colossians 3:18–4:1.

26. Schüssler Fiorenza, *In Memory of Her*, p. 236.

27. Schüssler Fiorenza, *In Memory of Her*, p. 265.

Women were called by God to be leaders in the early Christian movement, agents of reform and resistance.

The egalitarian ideal of the early Christian movement continues to inspire prophetic Christian theology and ethics today. However, ending patriarchy is an ongoing task. Many steps need to be taken to help liberate women. While we seek to dismantle patriarchal structures, we also have to cultivate a revolutionary consciousness. Rosemary Radford Ruether writes, "Liberation comes for women by breaking the chains of false consciousness that hold them in bondage."[28] Many times, women are not fully aware of their chains and the bondages that hold them down. "Breaking the chains of false consciousness" is an important part of forming feminist leaders to work toward healing the division between women and men, ushering in a more gender-just world.

New Global Voices

While white feminism cultivated a revolutionary consciousness among women in the theological academy and faith communities, it often did not deal with the problem of racism. Today, the "typical" Christian no longer lives in Europe or North America but in Africa, Asia, or South America. Thus, feminist theology needs to become anti-racist and intercultural, learning from women of color.

The center of gravity in the world Christian movement has shifted to the global South. Africa has the fastest-growing number of Christians, and by 2025, the Christian population in Africa, estimated to be 635 million, will surpass that of Europe. In 2050, only about one-fifth of the world's three billion Christians will be non-Hispanic white. This demographic shift presents new challenges as well as new opportunities to rethink what a new feminist Christianity should look like, a Christianity that is inclusive of various voices around the world.[29]

Since white feminist theology does not speak for all women, women of the global South need to be given a platform in the church, the academy, and society. As women spoke and addressed issues of women's equality, many

28. Rosemary Radford Ruether, *Gaia & God: An Ecofeminist Theology of Earth Healing* (New York: HarperCollins, 1992), p. 148. Ruether is interpreting the views of Mary Daly in the paragraph in which the quotation occurs.

29. Kwok Pui-lan, "A Postcolonial Feminist Vision for Christianity," in *New Feminist Christianity: Many Voices, Many Views*, ed. Hunt and Neu, p. 3.

women of color saw their ethnicity and specific cultural experiences being dismissed and disregarded by white feminist theologians. They soon realized that white women did not speak for them and they had to do their own critical analysis within their own subgroup.

The irony of our human situation is that in order to attain equality as political persons, we must stress and celebrate our differences of gender, culture, history, language, and economic class. This dialectic is at the heart of a theology of accepting differences, and of going beyond them. It is important to hear the voices of women living in all parts of the globe, especially the most vulnerable. The women who have been excluded from the table need to be invited back, celebrated, and empowered. The women who are viewed as the foreigner need to be embraced and the women who are trapped in subservient roles need to be welcomed so that all women's voices are united as a symphony for love, justice, and peace.

We need to move away from a patriarchal structure of the church, embodying a community of prophetic action for justice, reconciliation, and love. A patriarchal society needs to reexamine itself, as there are forces that are trying to oppose its hegemony and are working towards equality and justice. The patriarchal church will not last, so it needs to be reexamined, dismantled, and reorganized to become a healthy model of equality and social justice. All communities need to work towards social justice for all people. Equality must be achieved at all cost. New voices must be heard and welcomed to the table for deeper discourse and engagement. We cannot claim to have achieved social justice when more than half the people are not welcomed, and are relegated to the children's table.

Feminist theology needs to be at the subversive marginal spaces in the church and culture where new ideas, concepts, and understandings are formulated. Christian women have created and continue to create alternative spaces and developed their own organizations and movements. Women have exercised religious leadership and have impacted the church.[30] Women need to seek, create, and bring forth to the mainstream the different subversive spaces so that liberative spaces can exist for them.

The church as a movement will constantly reform itself. As it reforms, it must adjust to different circumstances, injustices, and situations.[31] This continual improvisation is necessary for the survival of the church. We need to listen to some of the different voices from around the globe and imple-

---

30. Kwok Pui-lan, "A Postcolonial Feminist Vision for Christianity," p. 5.
31. Kwok Pui-lan, "A Postcolonial Feminist Vision for Christianity," p. 6.

ment theological methods to work towards freedom, liberation, and justice. As the church moves to the global South, we need to recognize the various gender issues that exist in different parts of the world and act upon them to work towards a just world. As an Asian American feminist, I will explore what it means to be an Asian American woman as portal to a prophetic, feminist, intercultural future for Christianity.

Asian American Women

The terms "Asian" and "Asian American" are so common in the language of the Western world that we may forget that these terms are social and cultural constructs, arising out of particular historical stages of political struggles. The term "Asian" has an identifiable set of meanings: shared colonial and patriarchal history, multiple religious traditions, and rich, diverse cultures, with memories of immense suffering and poverty. One must keep all these struggles at the forefront as one engages in what we term Asian American women's theology.[32]

The term "Asian American" arose during the civil rights era in order to indicate inter-Asian group relationships, to identify this growing hybridity, and to mobilize a political movement for justice for all people of Asian descent. Thus the term "Asian American" came into usage out of a particular historical moment to bring to light a visible racial group trying to survive and thrive as racial minorities.[33] It is a term that emerged out of a difficult political struggle and social necessity.

From the time of its emergence, the terms "Asian" and "Asian American" have carved a space for themselves within the political, social, cultural, and religious sphere in North America. Within the field of theology, "Asian" and "Asian American" have been useful for creating a space for people of Asian descent who have experiences and cultures that are different from the dominant white Euro-American culture. Yet the terms "should not be essentialized or homogenized so as to hinder critical reflections on diversity" within the community, which is large and diverse.[34] This community

---

32. Kwok Pui-lan, *Postcolonial Imagination & Feminist Theology* (Louisville: Westminster John Knox Press, 2005), p. 24.

33. Kwok Pui-lan and Rachel A. R. Bundang, "PANAAWTM Lives!" *Journal of Feminist Studies in Religion* 21, no. 2 (2005): 149.

34. This excerpt is from "The Future of PANAAWTM Theology," written by Kwok Pui-lan, Seung Ai Yang, and Rita Nakashima Brock in July 2004 and is available at www.panaawtm

originated from the vast areas of South Asia and East Asia, which are different from one another politically, culturally, religiously, and historically. The diversity of Asian Americans must be noted, therefore, and recognized not only in general conversation but also in the particular exchanges of theological discourse and study. This diversity of Asian Americans is something to be celebrated rather than discouraged, welcomed rather than shunned. And it takes particular forms with women.

When Asian theologians call themselves Asian, they draw attention to their part in the history of groups of people who emigrated from Asia, especially China, Indo-China, Korea, Japan, Indonesia, and the Philippines. The term also references their participation in the myths, languages, and cuisines of Asian cultures. As Asian Americans, they see the world and themselves simultaneously from a particular vantage and disadvantage point. Asian American identity suggests a certain solidarity with the struggles and problems of a certain people. In the struggle, solidarity forms, and this solidarity works toward developing a better community, society, and world.

Asian American women are remarkably diverse socially, religiously, and culturally. In order to develop a meaningful and liberative theological voice, they address, critique, and embrace the hybrid experiences that inform their being and their theologies. Drawing on the deepest wells of our Asian cultural traditions, Asian feminist theologians are committed to collaborative theological construction for a more just and sustainable world.

What does it mean to be an Asian woman living across the ocean from her motherland in the multicultural and multinational society that is the United States? Certainly, not all women share the same experience of "being a woman." Even if all women are oppressed by sexism, we cannot automatically conclude that the sexism all women experience is the same,[35] as history, culture, and religion create different forms of sexism. Due to the diversity of women's experience, it is important to undermine any reductionist, essentializing definition of "women's oppression" as a universal female experience.[36] The experiences of Asian American women are different from Asian women

---

.org as cited by Rita Nakashima Brock, "Pacific and Asian Women's Theologies," in *Feminist Theologies: Legacy and Prospect,* ed. Rosemary Radford Ruether (Minneapolis: Fortress Press, 2007), p. 46.

35. Elizabeth Spelman, *Inessential Women: Problems of Exclusion in Feminist Thought* (Boston: Beacon Press, 1988), p. 14.

36. Ien Ang, "'I'm a Feminist but . . .': 'Other' women and Postnational Feminism," in *Feminist Postcolonial Theory: A Reader,* ed. Reina Lewis and Sara Mills (New York: Routledge, 2003), p. 191.

across the Pacific because the context is so different and expansive. Thus, it is important to recognize the difficulty in developing a liberating Asian American women's theology that reflects the experiences of and addresses all Asian American women.

Overall, Asian Americans who settle in North America experience a variety of difficulties. They are often viewed as not being part of North America even if they were born here or have been here for several generations. They are often never fully welcomed into the mainstream culture and context. Asian American studies has a name for this syndrome, that of the "perpetual foreigner."

Many Asian American women's social location as a *perpetual foreigner* is further marginalized by being a female who has to endure both the patriarchal attitudes of her Asian ethnicity and those of her U.S. context.[37] Being cast as a *perpetual foreigner* gives an uneasy feeling and makes one feel like a person on the run. No matter how hard one tries to feel that this is one's country and part of one's heritage, being viewed as a *perpetual foreigner* makes it hard for a person to call the U.S. home. The result is that many Asian American women feel caught in between their Asian ancestry and the new country and culture that do not accept them as their own. It is not uncommon for such women to say they feel like a lost child, like an orphan, living between spaces where one feels neither accepted nor welcomed.

For this reason, Asian American women theologians seek new ways of doing theology that will bear their true and complex identities. Asian American women need to lift up the multilingual nature of Asian traditions and begin new lines of theological inquiry by rearticulating theology through the liberating language of myths, stories, histories, and the rituals of women.[38]

The multireligious aspect of the Asian American community is very important to take into consideration when one engages in theology. Choi Hee An sees four different religions informing the religious experience of Korean woman: Shamanism, Buddhism, Confucianism, and Christianity.[39] Thus, religious pluralism is the matrix through which Korean and Korean Americans theologize. Given the religious diversity of Asia, Asian feminist theology is articulated in a multifaith modality.

37. Gale A. Yee, "Where Are You Really From? An Asian American Feminist Biblical Scholar Reflects on Her Guild," in *New Feminist Christianity: Many Voices, Many Views,* ed. Hunt and Neu, p. 79.

38. Kwok Pui-lan, *Introducing Asian Feminist Theology* (Cleveland: Pilgrim, 2000), p. 35.

39. Choi Hee An, *Korean Women and God: Experiencing God in a Multi Religious Colonial Context* (Maryknoll, NY: Orbis, 2005), pp. 9-44.

Recognizing the sacredness of our non-Christian historical and religious texts reminds us to develop a rigorous multifaith hermeneutic. In the context of religious plurality, we need to encourage theological authenticity, allowing for the emergence of new concepts and theological constructions. It is this kind of growth that will guide Asian American women to deeper understandings of personhood in touch with the divine Spirit. Asian American cultural, social, and religious diversity can add to the richness of the theological discourse, which is transient, permeable, and malleable.

We Asian American feminist theologians need to join other Asian theologians in highlighting the impact of socially entrenched cultural myths, rituals, and traditions on women's roles in society. Furthermore, we need to critically analyze the cultural and religious dimensions of oppression that impact the lives of Asian American women. We need to assess Christianity's role in supporting colonialism and patriarchy, because political independence for many of us happened only a generation ago.[40] We cannot blindly accept truths from Western society as the "truth." We must recognize that colonialism, imperialism, and white hegemony pervade Western theology and we must not take for granted that they are good for us. We must recognize that human greed has influenced Western theology. Instead of simply adapting that theology for our use, we need to seek ways of doing theology that fight against the destructive powers of colonialism, white supremacy, patriarchy, and racism. Theology that further perpetuates these systemic injustices is not good news to the poor (Luke 4:18).

Theology must be in touch with our own Asian American experience. If it is not, it is not and cannot be a living theology.[41] Korean theologian Chung Hyun Kyung offers a vision of the Spirit of God that draws on the spiritual legacies of Asian religious traditions. Chung's book *Struggle to Be the Sun Again* is a classic in Asian feminist theology. Given the pain and suffering of Asian women, the Spirit of God provides the foundation for a prophetic theology of healing and hope.

In "Holy Spirit — Renew the Whole Creation" delivered at the seventh assembly of the World Council of Churches in Canberra, Australia, in 1991, Chung Hyun Kyung advances pneumatology as a pathway for interfaith peacemaking and creation care. She proclaimed: "I rely on the compassionate God who weeps with us for life in the midst of the cruel destruction of

---

40. Kwok Pui-lan, *Postcolonial Imagination & Feminist Theology*, p. 152.

41. Jung Young Lee, *Marginality: The Key to Multicultural Theology* (Minneapolis: Fortress Press, 1995), p. 1.

life. The spirit of this compassionate God has been always with us from the time of creation."[42] When people cry out for life and liberation, the compassionate God is faithful and just to heal our wounds and bring us hope.

For Chung Hyun Kyung, Asian women's theology is a "cry, plea and invocation" to God in search of healing and justice from sexism and other inhibitions placed on women due to their race and gender.[43] It is an embodied, critical reflection on Asian American women's experiences, aimed at bringing about a community of harmony, peace, and love.

Asian American feminist theology is inductive and it does not begin with the Bible or Christian doctrines, but with the real and raw stories of the life experiences of women. The life experiences become a text to be exegeted as an important source of theology. Chung writes, "The text of God's revelation was, is, and will be written in our bodies and our people's everyday struggle for survival and liberation."[44] Asian feminist theology tells about the tremendous pain of sexism and racial discrimination that women bear. Therefore, theology must listen to women's stories and experiences of how they come to know God through their own personal and everyday experiences. This is a dynamic and experiential way of doing theology that is much closer to the experiences witnessed to in Holy Scripture.

Approaching God through spirituality is a way for people to come to know God by experiencing God[45] rather than through exegesis and theological discussion alone. This is an alternative to a typical modern Western method based solely on analysis, debate, and philosophical arguments.[46] Since Western theological methods often perpetuate patriarchy, colonialism, empire building, and racial discrimination, Asian feminist theologians have sought alternative forms of theologizing that are life-affirming and justice-seeking, animated by compassionate love.

While Chung Hyun Kyung highlights the centrality of the spirit of

---

42. Chung Hyun Kyung, "Come Holy Spirit — Renew the Whole Creation," *Signs of the Spirit: Official Report, Seventh Assembly, World Council of Churches,* ed. Michael Kinnamon (Grand Rapids: Eerdmans, 1991), pp. 39; 38-47.

43. Chung Hyun Kyung, *Struggle to Be the Sun Again* (Maryknoll, NY: Orbis, 1990), p. 99.

44. Chung Hyun Kyung, *Struggle to Be the Sun Again,* pp. 99-101.

45. Masao Takenaka, *God Is Rice: Asian Cultures and Christian Faith* (Geneva: World Council of Churches, 1986), p. 9.

46. Veli-Matti Kärkkäinen, "A Mapping of Asian Liberative Theology in Quest for the Mystery of God Amidst the Minjung Reality and World Religions," in *Asian Contextual Theology for the Third Millennium: Theology of Minjung in Fourth-Eye Formation,* ed. Paul S. Chung, Veli-Matti Kärkkäinen, and Kim Kyoung Jae (Eugene, OR: Pickwick, 2007), p. 109.

compassionate love within Asian feminist theology, W. Anne Joh's theological scholarship goes much deeper in investigating the spiritual psychodynamics of love. Joh's *Heart of the Cross: A Postcolonial Christology* offers a prophetic theology of love that is empowering for women and men trying to do the difficult emotional work of loving each other amid the alienation that is produced by consumer capitalism, and the legacy of violence of its colonial past. Drawing on the deep wells of Korean culture, Joh uses the Korean term *jeong* as way of describing the multiplicity of love in conversation with psychoanalytic theory. After Freud and Jung, we consider both the conscious and unconscious dimension of human existence, as we seek to understand and cultivate a more whole personhood. Joh finds the Bulgarian-French feminist philosopher Julia Kristeva a helpful interlocutor in constructing a theology of love. Kristeva uses the term "abjection" to describe acute suffering within humans, a suffering that sometimes seems unbearable with our individual psyches.

To engage the psychic problem of abjection, Joh appropriates the Korean term *jeong*, which describes the deep relationality between people, objects, and concepts within Korean culture. *Jeong* emphasizes love and connectedness, the vulnerability of one's self and one's heart. In the vulnerability of one's heart, one can still maintain a binding relationship with others due to *jeong*. This "sticky" love acknowledges that our human identity is deeply interconnected with the lives and love of our family, friends, colleagues, and even enemies.

Joh's insightful theological intervention is to bring together *jeong* and *abjection* in dialectical synergy focused on the cross of Christ. Joh writes: "On the cross there is a simultaneous presence of both the horror of violence as well as radical form of inclusive love, which I will link to *jeong*."[47]

Jeong captures the interconnectedness of people. *Jeong* offers an important resource for helping people to enter their places of pain and trauma, with the nurturing, supportive love of others whom they are connected to. The Song of Solomon says, "Place me like a seal over your heart, like a seal on your arm; for love is as strong as death" (8:6). *Jeong* is the affection, love, and connection between people that endures till death. *Jeong* is a frequently used word among friends and family when communicating one's connectedness or disconnectedness to each other. When a relationship should by rights be broken due to abuse and pain, often people attribute its continuance to

---

47. W. Anne Joh, *Heart of the Cross: A Postcolonial Christology* (Louisville: Westminster John Knox, 2006), p. xxv.

jeong. No matter how hard we try, we can't get away from each other. To love someone is to carry them with us throughout our life, whether in practice or memory, conscious or unconscious.

This Korean understanding of love and affection is a connectedness that brings one into an indissoluble intimacy with another. *Jeong* cannot be easily destroyed, eliminated, or taken away. It is a powerful force that sustains the bonds between people. Even though feelings for each other may fade over time, *jeong* keeps people connected.

Jeong is "sticky."[48] It holds together. It is a deep, intimate bond. When we experience love for someone, we are in some sense stuck to them. We become psychically dependent on each other, even when relationships are not healthy and whole. *Jeong* means we are stuck with each other.

It expresses the complex entanglement of emotion, conceptualized through Korean culture. Koreans are a passionate people who experience deep emotions and feelings of both love and pain in their heart of hearts. W. Anne Joh's work has deepened my understanding of the pyscho-dynamics of love and how our love is mediated through the love of Jesus. Through meditating on the suffering love of Jesus Christ, we are better able to see the self in the Other, opening ourselves up to a deeper intimacy in our relationships and wholeness in our communal life together.

While love is expressed through *jeong* in Korean, pain is expressed through the term *han. Jeong* and *han* express two dimensions of human existence that are inextricably linked in the human heart and experience of love. In my book, *Colonialism, Han, and the Transformative Spirit,* I discuss the suffering of people and the community of creation through the term *han.*[49] Given the cultural hegemony of the West through colonization, Asian Americans must acknowledge their painful wounds in order to be liberated to love. I find the term *jeong* can be a helpful window into working towards reconciliation between the oppressor and the oppressed, the colonizer and the colonized, women and men. As I seek to create the conditions for reconciliation between women and men, *jeong* shows that our strength to love must include an understanding of our powerful connectedness to each other.

Korean terms like *jeong* and *han* help us speak about the sexism we experience in our lives. *Jeong* and *han* give us new terminology to talk about the pain and love we carry in our hearts and community. Sexism deals with

48. Joh, *Heart of the Cross*, p. 121.

49. Grace Ji-Sun Kim, *Colonialism, Han, and the Transformative Spirit* (New York: Palgrave Macmillan, 2013).

gender roles, in which femininity and masculinity are assumed to be clearly delineated. The structural and regulatory forces of sexism effectively curb any desire to transgress boundaries of the binary of gender.

An anti-essentialist view should be adopted, as a person is not born a female but becomes one, and a person is not born as a woman of color but becomes one.[50] How society perceives and treats others will affect how we treat women and people of color. Labels keep minorities marginalized and subordinated. They keep certain people "in their place" and maintain the status quo.

These Western Eurocentric terms are social constructs created to separate the center from the marginalized, to keep the powerful from the powerless and the dominant from the subordinated. The understanding of color has become a useful construct by those who are born fairer skinned because it has been used politically, religiously, and socially by white people to retain their power. Therefore for many Asian American women, the color of their skin has become politicized and is often used to marginalize them. It has been also used to create tension among and between Asian American women, who vary in skin tone. Such stereotyping is used to keep women subordinated and subjugated. Furthermore, gender is "raced," as people of various racial and ethnic groups experience gender differently.

A wider conversation among scholars from all different racial and ethnic backgrounds is therefore needed today. Asian American women understand their gendered selves differently from other women of color. As a result, women's experience cannot be universalized and feminist theological vision should take seriously the ways in which becoming gendered infiltrates how we understand what it means to be equal human beings.[51] Since each racialized woman's experience of patriarchy is distinct and particular, every person needs to be understood, valued, and accepted as a unique child of God.

Structural and systemic oppression based on a racial hierarchy that perpetuates white power and privilege is part of North American history and our present reality. Racism and white supremacy prompted the colonization of this land and its people. White colonists defined who was more or less human, who had power and who did not, and in many ways these definitions were used by the dominant group to marginalize particular peoples, sustain the dominant identity, and create essentialist metanarratives about "them"

---

50. W. Anne Joh, "Race, Class, Gender, Sexuality," in *New Feminist Christianity: Many Voices, Many Views,* ed. Hunt and Neu, p. 55.

51. Joh, "Race, Class, Gender, Sexuality," p. 56.

and "us."[52] They pit one people of color against another group to perpetuate the marginalization and subordination of them all and to bring division. They perpetuate the Otherness of women and the racial stereotyping that continually endures in our society. White supremacy perpetuates the status quo, which benefits white, dominant, privileged people. Preserving and empowering the white structures makes people of color — and particularly women of color — deviant and problematic within society and culture. While women of color often internalize inferiority based on the white male power structures, we are called away from ways of thinking and life choices that are ultimately self-destructive and called to love ourselves and embrace the Other because the Spirit of God flows through all of us and the whole community of creation.

Concluding Thoughts

The history of women's oppression and subordination is long and deeply embedded in our culture, religion, and psyche. The subordination of women is already clearly evident in the Ancient Near East, as women were often treated as extensions of the men in the house and their primary purpose was to be faithful wives and childbearing mothers, bringing male heirs to honor their husbands. If women were unable to perform these familial functions they were viewed as unworthy. Women's sexuality was kept under tight control. Any form of breaking the marital covenant with her husband would be punished, often resulting in death. The egalitarian vision of the early Christian community, a discipleship of equals, created the conditions for women leaders to use their gifts and graces to help build a more just and loving church community and work to transform unjust social structures.

In the twentieth century, the feminist movement offered a focused, vigorous critique of masculine discourse, while offering a strategy to dismantle patriarchal social structures. The feminist movement inspired feminist theology, which became a powerful force for social transformation within the church. Feminist theology from its emergence worked towards women's liberation from debilitating patriarchal norms. As feminist theology made inroads within a male-dominated theological discourse, women of color began to recognize the limitations of feminist theology written by white women of European descent.

52. Joh, "Race, Class, Gender, Sexuality," p. 57.

Drawing on the spiritual legacies of Korean culture, Asian feminist theologians like Chung Hyun Kyung, W. Anne Joh, and myself have developed new theological paradigms that are life-giving, sustaining, and empowering to women, their male allies, and all people who are struggling to survive and flourish today. Women of color are increasingly leading the struggle to trouble the waters and heal the world. As Asian American women theologians work towards a society free of racism and sexism, we seek to reimagine our God who is leading us to freedom.

CHAPTER 5

Spirit God and Shalom Justice

God meets us in the margins. Since God dwells among the disinherited and dispossessed, we need to follow God's Spirit to the places of darkness and despair. The same Spirit that anointed the Hebrew prophets and Jesus who cared for the marginalized anoints us to be Spirit-filled prophets today. It is God the Spirit who gives the marginalized life and the moral courage to follow Jesus, to push against the constraints of marginalization, moving toward spaces of deep solidarity in a horizon of hope.

In this chapter, I develop an understanding of the Divine as Spirit God who empowers and liberates the marginalized. After discussing the situation of marginalization as the context of understanding the Spirit in Scripture and society, I analyze Spirit discourse in continental philosophy. While moving toward a more immanent understanding of the Spirit, Hegel and Nietzsche are still participants in the Western civilization project. It is vital today that we move away from the Western colonial captivity of the Spirit and reclaim the Spirit's vital work in indigenous, non-Western cultures, especially in the experiences of women.

Bringing together the vitalism of the Asian concept *Chi* and the biblical call to justice, Spirit God is a way to imagine God that captures the infinite energies of divine love that are the divine essence and permeate the community of creation. Our source of love and life, Spirit God heals the wound between women and men, blacks and whites, and every shade in between. As vessels of the Spirit, we bear prophetic witness to Spirit God, embodying shalom in and for the whole community of creation.

Theologizing from the Margins

In a broken world of misgivings, misrepresentations, and misunderstandings among the diverse human family created by God, we need to go to the margins to create a pathway toward healing and hope. As a poor Jewish peasant teacher from Nazareth, Jesus was marginalized and stood in solidarity with the marginalized throughout the Roman Empire. Jesus' incarnate life, kingdom teaching, and crucifixion on a Roman cross unveil God as a lover of justice, peace, and liberation.

While Jesus was a revolutionary, when Christianity became the official religion of the Roman Empire Jesus becomes reimagined as a supporter of empire. Classical theism in the West often emphasizes God as an Almighty Father. This patriarchal concept of God has often been wielded in destructive ways throughout the history of Western Christianity. Through European colonization, too often guided by a patriarchal image of God, indigenous cultures have been dominated and destroyed, Africans have been enslaved, Asians have been exploited, women have been abused, and the poor have been economically exploited. The male God image mediated through the Almighty Father has often had negative conscious and unconscious effects on women, especially women of color. God the Almighty Father has often been a theological tool used by white men of European descent to subjugate women and people of color.

Those in power often preach a gospel of an all-powerful God that is disconnected from the poor's daily struggles through which their community resists oppression and struggles to achieve fullness of life. The God of the privileged does not exist in the margins but rather remains in the center, safe and secure from all alarm. The God of the center may be spoken of in the margins, but never comes to live there, in the dire circumstances of dirt-poverty. The direct movement of coming towards the marginalized people with the intention of building deep solidarity with them as they "enflesh freedom" is an affront to the God of the privileged center.[1]

Asian Americans have been relegated to the margins of society. They have been neglected, discriminated against, and stereotyped since they arrived in North America. As discussed in Chapter 2, they have suffered and endured under the "model minority" myth. Yet as Asian American women seek the Divine in their marginalized existence, they realize that they are

---

1. See womanist theologian M. Shawn Copeland's *Enfleshing Freedom: Body, Race and Being* (Minneapolis: Fortress Press, 2009).

not alone. God has not abandoned them but, as the life of Jesus reveals, God exists in the margins with them.

Pushed to the margins, Asian immigrants have an attentive sensitivity to experiences of oppression. The deep wounds of Asian American women are raw and painful within a patriarchal world. As a Canadian of Korean descent teaching theology in the United States, I have experienced the negative effects of structural racism and patriarchy in my own life. It is through entering my own places of pain that my theological vision of healing and hope has emerged. The places of pain in our heart need to be honestly acknowledged and shared with others so that healing can occur and we can do our part to work for a loving, just, and sustainable world.

Theologizing from the margins entails acknowledging the deep wounds of our humanity. As Peter Heltzel writes, "Only through entering the pain of our deepest wounds will humanity heal and become whole once again."[2] It is through the healing power of God's Spirit that we can see the restoration of broken relationships and the rebuilding of broken systems.

While Asian immigrants experience marginality, it is a condition of oppression experienced by all people of color, including Native Americans, African Americans, and Latino Americans. As Jung Young Lee argues, in the "experience of marginality we find the common cord that gathers our ethnic and cultural differences into a mutual understanding, and can help to transform North America to be truly what it was meant to be: a nation of immigrants freed for the pursuit of happiness for all people."[3] Affirming the gifts and graces of our different cultures, we need to work together toward a prophetic intercultural future.

Traditional theologies posit that the God of the Center reaches out to the marginalized with inclusive love. Yet, in such theologies the center remains central command, determining who will be included and excluded. This creates an obvious structural disadvantage for those on the periphery. In many ways, church politics and theology still rely upon modern, masculine epistemologies[4] of the center and continue to institute

---

2. Peter Goodwin Heltzel, *Resurrection City: A Theology of Improvisation* (Grand Rapids: Eerdmans, 2012), p. 13.

3. Jung Young Lee, *Marginality: The Key to Multicultural Theology* (Minneapolis: Augsburg Fortress, 1995), p. 27.

4. Steven V. Sprinkle, "A God at the Margins? Marcella Althaus-Reid and the Marginality of LGBT People," *Journal of Religious Leadership* 8 (2009): 78, 79. Cf. Ivone Gebara, "Knowing Our Knowing: The Issue of Epistemology," in *Longing for Running Water* (Minneapolis: Fortress Press, 1999), pp. 19-66.

them.[5] Epistemologies of the center only perpetuate the status quo and keep power with those who are at the center. This center epistemology needs to be challenged and redefined so that the marginalized can claim their rightful seats at the table and voices in the dialogue.

We may ask, "What is the center?," as it appears to be an important question to those who are pushed to the margins. Marcella Althaus-Reid answers, "What we call the discourses of the centre are just the edited texts of the rich and powerful, hegemonically organizing people's lifestyles with promises of salvation which exclude, for instance, economic salvation."[6] Althaus-Reid unveils the ways in which "discourses of the center" are used to legitimatize power and privilege. The powerful define and maintain "the center" to their political and economic benefit. This has happened throughout history, and without clear opposition it will continue to go unchallenged.

It is important to recognize this collision of power and position in all aspects of society where the dominant are planted in the center, and those who do not "fit" into the dominant realm because of different physical looks, sexuality, gender, or class are pushed to the edges. This is disheartening in all aspects, as the marginalized are prevented from enriching the center and the center loses the benefits of diversity. When a homogeneous society resists change, there is no growth, modification, celebration, and reimagination, with the result that the society finds it lacks resources needed to survive dramatic changes in their environment. Such resistance to change at the center leads to stagnation and inactivity.

5. An example of "peripheral" epistemologies might be found in the Preface to an edition of David Brainerd's Journal, written by the Honourable Society (in Scotland) for Propagating Christian Knowledge (and not by Brainerd himself.) This Preface describes Brainerd's Indians ". . . who have for many ages dwelt in the grossest darkness and heathenism, and are brought to a cheerful subjection to the government of our divine Redeemer, who from generation to generation have remained the voluntary slaves of 'the prince of darkness.'" David Brainerd, *David Brainerd's Journal in Two Parts,* in *The Life and Diary of David Brainerd* (Peabody, MA: Hendrickson, Kindle Edition, 2013), location 5260 of 7127.

It also "assumes" a centrist morality when it describes "those that were sunk in the most degenerate state of human nature . . ." with the result that they ". . . at once, not only renounce those barbarous customs they had been inured to from their infancy, but surprisingly transformed into the character of real and devout Christians." Note that this is the opinion of Europeans, writing in Europe, not of Brainerd himself. Brainerd did not have universal success. The first entry in his journal speaks of his being disheartened by failed attempts in preaching to Indians around the Susquehanna River. Brainerd did find that these Indians often raised trivial and irrelevant objections. One might wish we knew what these *trivial* objections were.

6. Marcella Althaus-Reid, "The Divine Exodus of God," in *God: Experience and Mystery,* ed. Werner Jeanrod and Christoph Theobald, *Concilium* 2001/1 (London: SCM Press, 2001), p. 32.

Therefore, we need to ask the question, "Why does the center resist change?" It is due to their desire to maintain their power, property, and prestige. It is like people who anxiously climb to the top of the social and economic ladder only to see that it is not so grand after all. While rich with political influence, the elite within the consumer capitalist system are often depressed because they are unable to connect with the Divine; nor are they deeply connected with caring for those who are most in need. Yet, people seem to like being at the top and so people climb and cling to the top when it is reached, trying to hold onto their perch on the pyramid. Those at the top are understandably eager to maintain their power — even once they realize it can result in the loss of relationships, love, and spirit. A position of power means political influence and financial security, but often at the expense of moral height and spiritual depth.

The power elites of our society use two intentional strategies to subjugate the marginalized: 1) blaming the victim and 2) cultural subjugation. We hear the elite say "poor people are poor because they do not 'pull themselves up by their bootstraps.'" First, if poverty is conceived as merely an individual problem, rather than a system of economic oppression, poor individuals become easy targets of ridicule by the rich. The rich often see the poor as objects of their charity, instead of subversive subjects who can claim their power and organize their communities to become more equitable, sustainable, and just. Secondly, popular culture functions as a way of distracting the poor from their dire plight. From reality television to video games, alienated and underemployed individuals are often seduced by an entertainment culture that distracts them from overcoming the obstacles that prevent them from flourishing. Through these and other strategies the wealthy, white elite maintain their power, while the poor continue to struggle to survive.

How can we discuss the marginalized without exacerbating their victimized state, for certainly we must not reduce the victim to become a new Other? We must not play "blame the victim" with groups of people that society marginalizes.[7] This is a frequently encountered problem, as we tend to represent "Others" rather than paying attention to their own self-representation, so it is a matter that we must take seriously in our theological discourse.[8] Theology itself has led to discrimination and marginalization

7. William Ryan, *Blaming the Victim* (New York: Random House, 2010).

8. David Batstone, Eduardo Mendieta, Lois Ann Lorentzen, and Dwight N. Hopkins, eds., *Liberation Theologies, Postmodernity, and the Americas* (London: Routledge, 1997), p. 16.

of many groups of people. This needs to stop if we are to take seriously our commandment to love one another and celebrate our God-given diversity.

People who are oppressed often internalize the ideals and values of the oppressor. As a result, they live a life of continual oppression and subordination. This is more frequent with women who are more likely to accept their roles as subordinate due to their belief in Scripture as the revealed word of God. Because they have internalized and accepted a subordinate role, women can at times be highly resistant to feminist interpretations and accept the patriarchal understanding of Scripture and God.[9] This resistance to feminist and other interpretations that use Scripture to challenge the status quo needs to be analyzed and we need to develop new strategies for reaching out to women leaders, providing them with the tools to claim the power they have. Theologizing from the margins demands an intercultural hermeneutic that interprets Scripture from "the preferential option for the poor."[10]

The Spirit and Shalom Justice

The preferential option of the poor challenges both our interpretation of Scripture and our conception of God. Within the Hebrew Bible, God the Spirit is a primary way of conceiving divinity. In order to build a biblical foundation for my conception of the Spirit, I will always seek to understand the Spirit discourse in the Bible from the subject position of those on the margins.

From the creation of the world to the anointing of the prophets, the Israelites identified this Spirit as *ruach,* and understood its power, strength, and life-giving presence. God's Spirit rests upon the people Israel, a people of suffering sojourners often on the margins of oppressive economic orders like ancient Egypt. God tells Moses to go to Pharaoh and tell him that the Israelites should be liberated from slavery. As Moses leads Israel out of Egypt, he calls on *ruach* to separate the sea so the Hebrew people can escape the closing clutch of Pharaoh's army.

9. Monica Jyotsna Melanchthon, "Dalit Women and the Bible: Hermeneutical and Methodological Reflections," in *Hope Abundant: Third World and Indigenous Women's Theology,* eds. Kwok Pui-lan (Maryknoll, NY: Orbis, 2010), p. 103.

10. Gustavo Gutiérrez, "Preferential Option for the Poor," in *Gustavo Gutiérrez: Essential Writings,* ed. James B. Nickoloff (Maryknoll, NY: Orbis, 1996), pp. 143-46. Cf. Alexia Salvatierra and Peter Goodwin Heltzel, "Our Starting Place, the Call of the Poor," in *Faith-Rooted Organizing: Mobilizing the Church in Service to the World* (Downers Grove, IL: InterVarsity, 2014), pp. 42-64.

The presence of God was understood as *Shekinah* and they embraced its daily presence with them. This was no doubt a strong presence of God for them as they wandered in the desert, searching for a place to reside and trying to build their own identity as a people and a nation. "By day the Lord went ahead of them in a pillar of cloud to guide them on their way and by night in a pillar of fire to give them light, so that they could travel by day or night" (Exod. 13:21). A great prophet of Israel, Moses is a liberator and a law-giver. God gives Moses the Law to be a spiritual and moral guide to the people Israel (Exodus 20).

"Remember the Sabbath day by keeping it holy" is an important commandment, as practicing the Sabbath gives the people of God the opportunity to rest in the Lord, worship the Lord, and renew the community of creation (Exod. 20:8). According to the Torah rules of the sabbath Jubilee year: (1) slaves are to be freed, (2) debts are to be canceled, (3) the land is to lie fallow, and (4) the land (wealth) is to be returned or redistributed to its original holders (Lev. 25:23-24).

This vision of a sabbath Jubilee year offers a bold vision of *oikonomia tou theou,* the economy of God. The word "economics" is derived from the Greek word *oikonomia,* meaning household management. While there is division and injustice in the community of creation, the people of God are called to bring God's peace and justice to the world, being Spirit-led agents of healing and hope.

Shalom justice is the heart and soul of the vision of Hebrew Scripture. "Shalom justice is rooted in a worshipful acknowledgment that God the Creator is present in all creation and is graciously working for the redemption and reconciliation of the world . . . Shalom — communal and ecological well-being — is the outcome of the people of God embodying the justice and righteousness of God," writes Peter Heltzel.[11] When we do something wrong to one another, we are also doing wrong to God. God is in all of us.

Injustice is a violation against God. The social dimension of *mishpat* (justice) included many different types of social relations and referred to the relationship among Israelites within their tribe, the relationships between the tribes, their relationship with other nations, and their relationship with the community of creation. When nations would deal unjustly with Israel, Israel would cry out through passionate prayers for God's justice to be man-

---

11. Peter Goodwin Heltzel, "Shalom Justice: The Prophetic Imperative," in *Resurrection City,* pp. 22-23; cf. Michael Welker, "The Promised Spirit of Peace and Justice," in *God the Spirit* (Minneapolis: Fortress Press, 1994), pp. 108-82.

ifest. It was God, and God alone, who was the judge of the social dealings among the nations.

In Israelite history, whenever the people of God did not care for the marginalized, Israel was guilty of injustice and subject to God's judgment. God reminded Israel constantly of their obligation to care for those in need (Amos 5:21-24; Mic. 6:6-8; Isa. 1:17). Judges and kings were judged by how they treated the weakest and most vulnerable in society. Deborah sat under a palm tree, where the people came to her for *mishpat*[12] (Judg. 4:5). So highly valued was this *mishpat* that when people came to Absalom for it, he was able to "steal their hearts" (2 Sam. 15:2-6). The failure to deliver justice was especially despicable, as recorded in the book of Samuel. Samuel's sons "did not walk in his ways, but turned aside after gain; they took bribes and perverted justice *(mishpat)* (1 Sam. 8:3). Both the judges and kings were called to administer God's justice, but to also embody it in their own lives and families.

The word *mishpat* is used with *sadiqah,* "righteousness," which is the Bible's most common word pairing (e.g., Jer. 22:3-5; Isa. 28:17-18). *Sadiqah* calls the people of Israel to do what is right, and it becomes *mishpat* put into practice in the embodied life of God's people. Justice refers to how all people, especially the marginalized, are treated and accepted.[13] The marginalized in the world of the Israelites included the foreign women of color, the poor, the disenfranchised, and those who suffered from social structures that privileged the few rich people.

The Hebrew prophets demonstrate that Israel embodies shalom justice in the way that it treats its neighbors, especially people who have no one to take care of them. Israel's God is the defender of the poor and the oppressed (Jer. 9:23-24). Hebrew Scripture is clear in its constant clarion call to care for the widow, orphan, and stranger; and Zechariah adds the poor to this list (Zech. 7:10). The God of the prophets is concerned about the compassionate care of those with great needs. Whenever Israel lost its focus on caring for those who were victims of injustice and working toward a more equitable society, God would raise up prophets like Isaiah who said, "Is not this the fast that I choose: to loose the bonds of injustice, to undo the thongs of the yoke, to let the oppressed go free, and to break every yoke?" (Isa. 58:6).

---

12. *Mishpat Ivri* is that branch of Jewish Halaka (law) that deals with civil matters rather than matters relating to YHWH or cult practices. Therefore, such judgments were commonly made by the king or a magistrate.

13. Heltzel, *Resurrection City,* pp. 23, 24.

The prophet Micah calls Israel "to do *mishpat*," sharing what God has given, enacting God's will with a zealous determination to ensure that not one person is left out, in a spirit of humility and tender mercy (Mic. 6:8).[14] All persons need to be included in the work for God's justice. The Spirit of God's justice moves us to be mindful of everyone, even those we find most difficult to love and accept.

God's justice *(mishpat)* is not an idea or emotion; it is an action that God wants to be realized. It is something to be acted upon and lived out. If there is no action, justice becomes just a thought. We do not merely receive grace; we must put it to work. When grace is put to work, *mishpat* begins to happen. God expects the pursuit of shalom justice to be the *habitus* of the Hebrew people, the way lovers require one another, ever seeking to care and connect with their beloved through constant and creative love languages. Amos proclaims: "But let justice roll down like waters, and righteousness like an ever-flowing stream" (Amos 5:24). Amos's call to "let justice roll" is a metaphor of the river of redemption that flows through history. Justice troubles the calm waters of complacency, inactivity, and unawareness of social injustice. We cannot just sit back and be a passenger in the backseat, but must engage, rock the boat, and ensure that justice is achieved in all areas of life, which includes areas of social, racial, gender, economic, and environmental justice.

Inspired by the call for Jubilee justice (Lev. 25:23-24), Jesus inaugurates his ministry by reading the Isaiah scroll in the synagogue: "The Spirit of the Lord is upon me, because he has anointed me to bring good news to the poor. He has sent me to proclaim release to the captives and recovery of sight to the blind, to let the oppressed go free, to proclaim the year of the Lord's favor" (Luke 4:18-19). This gospel of freedom, heard as good news to the poor, sets the tone for his prophetic ministry that will include healings, exorcisms, miracles, and teaching the kingdom.

"The *basileia* of God has come near to you," proclaimed Jesus of Nazareth (Luke 10:9, 11). As a poor Jewish peasant teacher from Nazareth, Jesus' teaching of the reign of shalom justice would have been heard as hope for the poor, while being a threat to the Roman Empire. Jesus understands his identity and mission as a continuation of the prophets of Israel (Mark 8:27-28; Luke 24:19; Luke 13:33-4). While the Hebrew prophets anticipated God's coming reign of righteousness, Jesus announces that God's reign is here and

---

14. James C. Howell, *What Does the Lord Require?: Doing Justice, Loving Kindness, Walking Humbly* (Louisville: Westminster John Knox, 2012), pp. 26, 30, 31, 33.

now, and is manifested when people treat the deepest needs of the disinherited as if they are holy.[15]

Jesus' teaching revealed a new order in which the poor and the marginalized are welcomed and loved. Jesus lived and proclaimed God's identification with the people at the margins: "Truly I tell you, just as you did it to one of the least of these who are members of my family, you did it to me" (Matt. 25:40). Jesus teaches his disciples to search for him with the poor, the outcast, and the marginalized. When we reach out and stand with them, we stand with Jesus. The teaching and example of Jesus invites and challenges us to broaden our understanding and reimagine God, as God on the margins.

One day in his travels, Jesus encountered a Samaritan woman at the well (John 4:1-30). It was unpopular to talk with a Samaritan, and this encounter is somewhat unusual and unexpected. The Jews considered the Samaritans as foreigners and did not engage with them. Furthermore, it was unusual for a man to be engaged in conversation with a woman — especially a woman who had had five husbands. But this story is redemptive. As they conversed with each other and the woman learned who Jesus was, something extraordinary happened.

The Samaritan woman became excited, left her water jar, and went back to the city. She said to the people, "Come and see a man who told me everything I have ever done! He cannot be the Messiah, can he?" She decided to tell all her friends and family about Jesus who is the Messiah.

This is a story of a spiritual embrace and restoration of racial and gender division of that day. Jesus is engaged in risky vulnerable border crossing. He is engaged in restoring brokenness, troubling the waters, healing the creation and fighting in the spirit of justice. This is the vision of Spirit God, which is rooted in the scriptural narratives. Jesus energizes us and gives us life. This is the act of Spirit God which embraces us to move, act, and work for justice. It helps us walk in the power of love and justice in our lives.

After proclaiming his teaching of the Kingdom through the Galilean countryside, Jesus "turned his face like flint" to Jerusalem (Luke 9:51). With a large following, Jesus went to Jerusalem for the Passover feast with focused determination to challenge the hierarchical power of the Jewish temple elite and the leaders of the Roman Empire. Jesus' death on a Roman cross outside of the gates of the city points to a new reality and to a new community.

---

15. Obery M. Hendricks Jr., *The Politics of Jesus: Rediscovering the True Revolutionary Nature of the Teachings of Jesus and How They Have Been Corrupted* (New York: Doubleday, 2006); Howard Thurman, *Jesus and the Disinherited* (Boston: Beacon Press, 1976), p. 223.

After Jesus' resurrection and ascension, his followers kept his command and waited for the power from on high (Luke 24:49). Jesus had promised to send a "Helper, to be with you forever" (John 14:16). On Pentecost the early Christian community was baptized with "the Spirit and fire" (Luke 3:16; Acts 2), energizing them for the mission of love and justice.

At Pentecost the Spirit of shalom justice rests upon the early Christian community. As Peter Heltzel writes, "Emerging holistic pneumatology understands the Holy Spirit as the Spirit of justice-making that energizes Christian missional movements to actively proclaim and embody Christ's peaceable kingdom."[16] The description of the early church offers a powerful image of what the Spirit of shalom justice looks like in intentional community.

> All who believed were together and had all things in common; they would sell their possessions and goods and distribute the proceeds to all, as any had need. Day by day, as they spent much time together in the temple, they broke bread at home and ate their food with glad and generous hearts, praising God and having the goodwill of all the people. And day by day the Lord added to their number those who were being saved (Acts 2:44-47).

The early church modeled God's love as an egalitarian worship community and a democratic economic order. What is clear from this passage is that the early church was *koinonia* doxologically, socially, and economically. They ordered their economic relations in a manner that served the needs of all of the members of the community, privileging those who had need, who would have largely been women and children.

In the New Testament, the early followers of Christ experienced this Spirit of shalom justice in their life together. They understood the Spirit's wisdom, power, and life as being the infinite source of their life and love. It gave them hope as they sought for answers to their doubts and fears.

As a Korean American feminist constructive theologian, I want to build on the Spirit of shalom justice in the biblical narratives. In my book *The Holy Spirit, Chi, and the Other* I have described Spirit God as Spirit-Chi.[17]

16. Peter Goodwin Heltzel, "The Holy Spirit of Justice," in *The Justice Project*, ed. Brian McLaren et al. (Grand Rapids: Baker, 2009), pp. 44-50.

17. See Grace Ji-Sun Kim, *The Holy Spirit, Chi, and the Other* (New York: Palgrave Macmillan, 2011). Spirit-Chi is used to show the global aspect of our Christian understanding of the Spirit.

Chi is the Chinese term for energy force. We experience this energy force when we practice taekwondo or tai-chi. God is the source of this ubiquitous energy force. However, Spirit God is more than just the spirit of life; it is shaped by the scriptural shalom justice. We recognize that God dwells everywhere, but gives special attention to the poor, the outcasts, the marginalized, and the discarded persons of society. My conception of Spirit God integrates the vitalism of my earlier notion Spirit-Chi with the biblical call to justice, shaped by the concept of Chi that is central to my Asian cultural heritage. Before explaining my concept of Spirit God, I want to take a moment and consider pneumatological constructions in continental philosophy. This philosophy has deeply impacted how we view the Spirit and has essentially ignored the other voices around the world that also experience and live in the Spirit. Therefore, a glimpse of continental philosophy and its impact on theology will provide a window into how we can expand and open up the theological discourse on the Spirit. While Spirit discourse can be culturally contextualized, we must bring our prophetic intercultural feminist hermeneutic informed by postcolonial studies to the task of analyzing the pneumatologies of the West.

Hegel's Search for the Spirit

The son of a Lutheran pastor, Georg Wilhelm Friedrich Hegel used the concept *Geist* as a central theme in his philosophical account of history. Hegel's understanding of the Spirit is the notion that all of reality, including human history, is the expression of Spirit coming to its own self-realization and self-consciousness so that all we experience and perceive is Spirit. The world and especially history are the vehicles through which reason develops, gains self-awareness, and attains absolute truth. Spirit or reason is not something that exists over against the world; rather, the world process or history is the dynamic through which Spirit attains its fulfillment.[18]

History in the Hegelian system is not just the site of Spirit or reason's development. Spirit is also the *telos* that drives history, the internal essence of history that underlies all reality and history and that determines both the process and forms of its development. Spirit is that which is manifested in all reality and history. Spirit teleologically determines the direction and

---

18. Sheila Greeve Davaney, *Historicism: The Once and Future Challenge for Theology* (Minneapolis: Fortress Press, 2006), p. 39.

outcome of historical development. The Spirit comes to self-realization in history, which is the vehicle and manifestation of Spirit. This occurs not in some linear manner but by way of a dialectical movement in which Spirit develops through a process of disruption, contradiction, and reconciliation. Spirit's very life and nature are this ongoing expression and reconciliation of opposites.[19] The complexity of the Spirit cannot be denied; it must also be observed, embraced, and welcomed.

For Hegel, all of reality is the manifestation of Spirit and the universe is the Spirit's embodiment.[20] The Spirit is all and encompasses everything. It is what embraces life; in fact, it *is* life. It is especially within human history that Spirit comes to self-actualization. Every epoch and civilization is to some degree the manifestation of cosmic Spirit. The Spirit blows and moves as it wills and affects all humanity and history. Religion is a primary means by which worldly existence becomes conscious of the Spirit. In Christianity, the Spirit becomes fully manifest in the world through the incarnation. In the incarnation, the unity of the infinite and finite takes full conceptual form.[21] The Spirit is manifested in the world.

God is within the world. As Spirit immanent within the world, God interacts with and transforms the world. God is not a bystander but actively participates within the creation. God is present throughout the world and is seeking to transform it. After Hegel, constructive theologians need to give a deeper theological account of the intimate relationship between God the Creator and the created world. The Spirit is the key to this connection.

Zarathustra's Spirit in the Sea

It is not the case that the world is matter and God is Spirit; rather, there is continuity of being between God and the world. Thus we need to live justly and sustainably on our planet, as God is immanent within Creation. God's power of creative, redeeming, and sustaining love is closer to us than we are to ourselves. God's love is so great that God became incarnate in Jesus Christ to reconcile and restore the world. God is also manifested and dwells in the material world. God as Spirit penetrates and permeates the material world and everything in it. Therefore, it is our calling to be good caretakers

---

19. Davaney, *Historicism,* p. 39.
20. Charles Taylor, *Hegel* (Cambridge: Cambridge University Press, 1977), p. 87.
21. Davaney, *Historicism,* pp. 40, 41.

of the earth, the dwelling place of God. If we abuse the earth, we hurt not only God's beautiful creation — we hurt God the Creator.[22]

Spirit God is the source of power and love in which our world exists. Spirit God is the life, love, truth, goodness, and beauty that empower the universe and shine out from it. Spirit God is the reality of everything that is in the world. Without Spirit God nothing exists. As humans we have a deep and restless yearning to be lost in the awe-inspiring beauty of creation. Friedrich Nietzsche, in *Thus Spoke Zarathustra,* captures the restless spirit of humanity that seeks to improvise as a way to transfigure the tragedy of human existence. While Hegel saw *Geist* as the dialectical driver of history, Nietzsche naturalizes the spirit discourse. Nietzsche imagines the Spirit through naturalistic ways of looking at the earth and the material realities of human existence. Nietzsche brings us even closer to the palpable, physical earth. For him, the transformation of man happens in a very tangible manner: "Verily, a polluted stream is man. One must be a sea to be able to receive a polluted stream without becoming unclean. Behold, I teach you the Overman: he is this sea; in him your great contempt can go under."[23] In this passage Nietzsche compares the Overman to the sea, which is so ubiquitous and deep it can never be contaminated and destroyed.

The metaphor of the sea as a window into the subjectivity of Nietzsche's ideal person is captured when he writes: "Verily, like the sun I love life and all deep seas. And this is what perceptive knowledge means to me: all that is deep shall rise up to my heights. Thus spoke Zarathustra."[24] The sea for Nietzsche represents new possibilities, just like the Overman (who is really replaced by Nietzsche, in his later writings, by the "free spirit"). The free spirit or Overman is able to move beyond human life as we know it and liberate himself. Not everyone, it would seem, is able to carry out such a project. So Nietzsche thinks that only certain individuals have this potential. The sea is where we can be "cleansed" from all that holds us back (including, of course, *ressentiment*).

Nietzsche in his poetry often uses both the heights of mountains and

---

22. In an earlier work I use the Korean term *han* to describe the pain of the oppressed, the pain of creation, and the pain in the heart of God. Grace Ji-Sun Kim, *Colonialism, Han, and the Transformative Spirit* (New York: Palgrave Macmillan, 2013), pp. 50-59. See also Andrew Sung Park, *The Wounded Heart of God: The Asian Concept of Han and the Christian Doctrine of Sin* (Nashville: Abingdon, 1993).

23. Friedrich Nietzsche, *Thus Spoke Zarathustra,* in *The Portable Nietzsche,* trans. Walter Kaufmann (New York: Penguin Books, Kindle Edition, 1982), p. 125.

24. Nietzsche, *Thus Spoke Zarathustra,* p. 236.

the depths of seas to represent greatness that is as yet unobtained. He writes
of that greatness becoming an equilibrium, a balance of powerful forces.
For example:

> My soul itself is itself a flame:
> insatiable for new distances
> blaze upwards, upwards your still glow.
> Why does Zarathustra flee from animals and man?
> Why does he flee from dry land?
> Six solitudes, he knows already,
> but the sea itself was not lonely enough for him,
> the island lets him climb — upon the mountain he becomes a flame,
> toward his seventh solitude. . . .[25]

Zarathustra symbolizes the human being's efforts to overcome the multi-
dimensional challenges of human existence through existentially entering
the dark abyss of solitude. Zarathustra's ascent to the "seventh solitude" is
a search for inner peace and dynamic power in a world full of sickness and
suffering.

For Nietzsche, there is nothing beyond the natural world (he accuses
philosophers and Christians of being "otherworldly"). For Nietzsche, there
is just this world. Nietzsche tells us that, when he uses the term "soul," he
simply means another aspect of the body. Hegel's *Geist* simply disappears in
Nietzsche's philosophy.[26] While Hegel sees all things unified by one Spirit,
Nietzsche revels in the diversity, the ebb and flow of forces, represented differently by different peoples. Perhaps for Nietzsche, "Spirit" is one of those tired
metaphors about which Sallie McFague speaks;[27] McFague believes Nietzsche
anticipated tired metaphors in his statement that truth is "[a]n army of metaphors, metonymies, anthropomorphisms . . . which . . . are illusions that are

25. Friedrich Nietzsche, "The Fire Sign," in *The Peacock and the Buffalo: The Poetry of Nietzsche*, trans. James Luchte (New York: Continuum, Kindle Edition, 2010), 1199 of 1590.

26. The eclipse of the spirit in Nietzsche's thought is complicated by the fact that Nietz-sche adopts Dionysus as his god, as argued by Bruce Ellis Benson in *Pious Nietzsche* (Bloom-ington: Indiana University Press, 2008). Dionysus is not otherworldly but very this-worldly. Dionysus could not be a spiritual entity for Nietzsche (except in the sense that the word "soul" is another name for the body). So, Dionysus is another word for this world and gets at Nietzsche's affirmation of life in the material world.

27. Sallie McFague, *Models of God: Theology for an Ecological, Nuclear Age* (Minneap-olis: Fortress Press, 1987), p. 189.

no longer remembered as being illusions, metaphors that have become worn and stripped of their sensuous force. . . ."[28]

But our theology proclaims that God is greater than what our minds can imagine. Therefore when we experience a new revelation of God, we should be able to add it to our various understandings of God. The more images and depth that we can imagine, the more profound our understanding of God and the deeper our union and communion with God. God's Spirit is vast and we can only comprehend a small segment of God's vastness.

Reckoning with Nietzsche's philosophical vision, Sallie McFague poses the provocative question ". . . what if spirit and matter were not entirely different? What if all life, God's and ours, as well as that of all others on earth — was seen to be on a continuum, more like a circle or the recycle symbol than like a dualistic hierarchy? What if spirit and matter were intrinsically related rather than diametrically opposed?"[29] It's time for prophetic Christian theology to move beyond a social framework based on "dualistic hierarchy" toward a framework based on such wholistic interdependence.

While the dualism of Greco-Roman philosophy has dominated Western theology, the apocalyptic fragments of Nietzsche's vision open up new possibilities for a more earth-affirming theology. Nietzsche writes, "The two most extreme modes of thought — the mechanistic and the Platonic — are reconciled in the eternal recurrence: both as ideals."[30] Within our dualistic frame of mind, we have a tendency to dichotomize opposites. It feels like a parallel existence for many concepts. In dualisms, concepts stay separated and cannot be joined together. They are one or the other and not both at once. McFague challenges us to consider that perhaps spirit and matter are not totally different. God became incarnate in Jesus and was like us. God became matter. Why are we so set on the notion that God and matter are opposites? Perhaps they can be understood as complementary of each other. Body and spirit are dimensions of the same reality. If we can approach nature in an integrated manner then we are in a much better position to construct a broader understanding of God. While Nietzsche's naturalism provokes a more immanent understanding of the Spirit, Nietzsche and Hegel are still

28. Friedrich Nietzsche, "On Truth and Lie in an Extra-Moral Sense," in *Writings from the Early Notebooks*, ed. Raymond Geuss and Alexander Nehamas, trans. Ladislaus Löb (Cambridge: Cambridge University Press, 2009), p. 257.

29. Sallie McFague, *A New Climate for Theology: God, the World and Global Warming* (Minneapolis: Fortress Press, 2008), p. 65.

30. Friedrich Nietzsche, *The Will to Power*, trans. Walter Kaufmann and R. J. Hollingdale, ed. Walter Kaufmann (New York: Alfred A. Knopf, 1968), location 11188, paragraph 1061.

participants in the Western civilization project and its violent legacy of oppression. Today we must liberate the Spirit from its Western colonial captivity, wisely discerning the movement of the Spirit in indigenous coultures outside of the West.

When we consider theology's broad global context, we see indigenous ways of imaging God that are similar to McFague's cosmic Christian vision. We learn from indigenous folktales that people's stories are deeply rooted in what is tangible to them, such as the wind, the clouds, the forests, the plains, and the animals. How different is learning from all of these than learning from a God who became flesh? But such learning becomes easier if one studies the stories of other cultures, and how they vary. Even within Native American thought, there are many stories about how the earth was created and how humanity came to be. They accept the truth that each story has to offer and understand that all theology is localized and we all are limited in our views. Many of these stories put humans and animals on the same level, where all creatures have the power of speech. And among all these stories, some involve Spirit[31] and some do not.[32] However, the assumption is always that Spirit is present even when not mentioned.

A remarkable fact about many Native American stories is that Spirit is encountered as the spirit of an animal or a deceased person, and as the "Great Spirit" we hear of in John Ford films about the "Wild West." Randy Woodley writes, "Indigenous North American tribes' understanding of a personal spirit being who indwells all creation," or their understanding of creation indwelt by a panentheistic force — either understanding is "fully spiritual, fully tangible and immanent."[33] It may be an especially good model to see how so many different understandings of the spiritual coexisted in the Americas. As spaces and ideas collide, it is important to acknowledge that there should not be such a great distinction between traditionally conceived dualistic concepts. Perhaps the distinction resides only in two ways of seeing, and not in two ways of being.

This will shape our understanding when it comes to matter and Spirit.

---

31. "Coyote and the Origin of Death," in *American Indian Myths and Legends,* ed. Richard Erdoes and Alfonso Ortiz (New York: Pantheon, 1984), p. 470.

32. "How Coyote Got His Cunning," in *American Indian Myths and Legends,* ed. Erdoes and Ortiz, p. 382.

33. Randy Woodley, email correspondence, September 15, 2014. For an extensive discussion of the relationship between the Native American Harmony Way and Jesus' teaching of Kingdom, see Randy Woodley's *Shalom and the Community of Creation: An Indigenous Vision* (Grand Rapids: Eerdmans, 2012).

These two should not be separated but instead synthesized in a cosmic constructive theological vision. With such an understanding, it becomes easier for us to talk about God. God is not at some nebulous distance, but is close to us, right here and right now, in the vulnerable flesh of our bodies. God's Spirit is actualized in the everyday objects we see and touch in this world. We experience the presence of God within our world today. We can find deep comfort in the close presence of God who is right next to us in the stranger and friend. The mighty Spirit of God dwells within all of us.

The Spirit "dwells deeply within all that exists, energizing, animating and sustaining everything in the process of being and becoming."[34] God's Spirit is always within us, giving us life and sustaining us throughout our daily lives and routines. We are all the holy temples of God and this knowledge can make all the difference in how we treat ourselves, others, and nature. By recognizing that God is within us, we will begin to treat ourselves, others, and nature with respect, compassion, and love.

The Spirit needs to be understood as movement. The Spirit, who goes between, moves through the borders and boundaries of space and time.[35] The Spirit can move into the in-between spaces that marginalized people occupy; the hybrid spaces to which the marginalized are relegated. Because the Spirit is able to move into all places, the Spirit can reach these hard-to-get-to spaces and bring healing and wholeness to the marginalized. As the Spirit moves into these marginal spaces, wonderful things begin to occur.

Spirit God challenges the Euro-American Christian community to open itself up to deep solidarity with the counter-traditions in the margins, and see itself in light of the Other being oppressed by patriarchy, white supremacy, and economic exploitation. Spirit God transforms women who have internalized inferiority, and transforms men who have internalized superiority so they can achieve a psychoanalytic relational healing, working toward an ethic of mutuality and hope. The Spirit-led Christ community recognizes that Spirit God brings liberation, new life, sustenance, empowerment, flourishing, life-balances, and life abundant. Life is good and it is the Spirit that makes it good. The Spirit provides the sustenance and flourishing that leads to wholeness. The Spirit transcends the time and space that confine us, and brings meaning and understanding into our lives.

---

34. Diarmuid O'Murchu, *In the Beginning Was the Spirit: Science, Religion, and Indigenous Spirituality* (Maryknoll, NY: Orbis, 2012), p. 96.

35. Sigurd Bergmann, "Invoking the Spirit amid Dangerous Environmental Change," in *God, Creation and Climate Change* (Minneapolis: Lutheran University Press, 2009), p. 173.

Global Understandings of Spirit God

Being radically open to the cosmic character of Spirit God and a multiplicity of forms, we witness the movement of the Spirit all over the world. The understanding of God as Spirit becomes liberating and empowering for many around the globe. In Asia, it is understood as Chi and has been part of Asian tradition for thousands of years as the life-giving power of all created things. It is what gives life, power, and sustenance. Although manifested, experienced, and understood in various ways, we Christians recognize it as the one Spirit of God.

The breath of God (*ruach ha kodesh* in Hebrew, *Spiritus Sancti* in Latin) is synonymous with the Spirit. A similar idea is expressed in the holy scripture of Islam, the *Qur'an* (Koran). The words *nafas,* which means Allah's breath, and *ruh,* which means Allah's own soul, are used to convey that human breath and human soul-confirming are originally from Allah. Breath is a divine energy that regulates human emotions and the equilibrium of the body. Both the quantity and quality of breath have a definite and direct effect upon human health.[36] This connection of Spirit, breath, and Allah may help us develop a global understanding of the Spirit.

In Africa, the word is different, but the concept is the same. For example, among the Kung San, the indigenous people of Africa's Kalahari Desert, life energy is *num.* The *num* is stored in the lower abdomen and at the base of the spine and can be made to "boil" through various ecstatic dances. Moving the body according to the rhythms and movements of traditional dance releases the *num,* producing new energy that allows one to love and that gives one a deep inner peace. The "*num* enters every part of your body, right to the tip of your feet and even your hair."[37] *Num* makes the spine tingle and can make the mind empty without thoughts.[38] Diseases can sometimes be cured by accumulating *num* or increasing the inner reserves of healing power.[39] It is important to make the connection and understand that healing power can come from within us through the Spirit.

In India, the life energy, *prana,* is described as flowing through thousands of subtle-energy veins, the *nadis.* One of the goals of yoga is to accumulate more *prana* through breath control exercises *(pranayama)* and

---

36. Kenneth Cohen, *The Way of Qigong: The Art and Science of Chinese Energy Healing* (New York: Random House, 1997), p. 23.

37. Richard Katz, *Boiling Energy* (Cambridge, MA: Harvard University Press, 1966), p. 42.

38. Katz, *Boiling Energy,* p. 42.

39. Cohen, *The Way of Qigong,* p. 24.

physical postures *(asana).*[40] Furthermore, some fifty or sixty thousand years ago, long before the Chinese spoke of Chi, Australian Aborigines were cultivating life energy as a key to healing and spiritual power. People who had this energy could communicate telepathically across vast distances, and in this manner they formed the "aboriginal telephone line."[41]

Native Americans make a deep connection between breathing and the soul. In the Lakota (Sioux) language, the word for soul, *waniya,* is derived from the word for breath, *ni.* It is the same as breath and gives strength. All that is inside a person's body *waniya* keeps clean. If *waniya* is weak it cannot clean the inside of the body. A person will die if *waniya* goes away.[42] The Lakota sweat lodge healing rite is called *inipi* because it purifies the *ni.* Sitting in darkness with hot burning stones purifies both the body and soul of each individual present in the context of a collective catharsis. After the "sweat," the participants can breathe easier and return to their lives with fresh vigor and a wider perspective on their lives.

The Japanese have a similar term and call this energy *Ki.* This *Ki* is part of other words such as *Reiki* and *Aikido,* which deal with this energy. Very often this energy is connected in the external world with wind and internally with breath.

In Hawaii, the word for breath is *ha.* Many visitors to Hawaii are presented with a flowery wreath and the greeting *Aloha* which is translated as the "meeting face to face *(alo)* of the breath of life *(ha)*."[43] The sacred healing breath, *ha,* can be absorbed at power places in nature *(heiau)* and through dance (such as the hula) and deep-breathing exercises. The Hawaiian word *Aloha,* often used as a respectful, heartfelt greeting, also means "love."[44] In short, many cultures have words to articulate similar ideas of breath, life, and vital energy expressed by the Christian understanding of the Holy Spirit.

The Holy Spirit is vital and elusive, escaping all our attempts to capture its power in one symbolic valence. As Dwight Hopkins argues, "the Spirit cannot be contained within one human symbol."[45] Because one sym-

40. Cohen, *The Way of Qigong,* p. 26.

41. Cohen, *The Way of Qigong,* p. 25.

42. James R. Walker, *Lakota Belief and Ritual* (Lincoln: University of Nebraska Press, 1980), p. 83.

43. Robert Cook, "Alternative and Complementary Theologies: The Case of Cosmic Energy with Special Reference to Chi," *Studies in World Christianity* 6 (2000): 176.

44. Cohen, *The Way of Qigong,* p. 26.

45. Dwight Hopkins, *Heart and Head: Black Theology — Past, Present, and Future* (New York: Palgrave Macmillan, 2003), pp. 99, 100.

bol cannot contain it, we have freedom and liberty in how we experience and understand the Spirit. There can be no white European stronghold on how we experience and are to view and understand the Spirit. This has been the historical practice within Christianity, as European Christianity has believed it had a monopoly on the world's understanding of the Holy Spirit. Anything that is nonwhite or non-European was termed "bad" Spirit. However, this goes against what the Scriptures and our Christian tradition have proclaimed. The Scriptures are clear that the Spirit cannot be tied down or understood. We need to become open and vulnerable and allow the Spirit to overwhelm us.

Jesus said the Spirit would come to us, guide us, and explain things for us after he was gone (John 16:13-14): "When the Spirit of truth comes, he will guide you into all truth; for he will not speak on his own, but will speak whatever he hears, and he will declare to you the things that are to come. He will glorify me, because he will take what is mine and declare it to you." In the Christian tradition, Spirit God is a spirit of truth. It is one with the truth incarnate in Jesus of Nazareth, the fully human and fully divine Son of God. The Gospel of John emphasizes that the Father and the Son "are one" (John 10:30), expressing the ontological unity between the Father and the Son. When Jesus speaks of the Holy Spirit as the "Spirit of truth" (John 16:13) he is acknowledging that the Spirit, too, is one with the Father and the Son. Thus, Spirit God is a Spirit that guides us into all truth and wisdom, but in the context of being part of a triune communion of love. Within prophetic Christian theology, Spirit God is more than a vital life force; it is the Spirit of love.

The premise of a global understanding of the Spirit frees us to explore new ways of understanding the Spirit and allowing the Spirit to come to us. Our finite minds are limited and incapable of understanding the fullness of the Divine. Therefore, we should stop pretending that we have the only answer, the only image, or the only symbol conceptualizing the Divine. The conception of God in the Christian West is one approach to the Divine, but it is marked by the patriarchy of the tradition that gave it birth. We need to build on biblical insights about the Holy Spirit and deepen them through the wisdom of other religious traditions.

The Spirit came upon Jesus' disciples with flames of fire. "When the day of Pentecost had come, they were all together in one place. And suddenly from heaven there came a sound like the rush of a violent wind, and it filled the entire house where they were sitting. Divided tongues, as of fire, appeared among them, and a tongue rested on each of them" (Acts 2:1-3). As we seek to penetrate the mysteries of the Spirit, we keep our eyes on the fire of God. Carl Jung writes, "I have my eye on the central fire, and I am trying to put some mirrors around it to show it to others. Sometimes the edges of those mirrors leave gaps and don't fit together exactly. I can't help that. Look at what I'm trying to point to!"[46] Like Jung's fire, and like the fire in Plato's analogy of the cave, it is only through meditating on the fire as the source of truth that we can see the dark shadows in our psyche and be liberated to live as light and love in the world.

We cannot possibly conceive the entirety of who and what God is. As created beings, we are unable to grasp the fullness of our Creator. Clear and complete theological knowledge is an impossibility. Therefore, we need to recognize our own inability to have such complete knowledge and proceed forward nonetheless. We are limited in our ways of understanding God. Therefore, we must honestly confess our limitations and allow others around the world to enter the discussion so that we can have a richer understanding and a deeper understanding of who the Divine is. Limiting the sense of the Divine to a single image denies the mysterious and ubiquitous nature of God and the ongoing challenge of naming the Divine.

Chi and the Transformative Power of Spirit God

Constructive theology is written from a particular cultural-linguistic context. Theology is deepened and limited by the language that we speak. Each community of people uses the terms, words, and languages that are available to them to talk about God. As theology became more Eurocentric, theologians used the German term *Geist* to express the Spirit of God. As theology becomes more global and moves away from domination by European theology, we seek new communities of faith to help us articulate the Divine, which cannot be limited or constrained by our language. As an Asian American woman theologian, I turn to my Asian heritage to seek new ways of speaking about God that will affirm the experiences of our people. As I explore feminist Asian American understandings of God, I recognize the richness of our Asian religious, cultural, and historical heritage. The Spirit is not a new concept. It has always existed in our Asian identity. We closely identify our personal being with the amount of Spirit within us. We talk about how low

---

46. Murray Stein, *Jung's Map of the Soul: An Introduction* (Chicago: Open Court, Kindle Edition, 2010), p. 11.

or great our Spirit is on a daily basis. The everyday word used by Asians to talk about the Spirit is the word "Chi."

Along with the Christian understanding of *ruach* and *pneuma* as Spirit, there is also the understanding of Chi as Spirit in various Asian traditions. Chi can be found in Taoism, Hinduism, and Buddhism[47] and has similar characteristics to the Holy Spirit. Within Asian tradition, it is understood that the universe originates in Chi, which is both the source of the universe and the driving force of endless changes. All things in the universe are based in and formed by one and the same Chi. This Chi then begins to contract and consolidate because of the interaction between yin and yang.[48]

Chi is the Chinese word for "life energy." Chi is the animating power that flows through all living things; a living being is filled with it. A dead person has no more: the warmth and the life energy dissipate. A healthy person has more Chi than one who is ill. Health implies that Chi in our bodies is clear, rather than polluted and turbid, and flowing smoothly, like a stream, not blocked or stagnant. It is also the life energy one senses in nature. Earth itself is moving, transforming, breathing, and alive with Chi. Some modern scientists speak the same language as ancient poets when they call the Earth "Gaia," a living being. When we appreciate the beauty of animals, fish, birds, flowers, trees, mountains, the deep ocean, and floating clouds, we are sensing their Chi and feeling an intuitive unity with them.[49]

In ancient times, people in East Asia believed that heaven and earth, as well as all beings, breathed Chi. The universe is generated and sustained by the holistic matter-energy of Chi.[50] Chi sustains all things on the earth and gives them fulfillment and life. This is important to comprehend as we strive to understand the root of why the people wanted Chi and thought it was crucial for a good life.[51] As the life force, Chi interpenetrated not only living beings but also all natural objects. Chi is the ever-present force of the life that has always been existent, an important force within our universe.[52]

---

47. Bede Bidlack, "Qi in the Christian Tradition," *Dialogue and Alliance* 17, no. 1 (2003): 51.

48. Paul S. Chung, "The Mystery of God and Tao in Jewish-Christian-Taoist Context," in *Asian Contextual Theology for the Third Millennium: Theology of Minjung in Fourth-Eye Formation,* ed. Paul S. Chung, Veli-Matti Kärkkäinen, and Kim Kyoung-Jae (Eugene, OR: Pickwick, 2007), p. 261.

49. Grace Ji-Sun Kim, *The Holy Spirit, Chi, and the Other,* pp. 13, 14.

50. Rosemary Radford Ruether, *Integrating Ecofeminism, Globalization, and World Religion* (Lanham, MD: Rowman & Littlefield, 2005), p. 62.

51. Chung, "The Mystery of God and Tao in Jewish-Christian-Taoist Context," p. 261.

52. Grace Ji-Sun Kim, *The Holy Spirit, Chi, and the Other,* p. 12.

Chi is a life-giving energy whose source is Spirit God. Like the *Ruach* that hovered over creation, Spirit God nourishes, sustains, and maintains life throughout the community of creation. When shalom was shattered in this community, humans were called to restore shalom between humanity and God, men and women, and humanity and the rest of creation. The Hebrew prophets cried out for shalom justice. Jesus, the Prince of Peace, led a Spirit-led movement for shalom justice in the midst of the Roman Empire. In the spirit of Jeremiah and Jesus, we need to use the breath God has given us to work toward reconciliation, solidarity, and hope.

Shalom justice offers the moral imagination through which disciples of Jesus seek to embody our life together. Since Spirit God is the source of Chi, we need to channel our Chi toward the common good. The scriptural vision of shalom provides the values that guide our Spirit-led activism in and for the world, especially among those divided by race, class, gender, and sexuality. Since women, especially women of color, have been marginalized in the modern world, Christians have an urgent call to work for gender justice. The healing between women and men through the power of Spirit God is vital to the Christian call to trouble the waters and heal the world.

Concluding Thoughts

As Asian American women, in solidarity with other women of color, seek to move away from the marginalized segments of society, we reimagine a God who is with them in the margins and energizes them to work for a just and sustainable world. While Spirit God emerges from within, it propels people to engage in the long-term work of dismantling outward evils such as racism and sexism.

These problematic systematized structures are so deeply embedded in our society that they become unrecognizable. Much of our Christian theology is developed by colonial perceptions that further perpetuate this racism and sexism against women and people of color, including Asian American women. We need to begin recognizing these structures of powers that subordinate the weak, women, the disenfranchised, and people of color. But we also need to recognize the power of Spirit God to bring in shalom justice to eliminate racism and sexism from our social structures and consciousness.

As Asian Americans practice multi-faith hermeneutics, we are encouraged to search within our own rich heritage and backgrounds to discern and deploy liberative elements that empower the work of shalom justice.

As we search for meaning, life, and love, Asian American women recognize that Spirit God is present in our bodies, our religious heritage, and our communities. As we tap into these vitalistic energies in the deep wells of our humanity and cultures, we are then able to deepen our understanding and experience of Spirit God. Tied in with Spirit is the concept of Eros that interconnects human beings to others and to God. The last chapter will examine the concepts of Eros and erotic power. By joining us to one another and our God, the transformative Spirit of love empowers people to work for reconciliation between men and women to create gender justice and shalom in the community of creation.

CHAPTER 6

The Transformative Spirit of Love

The healing and restoring of the world is happening through the transformative Spirit of love. With restless hearts we long to connect with God, the Other, and the community of creation. Through the practice of prayer to the triune God our erotic longing is transformed into a Spirit of love. More than merely a longing for sexual ecstasy, our erotic power is a life energy that gives us spiritual strength to love God, love our neighbor, and love all of creation.

The communion of the three persons of the Trinity is the primal source of human love. Together these three persons form a dynamic communion of love, which flows out into the world as an ever-flowing stream. The gracious love of the triune God can be an infinite source of loving restoration between women and men. Challenging patriarchal discourse and social structures, the notion of Spirit God helps us reimagine divinity as the transformative Spirit of love who embraces us all.

As we work out our differences and difficulties as people of color and whites, as men and as women, we understand that it is Spirit God who can reconcile us and bring us together. As a step towards a loving community and intimate relationship with each other, we must consider other possibilities of experiencing care, acceptance, and love. For there to be a healing and reconciliation between men and women, we must embrace our erotic power in healthy, whole relational ways.

Spirit God liberates the erotic energy of both women and men to have conflict-resolution conversations where we go to the places that divide us, talk about the issues with nonviolent empathetic listening, mutual understanding, and heartfelt prayer. Spirit God connects us to each other, opens us up for an exchange of hearts, heals the curse between men and women that goes back to Adam and Eve, and is a source of perpetual soul repair and bodily renewal as we love into a deep and disciplined spirituality that can sustain the movement to incarnate God's justice and shalom, on earth as it is in heaven.

Eros and the Spirit of Love

Eros was the Greek god of love, and one of the Greek words meaning love, with a tendency to suggest the sensual, erotic, and visceral aspects of the experience of love. Eros connotes intimacy through the subjective engagement of the whole self in a relationship, in the absence of doubt, decorum, or duty. It is sometimes considered synonymous with lust or sexuality. While erotic feelings include those experienced with lust, they are also related to the notions of *anima* and *animus*. The erotic bridges the passions of our lives — the physical, emotional, psychic, mental, and spiritual elements. The erotic can be felt through our presence and the presence of others to us. The erotic underlies all levels of experience and compels and propels us to be hungry for justice at our very depths. The raw spiritual hunger pangs that develop deep within us will motivate us to work for justice and change.

Filled with the power of the erotic, we can reject all that makes us numb to the suffering, apathy, and hate of others. When we allow the empowering Spirit to work in us, energizing us and giving us abundant life, we are able to stand up against all forms of oppression. Through the erotic as power we become less willing to accept powerlessness, despair, depression, and self-denial. The erotic binds wounds and gives life and hope. It connects us to one another and even to ourselves. This connectedness is important as we try to live in community, neighborhoods, family, and society rather than in isolation from one another. Just as Eros enables all of us to connect to each other, it also connects us to the earth.[1] It is the Spirit that moves in us in response to seeing a sunset over the ocean or a range of snowcapped mountains, a family of wild animals or a flock of birds. This connection empowers us to work for justice within our communities, our countries, and in our world.

Rita Nakashima Brock was one of the first feminist thinkers to articulate the possibilities of erotic power. Her understanding of Eros is provocative and powerful:

1. Rita Nakashima Brock, *Journeys by Heart: A Christology of Erotic Power* (New York: Crossroad, 1992), pp. 40, 41.

Feminist Eros is grounded in the relational lives of women and in a critical, self-aware consciousness that unites the psychological and political spheres of life, binding love with power. In addition, Eros involves an appreciation of concrete, embodied beauty and a sense of the tenuousness and fluidity of life. . . . Erotic power is the power of our primal interrelatedness.[2]

Erotic power brings together people and reminds us of our interrelatedness to each other and the interrelatedness of all creation.

Brock reminds us of the power that exists within Eros:

Erotic power, as it creates and connects hearts, involves the whole person in relationships of self-awareness, vulnerability, openness, and caring. Erotic power as an ontic category, as a fundamentally ultimate reality in human existence, is a more inclusive and accurate understanding of the dynamics of power within which dominance and willful assertion can be explained. . . . Hence all other forms of power emerge from the reality of erotic power.[3]

This power needs to be harnessed in order to work towards transformative justice. The power that emerges from erotic power illustrates the interconnectedness of all beings and the need to work for shalom justice by embracing those who are pushed to the margins.

The notion of Eros is a powerful one that can help illuminate our conception of God as Spirit. Feminist theology adds a new dimension to the work of liberation, salvation, and justice in the world by examining the notion of erotic power and force. The Spirit can be understood as possessing this erotic power that transforms us and the world. This erotic power is found within some Asian concepts and understandings associated with the Divine. Asian understandings of the Spirit often associate Chi with it. Chi possesses the same qualities as those described by the biblical understanding of the Spirit. Therefore, it may be meaningful to speak of Spirit-Chi.[4]

The idea of Spirit-Chi plays on the notion of the birth of the world in creation. In classical Christian spirituality, such as those of the New

2. Brock, *Journeys by Heart,* pp. 25, 26.
3. Brock, *Journeys by Heart,* pp. 25, 26.
4. For further discussion on Spirit-Chi, see Grace Ji-Sun Kim, *The Holy Spirit, Chi, and the Other: A Model of Global and Intercultural Pneumatology* (New York: Palgrave Macmillan, 2011).

England Puritans and the early Greek ascetics, the erotic denotes primitive instinctual desires — a wild, uncontrolled passion, with daemonic sexual desire as one of its primary expressions. Within such theologies, Eros denotes the disorderly and the source of temptation that could drive humans to insanity.[5] It is presented as an undesirable aspect and is often viewed as unpredictable or unreliable, unlike "logos."[6] However, much of this negativity can be attributed to a dualism that works to benefit a white Eurocentric male perspective. Therefore it is no surprise that some perceive reason to be superior to emotion, male to female, logos to Sophia, and logic to Eros. However, if we are willing to reexamine Eros, it can allow us to become open to the positive opportunities and engagement that Eros can provide to feminist theological discourse. The issues created by dualism need to be overcome so that our God-created diversity leads not to division but to cohesion. The feminine impulse, perhaps the same as Carl Jung's *anima* (and *animus*), encompasses the "life force" and is an energy that comes from the desire for creation with purpose.[7] It integrates

5. Diarmuid O'Murchu, *In the Beginning Was the Spirit: Science, Religion, and Indigenous Spirituality* (Maryknoll, NY: Orbis, 2012), p. 157.

6. Grace Ji-Sun Kim, *Colonialism, Han, and the Transformative Spirit* (New York: Palgrave Macmillan, 2013), p. 74.

7. Regarding the feminine impulse: It may be confusing to name the feminine impulse *Eros*, since in Greek mythology Eros was male.

Regarding *anima* (and *animus*): Jung (according to Murray Stein, *Jung's Map of the Soul: An Introduction* [Chicago: Open Court, Kindle Edition, 2010], p. 9) is not compulsively consistent and Jung admitted as much to his students. Therefore, in some places *anima* may appear to be a female impulse while *animus* is an analogous male impulse. In other places in Jung's writings, it appears that females and males have both *anima* and *animus*.

Jung's *anima*, according to his biography, is akin to a female, who relays to him inspirations driving his creations, in the manner that art is created, far more than it is an empirical investigation composed of repeatable experiments, in the fashion of Bacon or Mill. See Stein, *Jung's Map of the Soul,* reporting an event in Carl Jung's *Memories, Dreams, Reflections*, ed. Aniela Jaffe, trans. Richard and Clara Winston (New York: Vintage Books, Kindle Edition, 1989), 278 of 7243, where a servant girl to Jung's family "became a component of my anima."

Later, Jung says women have a special talent and "at times see also into men's anima intrigues. They see aspects that the man does not see" (2397 of 7243). Later still, Jung says that blind "Salome is an anima figure . . . Elijah . . . represents the factor of intelligence and knowledge; Salome, the erotic element. One might say that the two figures are personifications of Logos and Eros. But such a definition would be excessively intellectual" (3217 of 7243). Further, Jung attributes the name anima to the soul, and comments that it is "thought to be female . . . which plays a typical . . . role in the unconscious of a man, and I called her the *anima*. The corresponding figure in the unconscious of woman I called the *animus*" (3283 of 7243).

One way of imagining Jung's anima is to see the imaginary character Natalie Vincent in

the sensual and the rational, the spiritual and the political. Eros is both love and power.[8]

Feminist Eros for a long time has been associated with sexuality and thus has been ignored and dismissed within our Christian tradition. Within the dualistic framework, the spiritual is more desirable than the carnal, which was often linked to the sexual. However, feminist Eros is far more than sexuality; it is the passion of a quest for beauty. This beauty can be found within creation, in the cycles of the seasons, and in all of our representations of life. Eros tries to connect love with power and is a sensuous, transformative, whole-making wisdom. Love and wisdom are bound together and closely associated. Erotic power creates and connects hearts through vulnerability and caring.

Today this connection is lost in our world as we become more individualistic and care only for ourselves. In recognition of Christ's message of embracing the Other and welcoming the poor, we need to regain this lost sense of connection with each other and to each other. Erotic power is about inclusion and embracing of others. When this occurs, other forms of power emerge from it.[9] This erotic power is important and necessary to acknowledge within our own lives and in the world. As power emerges from the erotic, we need to recognize the erotic power of the Spirit. Both the female anima and the male animus explain Jung's notion of difference, a term he uses to describe the elemental power within all of us that can motivate us to lead collective movements for the common good.[10] In a broken and hurting world, this erotic power of the Spirit is deeply needed and cherished. It will bring healing to the brokenhearted, and comfort to the distraught, and wholeness to a world that has been so wounded by hate and despair. Our erotic longing is grounded in Spirit God who deeply desires us. As we

---

the TV series *Perception*. This schizophrenic imagining often helps the lead character to solve crimes. Jung describes his similar sense of the anima as he thought and wrote about it: "At first it was the negative aspect of the anima that most impressed me. I felt a little awed by her. It was like the feeling of an invisible presence . . . Then . . . in putting down all this material for analysis I was in effect writing letters to the anima, that is, to a part of myself with a different viewpoint from my conscious one" (3290 of 7243).

Be especially careful in pushing the comparison between Eros and *anima*. *Anima* is a female impulse, but it is found in males. *Animus* is a male impulse, found in women. It may be more accurate to map Eros to the set of (anima, animus).

8. Haunani-Kay Trask, *Eros and Power: The Promise of Feminist Theory* (Philadelphia: University of Pennsylvania Press, 1986), pp. 92-93.

9. Brock, *Journeys by Heart*, pp. 25, 26.

10. Grace Ji-Sun Kim, *Colonialism, Han, and the Transformative Spirit*, p. 75.

allow our Chi to rise we are able to love with vulnerable, open intimacy and engage the powers and principalities in the spirit of nonviolent love. Spirit God's erotic love helps us to love those who have hurt us and damaged us. It helps us to overcome alienation and separation towards reconciliation and embrace.

Divine Eros

The Eros of the Triune God is the source of our own erotic energy. There is beauty and life in the Divine Eros and love expresses its healing power. Love is expressed in the incarnation. The incarnation is powerful because it reveals and heals. This in turn expresses the singularity of love in the world. Lovers of the Divine in the past and the present, many of whom are despised by the institutional church, bear witness to this nonviolent love. It is important to engage in practices of love that are divorced from all separating dualisms created by our arrogance and insistence on the virtues of "my way of knowing" as we inquire into the meaning of incarnation. Such practices of love help us to better recognize the idols we have been worshiping as, at best, representations of that which we call the Divine. Love and compassion expose our inner tendencies to do violence to the face of Christ shining in those sisters and brothers of ours that we allow the church to despise.[11] We must allow love to flow through us to eliminate the dangerous acts of segregation, hatred, and anger from our lives.

The Spirit is pervaded by love. This love is emancipatory, liberating, and courageous. And it is prophetic. It compels us to act. It encourages us to seek to love rather than to give in to hate. It provokes us to work for justice rather than be a silent bystander. Confronted by systems that wound our sisters and brothers and violate God's creation, we need to act courageously. This can only come from the Spirit that enriches and sustains us. It frees us to act in positive ways, once the barriers of conflicting articles of faith, and the motives of politics and wealth, are laid aside.

The Spirit awakens, stimulates, arouses, and engages processes of creativity with passion and intimacy. The erotic foreplay for the birthing of possibilities is a prerogative of the Spirit. Several indigenous cultures view the Spirit in this way, as does the Asian notion of the Spirit as a Great

---

11. Wendy Farley, *Gathering Those Driven Away: A Theology of Incarnation* (Louisville: Westminster John Knox, 2011), p. 38.

Mother.[12] The Divine Eros can also help us to understand the incarnation, as it is within the Divine Eros that the incarnation comes forth.

Feminist theologian Wendy Farley speaks of Divine Eros as a dimension of reality that is monadic, wordless, and yearns to realize itself in creation. It is in the sublime intimacy of being filled with the Spirit that one experiences Eros. It is in this Spirit that the wordless energy of all that is and the deepest truth of the human soul can be experienced and lived out. Farley states that it is this erotic groundlessness that constitutes our own image of the Divine. This in turn prevents us from creating unworthy concepts of God and helps us avoid the way of negation — the practice of naming that excludes.[13] This Divine Eros is powerful and it is in this intimate relationship of the Spirit that we can experience love.

When we talk about the Divine, we confront a great mystery, and this should not be taken lightly. For some, wrestling to understand the divine mystery is the heart of one's faith and theology and also part of one's contemplative practice. Seeking the Divine becomes a daily journey. We can perhaps begin to reflect on the Divine Eros incarnate in Wisdom and in Christ.[14] For so long we have dichotomized wisdom and logos as if they were two separate entities. The movement away from dualism will allow us to see that they are not separate. The Divine Eros embodies both the logos and the Sophia. "With Jesus as Sophia, one encounters the mystery of God who is neither male nor female, but who, as Source of both and Creator of both in the divine image, can in turn be imaged as either."[15] The Divine Eros embodies the Spirit and Wisdom of God, and it is this unity that enables us to build bridges and connect with people we have marginalized. If we can recognize the foreignness within our individual selves, we can recognize and accept the foreignness in the Other. This recognition encourages us to welcome and embrace the Other.

Imagining the Divine is difficult. We have created limiting concepts of God that have lasted centuries. If it serves the purpose of legitimating those who are in positions of power, such unbalanced images will continue to perpetuate and bring negative feelings to those who are on the outside as well as those who are relegated to inferior roles. We need to be able to reimagine God in ways that embrace all people and liberate those who are

---

12. O'Murchu, *In the Beginning Was the Spirit*, p. 157.

13. Farley, *Gathering Those Driven Away*, p. 66.

14. Farley, *Gathering Those Driven Away*, p. 88.

15. Grace Ji-Sun Kim, *The Grace of Sophia: A Korean North American Women's Christology* (Cleveland: Pilgrim Press, 2002), p. 134.

in bondage. As we work towards such a goal, we are struck by the power of love. Erotic love is powerful and transformative. It can change lives and give us new ways of understanding and being. We need to unleash this power and work towards liberty and shalom justice. This is a very interesting exploration of how we can imagine the Divine. It is not something we can fully conceptualize with our finite minds.

We must leave room for mystery in our theological discourse and journey. As we meditate on the Divine, we can be open to the apophatic depth of mystery, the incomprehensible and unthinkable abyss into which reason and experience and language fall. If we do not allow mystery, then our religions can become idolatrous and our faith can become a consoling fiction. The unthinkable abyss is the spiritual Eros. The Wisdom in the Divine enacts the richness of this Erotic Abyss. Wisdom or Sophia discloses immeasurable Eros to itself.[16] Sophia and Eros are inseparable. Both make Spirit God. It is what we witness in the incarnation and the ongoing experience and revelation of the Spirit. The Spirit is fed and nourished by this deep mysterious Eros that electrifies us and gives us power to act for change. It encourages us to act prophetically, to join God in building God's reign here on this earth. God is the powerful Spirit who moves us to work for justice and goodwill. The Spirit never leaves us, but rather clings to us, lives within us, and manifests our total being. We must allow this erotic power of the Spirit to work for change.

The twentieth-century renaissance in Trinitarian theology was inspired by a recovery of interest in Greek patristics, especially the Cappadocian theologians. In the Russian Orthodox theologian Sergei Bulgakov we find an affirmation of Sophia as illuminating the love in the immanent Trinity expressed generously to the whole community of creation. Bulgakov understands God as Love by bringing in Sophia. God is Love not "in the sense of a quality or a property peculiar to God, but as the very substance and vigor of his life. The tri-hypostatic union of the Godhead is a mutual love, in which each of the hypostases, by a timeless act of self-giving in love, reveals itself in both the others."[17] It is a loving Trinitarian understanding of God that centers on mutual love. Sophia like Spirit is an integral part of the Trinity. Bulgakov believes that "the divine hypostases alone do not constitute the only personal centers of this love, for Ousia-Sophia likewise belongs to the

---

16. Farley, *Gathering Those Driven Away*, p. 123.

17. Sergei Bulgakov, *Sophia: The Wisdom of God, An Outline of Sophiology* (New York: Paisley Press, 1937), pp. 34, 35.

realm of God's Love. It is loved by the Holy Trinity as life and revelation, in it the triune God loves himself."[18] There is a mutual understanding and experience of love within the Godhead. God loves Sophia and Sophia loves God. Since love is the animating center of the Triune God, the Erotic Divine gives power to transform lives and empower those who are in the margins.

Bulgakov offers a Trinitarian theology that takes Sophia seriously. He states, "This unity of all with all and in all is the ground of the energy of love within the Godhead. Sophia, as the 'world' of God, represents a 'pan-organism' of the ideas of all in the all, while vital power of this organism is derived from the Holy Spirit. That, in effect, is what the Godhead is for God."[19] There is a connectedness between Sophia and the Spirit. "Sophia changes the theological and spiritual landscape for all who recognize her presence."[20] This understanding of the Trinity includes Sophia and Spirit God and in doing so embodies and exposes a vulnerable love so that we can experience God's love and be erotically energized for the work of reconciliation and transformation. Sophia and Spirit are internal to the immanent Trinity, the Godhead within God.

The Divine Eros can eliminate the darkness and bring wholeness to our lives. Wendy Farley reminds us that there is nothing more joyous than the divine presence. The Divine Eros is a kind of intoxicating overabundance of life and all that life has to offer. This is the power that flows through Jesus of Nazareth,[21] the joy of sustaining the sense of the mystical without interruption. The Divine Eros exudes joy regardless of one's race, ethnicity, and gender. This love that comes from the flow of God's energy erases doubt and relieves the mind from suffering.

When we abandon abuse and unkindness, our bodies can become instruments of joy: this is the ongoing power of Erotic Divinity. We need the Divine to melt away the institutions that take beauty and life away from all of us, those "thousand natural shocks that flesh is heir to!"[22] Sexism, racism, homophobia, and patriarchy all defraud us and make us inhuman.[23] We are the embodiments of the erotic love that we are able to display in our day-to-day living. We need to succumb to it and allow it to move and shake our lives. Joy needs to overflow from our lives and flow through life. The Spirit of God

---

18. Bulgakov, *Sophia: The Wisdom of God*, pp. 34, 35.
19. Bulgakov, *Sophia: The Wisdom of God*, p. 59.
20. Grace Ji-Sun Kim, *The Grace of Sophia*, p. 147.
21. Farley, *Gathering Those Driven Away*, p. 222.
22. Shakespeare, *Hamlet*, Act III, Scene I.
23. Farley, *Gathering Those Driven Away*, p. 224.

empowers us to work for change. Danger, hatred, and prejudice need to be dismantled so that the Divine Eros can overflow and embrace the goodness of life and so that all people and creation can experience God's presence and reign. Embracing the Other begins in the heart.

Embracing the Other

My baptism into embracing the Other took place in India in 1989. I spent twelve hot weeks there as a summer intern (sponsored by the mission office of the Presbyterian Church in Canada). I landed in New Delhi around one in the morning. When my missionary contact came to pick me up, I noticed dozens of people lying on the sidewalks and beside the road. Only later did I realize that these were homeless people sleeping outside under the night sky. It was in this place so foreign to me that I began my heart journey to embrace the Other.

This was a summer of new experiences. I tried on a sari. I tasted "lady's fingers" — okra — for the first time. And I visited the Taj Mahal, which overwhelmed me with its majestic, astonishing, mysterious beauty.

I was also confronted with new challenges. The streets of New Delhi and Calcutta were full of poor people begging for economic survival. Among them were lepers, who elicited my deepest fears. The fear of the unknown prevented me from approaching them and talking with them, much less embracing them.

When I visited Mother Teresa's Missionaries of Charity in Calcutta, I witnessed many of the sisters and volunteers feeding and otherwise helping the lepers. But even there I couldn't bring myself to get close to them, let alone embrace them.

These memories have haunted me for over twenty-five years. Jesus taught us about the importance of caring for lepers. In fact, in the Gospel of Matthew, a leper approached Jesus and asked to be healed, saying, "Lord, if you choose, you can make me clean." Jesus reached out his hand and touched the leper, saying, "I do choose. Be made clean!" (Matt. 8:1-3). Jesus welcomed those who were different — the ill, the outcast, the foreigner, the marginalized. And he challenged everyone to do likewise.

My experience in India raised larger questions. As a Korean American seeking to embrace the Other, I was forced to do some deep soul-searching. I raised the question that most troubled my heart: "Can I embrace the Japanese, who have invaded my homeland too many times?" During the Japanese occupation (1910-1945), many Koreans lost their lives. But even those who survived lost their former lives: they lost much of their Korean identity, culture, history, and society. For example, my grandmother had to change her name to a Japanese name to survive. Other women faced even more traumatic challenges: some were kidnapped by the Japanese and forced to become "comfort women" before and during World War II.

Comfort women were women and girls forced into sexual slavery by the Imperial Japanese Army. The number of women taken as sexual slaves is estimated to be over 400,000. Many young Korean girls were abducted from their own homes or were lured with promises of work in factories or restaurants. They were then locked up in what were called "comfort stations" and placed in small quarters, where they were repeatedly raped day and night. Each woman was "servicing" about fifty men a day.

About three-quarters of these "comfort women" died. They suffered tremendously under this oppressive system: besides being raped, they were physically tortured and mentally abused. The survivors often became infertile because they had contracted venereal diseases. After the war, many women couldn't return to their families because of the shame it would bring to them.

This horrific experience cast a long, dark shadow over many Korean communities. As I argued in Chapter 3, the legacy of Korean "comfort women" during the Japanese occupation of Korea created the conditions in which Korean women could be "Orientalized" and exploited again by U.S. servicemen through militarized prostitution in the late twentieth century. Given the dark period in our history created by the Japanese occupation, how can we embrace this enemy, who destroyed innocent lives and our sacred culture and folkways?

Sometimes we take Jesus' challenges to heart, but in most cases, we do not. We find it too difficult to follow Jesus and do what he did during his ministry on earth. But the challenge remains for us: How do we truly and vulnerably embrace the Other?

First, we need to overcome any doubt about whether Jesus really wanted us to embrace the Other. Did he mean it, or was it merely a way to dramatize a point? It is the same way we approach the passage about the rich man giving up his wealth to follow Jesus. "Jesus, looking at him, loved him and said, 'You lack one thing; go, sell what you own, and give the money to the poor, and you will have treasure in heaven; then come, follow me'" (Mark 10:21). Many Christians just take this passage as a dramatization of a point and do not necessarily follow it. They believe that Jesus didn't really mean it. But if this was a command that Jesus gave us, it is crucial to obey it. When wealthy people give their money to the poor, they enter into a deep solidarity with "the least and the lost" that we are called to care for. We enter into a similar solidarity when we embrace the Other.

Second, we fear the unknown. We are afraid to love and embrace those who are different from us. We are often scared of those with a disease or those who don't look like we do. When I was in India, I didn't embrace the lepers because I was young and all by myself, and I was afraid that I might contract leprosy. Yet my deepest fear was the fear of the unknown — a fear that most of us share. Many white Americans, for example, are fearful of people from different countries and of different races and religions. People from other countries, from Muslims to Asians, are often called "foreigners," which distances them from the white norm. Let's face it: we're afraid of those whom we do not know. Subterranean fears prevent us from taking the bold and risky step of embracing the Other.

Third, it takes time, energy, and commitment to truly embrace the Other. Embracing is not a verbal proclamation. It is not a simple act of getting to know the Other. It requires more than that. It requires patient and persistent love. It requires that we get to know them and accept them, and then embrace them fully with our body, heart, and soul.

Fourth, we need to open ourselves to Spirit God, who moves within us to move us to embrace the Other. Jesus sent the Spirit as "the helper" to lead us as we seek to love and be reconciled with the Other (John 14:16). The work of reconciliation is fundamentally spiritual work. Spirit God transcends culture, race, and religion and is the wellspring of healing and hope. As we recognize that the Spirit is in the Other, we will be more able to share our whole soul with the Other. It is through the presence of the Spirit that the wounds between countries, between races, between faiths, between women and men can be healed and new prophetic partnerships can be forged. While the Spirit is mysterious, it helps us overcome our deepest fears, enabling us to take the risk of opening ourselves to be intimate with the Other. Our openness to the Spirit is crucial in our step toward embracing the stranger, the foreigner, the outcast, the marginalized. Spirit God empowers us to welcome, embrace, and love the Other.

Croatian Protestant theologian Miroslav Volf discusses the complexity of embrace in his theological classic, *Exclusion and Embrace*. To get at a deeper understanding of embrace, Volf first defines exclusion. According to Volf, "Exclusion can entail cutting of the bonds that connect, taking oneself out of the pattern of interdependence and placing oneself in a position of sovereign independence."[24] Volf believes that Christ's work involves not allowing an enemy to remain an enemy but rather trying to create a space for the enemy to come in. "Having been embraced by God," he says, "we must make space for others in ourselves and invite them in — even our enemies."[25] As we offer hospitality to the enemy, allow them to come into our lives, we are doing the difficult work of moving toward embracing the Other.

As Volf notes, we need to desire to engage the Other. When we stretch out our arms in embrace, we signal this desire, create space, and open boundaries. An embrace is one of the engagements needed to make a change for the better in society. Without true embrace, true engagement, "meeting" the Other becomes something shallow and non-committal.[26] Embracing the Other demands deep existential commitment and persistent love to achieve reconciliation, justice, and peace.

From my perspective as a Korean American feminist theologian, I pose three challenges to Volf's theology of embrace. First, the work of reconciliation begins with our wounds, which affect the deepest areas of our heart. If we are to work for justice and reconciliation, we need to have the courage to enter the places of our greatest pain in order to be instruments of peace in the world. This will mean a deeper account of the psychological effects of trauma on the victims of disaster, war, and sexual violence. Second, we have to tap into the dark abyss of our erotic power in order to claim our power as public leaders who seek to be agents of reconciliation, healing, and hope. Erotic power produces both conflict and resolution in relationships between women and men. Open acknowledgment of the erotic dimensions of our relationships will foster the conditions for channeling our Chi toward deeper intimacy and the struggle for the common good. Third, we need a sharper analysis of the structures of exclusion in our neo-liberal global capitalist regime, where women of Asian descent are often objectified and commodified in sex trafficking rings and sweat-shop factory work and domestic work abroad. It is the *han* or unjust suffering of this trans-national Asian sisterhood that I feel in my heart and soul, and that is why I am committed to an analysis of power that unveils the power differential between women of Asian descent and men of European descent as integral to the work of reconciliation and embrace. With a clear analysis of the power of patriarchy and racism in North

24. Miroslav Volf, *Exclusion and Embrace: A Theological Exploration of Identity, Otherness, and Reconciliation* (Nashville: Abingdon Press, 1996), p. 67.

25. Volf, *Exclusion and Embrace*, p. 129.

26. Volf, *Exclusion and Embrace*, p. 141.

American society, we will be in a better position to channel our erotic energy toward deep interpersonal healing and systemic transformation.

Spirit God energizes both women and men to have conflict-resolution conversations in which we courageously go to the places of deep division and traumatic wounds. Embracing the Other entails talking about the issues with nonviolent, empathetic listening, mutual understanding, and heartfelt prayer. Spirit God connects us to each other, opens us up for an exchange of what is in our hearts, heals the curse between men and women that goes back to Adam and Eve (Gen. 3:14-19), and is a source of perpetual soul repair and bodily renewal as we move into a deep and disciplined spirituality that can sustain the movement to incarnate God's justice and shalom, on earth as it is in heaven.

God took the first step to embrace us. We ought to follow that example by taking the first step to embrace the Other. The Spirit of God which dances in our lives — connecting us, challenging us, and comforting us — asks us to treat those who are different as ourselves. The Spirit of God teaches us to join the divine dance of love.

Perichoresis and the Dance of Love

The classical Trinitarian concept of *perichoresis* (περιχώρησις in the Greek or *circumincessio* in the Latin) can inspire us to embrace the Other. *Perichoresis* is the mutual indwelling and interpenetration of the three persons of the Trinity. The eighth-century theologian John Damascene coined the term to express the intimate relationship between the three persons of the Trinity. *Perichoresis* connotes that each person of the Trinity is never an isolated entity but is always dependent upon the other two persons of the Trinity.[27] The Trinity exists in an interrelatedness, interpenetration, and codependence. *Perichoresis* describes this mutual indwelling, dependence, love, and synergistic collective action. It is an example that we humans can imitate.

Perichoresis exemplifies how we are to engage in relationships with one another. We are to be always dependent upon each other; we do not exist alone. Like ballet dancers, we become one as we move together in an artful, flowing form. This codependency is vital to our spiritual growth and development, and specifically to our growth in love, forgiveness, and acceptance.

27. Patrick S. Cheng, "A Three-Part Sinfonia: Queer Asian Reflections on the Trinity," *Journal of Race, Ethnicity and Religion* 3 (2012): 19.

Perichoresis provides an image of the three persons of the Trinity engaged in a joyful, intertwined dance. The word *perichoresis* actually is derived from the Greek root word for dancing, evoking an image of an eternal and ecstatic dance of love and mutuality.[28] The bond between the persons of the Trinity is so strong that it cannot be broken or severed. This strength and unity allows it to create new things.

Theorists such as Michel Foucault and Judith Butler have challenged fixed, static, or essentialist notions of ourselves. In the same manner *perichoresis* challenges a fixed, static, or essentialist notion of each person of the Trinity. *Perichoresis* describes the boundaries of each triune person as being in a continual state of flux, constantly being interpenetrated by the other two persons. This blurred relationship among the three persons of the Trinity is helpful to our own understanding and perception of ourselves. It is similar to notions of hybridity within postcolonial discourse that remind us we are not fixed beings but are forever changing, moving, and in flux.[29] In our fluid state, we change and move as the Spirit leads.

This Spirit God has the capacity and power to make us into new beings. The Spirit is full of life, encouragement, and love. Life needs to be fruitful and giving, and it is only this Spirit of God who can accomplish this. As we recognize this, it is almost a plea that we surrender to the power of the Spirit, which embodies the erotic power of love and can show us how we are to live in mutuality, love, care, forgiveness, and Eros. God creates us to celebrate life and not destroy it. We are to enjoy and take care of life.

Spirit God who embraces life is in a divine dance with Sophia. This divine dance unveils a dynamic erotic energy within the Godhead, which integrates the three forms of love: Agape, Eros, and Philios. Bulgakov believes that there is more to the love energy in the Trinity than simply the *perichoretic* communion between the Father, Son, and Holy Spirit. There is an actual divine dance that occurs between the Holy Spirit and Sophia in the dark abyss of the "Godhead of God." It is this divine dance of love that we are able to experience and share with each other. This leads to empowerment and hope for the weary, the marginalized, and the outcasts.

Asian American theological discourse needs to re-imagine the Trinity, conceiving the Divine primarily as Spirit. Spirit connects us to God through ecstatic prayer. Anglican theologian Sarah Coakley reminds us that "the 'Trinity' *is* the graced ways of God with creation, alluring and conforming

---

28. Cheng, "A Three-Part Sinfonia," p. 19.
29. Cheng, "A Three-Part Sinfonia," p. 20.

that creation into the life of the 'Son.' ('When we cry "Abba, Father," it is the Spirit bearing witness with our spirit that we are children of God' [Romans 8.15-16].)."[30] We experience grace through the Trinity. The Trinity helps us understand how Spirit God works in our world. Coakley writes that "the 'Spirit' is that which, while being nothing less than 'God,' cannot quite be reduced to a metaphorical naming of the Father's outreach. It is not that the prayer is having a conversation with some distant and undifferentiated deity, and then is being asked (rather arbitrarily) to 'hypostatize' that conversation (or 'relationship') into a 'person' (the Spirit)."[31] Since Spirit is God, opening our bodies up to be inhabited by the Spirit deepens our communion with the Triune God, with the Other, and with the community of creation.

Sergei Bulgakov explains the relationship within the Trinity this way: "[The first postulate affirms that] the Father, the Son, and the Holy Spirit, who are three distinct divine persons, together constitute one God. The second postulate is concerned with the consubstantiality of the Holy Trinity, which has but one substance or nature (*ousia* or *physis, substantia* or *natura*)."[32] Bulgakov discusses the Trinity with Sophia, which ultimately helps move towards a liberative theology, especially for women. Bulgakov believes that "[t]he Holy Trinity is consubstantial and indivisible. The three persons of the Holy Trinity have one life in common, that is, one Ousia, one Sophia. Nevertheless this unity of divine life coexists with the fact that the life of each of the hypostases in the divine Ousia-Sophia is determined in accordance with its own personal character, or specific hypostatic features."[33] The three are one. Sophia and Spirit-Chi give life to the work of reconciliation and embrace, unveiling the mystery of the Triune God.

As I have sought to deepen my account of a Trinitarian ontology of reconciliation, I have found Hyo-Dong Lee's *Spirit, Qi, and the Multitude* illuminating. We both affirm the importance of Spirit-Chi as an ontic connection between the Trinity and the world. With an Augustinian inspiration, Lee unveils the mystical union between the Spirit and the Father, writing, "[The first postulate affirms that] the Spirit, who eternally proceeds from the Father and the Son as their mutual love, one pole of which is originary and the other derivative, comes to embrace the multitude of creaturely spirits only with the Father's decision to create the material world ex nihilo

---

30. Sarah Coakley, *God, Sexuality and the Self: An Essay "on the Trinity"* (Cambridge: Cambridge University Press, 2013), p. 112.

31. Coakley, *God, Sexuality and the Self,* p. 112.

32. Bulgakov, *Sophia: The Wisdom of God,* p. 23.

33. Bulgakov, *Sophia: The Wisdom of God,* pp. 37, 38.

and send the Son into the world in the 'economy' of salvation history."[34] Our participation in the gracious unity of the Trinitarian God is what saves us. Mystically shaped by this triune communion of love, Lee notes, we are pushed toward a materialization of justice in the political sphere. Moments of materialization in the multitude's attempt to embody democracy offer traces of the Trinity. Spirit God provides the ontic link between the triune economy and the *oikonomia*. This *oikonomia*, or whole inhabited earth, is the place where God's Spirit dwells. As we receive the embrace of Spirit God, we are enabled to embrace the Other.

Hyo-Dong Lee further explains the Trinity by affirming the common divine substance among the Godhead:

> Granted, insofar as the Father's eternal, "immanent" relations to the Son and the Spirit are concerned (i.e., within the so-called "immanent Trinity"), the classical doctrine has always adamantly affirmed the equality of the divine persons. The three divine persons share a common divine substance or essence equally, because the Father communicates to the Son and the Spirit the totality of the divine essence without any diminishment.[35]

The unity of the Trinitarian God is what saves us. Spirit God, which is in the Trinity, continues to work within the Godhead to save us. It is ultimately the work of the Trinity that saves, empowers, and liberates us to experience human flourishing and new life.

The concept of the *perichoresis* can help Asian American women resist the notion that we are hopelessly trapped by our marginalized identities as Asian, immigrant, and woman. *Perichoresis* allows us to appreciate the fact that, rather than being limited by these identities, our beautiful inner life is always changing and becoming new and renewed. As each of the three persons of the Trinity constantly interact in a mutually interpenetrating dance, so too Asian American immigrant women are interacting with and embracing each other and others in society.[36] New places of encouragement and life-giving elements open up as we try to coexist in places of in-betweenness and hybridity created by our three identities on society's margins. *Perichore-*

34. Hyo-Dong Lee, *Spirit, Qi, and the Multitude: A Comparative Theology for the Democracy of Creation* (New York: Fordham University Press, 2014), p. 10.

35. Lee, *Spirit, Qi, and the Multitude*, p. 11.

36. Cheng, "A Three-Part Sinfonia," p. 20.

sis affirms that each of these three identities is intertwined in a unique way. The interplay of these three identities is a reflection of the joyful dance of *perichoresis.*[37] It is Spirit God that moves in between these crevices to bring hope, life, and abounding joy.

As Asian Americans recognize that our place of marginality can be a site of empowerment, we become further encouraged, enlightened, and liberated. We are complex beings and therefore a simple categorization or essentialization will only work negatively. We must accept the complexities of Asian American immigrant women and understand that it is within this complexity that we experience the mysterious understanding of the Divine. Mystery engulfs the being of God. In the mysterious Abyss between God and us, we come to experience the erotic power that will give us new life and encourage us to create new life in others. It is this empowering erotic power of God's Spirit that will transform our lives so that we can live a prophetic life within a broken world, a world torn apart by differing understandings of race, gender, and sexuality.

Spirit God through the erotic power of prophets of revolutionary love can break down the walls and cross the boundaries that separate us. The boundless and free erotic power moves in between and among spaces within and between people. The erotic power that exists between people and among communities can help dislocate the systems that maintain boundaries of privilege and exclusion created by systems of racism, sexism, and capitalism. These boundaries are set up intentionally to maintain and contain power by, and for, the powerful. They establish and maintain continual discrimination, prejudice, and subordination. The oppressive structures create spaces of marginalization and exclusion. To address the issues of discrimination, prejudice, and subordination, the structures that maintain the marginal spaces need to be dismantled.

As we continue to seek a theology that will liberate Asian American women, it is apparent that Spirit God can disrupt this reality and change the dynamics of power. Spirit God is present in these spaces. It is not a divine God who lives in the center and visits the margins. Rather Spirit God resides in the margins and is present with the marginalized. Just as the *perichoresis* of the three persons of the Trinity involves a dance, Spirit God engages in a joyful, intimate movement of dancing with marginalized people seeking justice and liberation. Spirit God disrupts, contradicts, and also reconciles. Spirit God empowers marginalized people to challenge the center and ex-

---

37. Cheng, "A Three-Part Sinfonia," p. 22.

pand the boundaries that keep them excluded. Spirit God contests the walls and boundaries to set up new ways of being together in a broken world. The dynamics of power become altered so that new energies and creativities can be explored and released. Gordon Fee points to the reality when he lifts up ". . . the Holy Spirit as *person,* the person of God himself; the Holy Spirit as God's personal *presence;* and the Holy Spirit as God's *empowering* presence."[38] God's personal and empowering presence is both the motivation and the modality of embracing the Other. It is only through Spirit-led reconciliation that deep healing can occur between victim and victimizer, oppressed and oppressor, as they work together to dismantle systemic oppression in our society today.

When "justice rolls like a river" (Amos 5:24) for the powerless, the powerful are not just abandoned. The people who benefit from oppressive systems can experience healing and wholeness from Spirit God. Once they experience healing, they in turn will discontinue their participation in such oppressive systems. They can then join hands with the marginalized and walk hand in hand. This can all be accomplished through the erotic power of Spirit-Chi. The power of the Spirit is influential and persuasive. As Fee elaborates, "the personal presence of God, the Spirit is not merely some 'force' or 'influence.' The living God is a God of power; and by the Spirit the power of the living God is present with and for us."[39] The Spirit is present to all people, bringing healing and hope.

Spirit God can disrupt spaces and bring wholeness to both the marginalized and the oppressors. As Spirit-Chi dances with Sophia in the Godhead, it brings holiness and wholeness to the people. It is prophetic and grounds itself in shalom justice in the Godhead. It dwells among us. It is the life-giving force that changes us and moves us to work for justice. It stirs the erotic power within us to care for each other and to work together for shalom justice.

The *perichoresis* of the Triune God reminds us of the ultimate fluidity of our racial, sexual, and spiritual identities, and this identity connects us to God. The Spirit is fluid and can move into places that are usually bound and limited. The boundaries and borders created by people with power to provide privilege for people with power can be dismantled as the Spirit's presence enters and transforms them. We need to be open to the transformative power

---

38. Gordon D. Fee, *God's Empowering Presence: The Holy Spirit in the Letters of Paul* (Peabody, MA: Hendrickson, 1994), p. 5.

39. Fee, *God's Empowering Presence,* p. 8.

of Spirit God that both disrupts and interrupts power structures and that challenges and transforms systems, communities, people, and our entire world. It carries out the holy work of building shalom justice in a world broken, torn apart by unjust structures, and it welcomes us to join in that work. The Spirit restores what is broken.

Through it all, it is by grace that God redeems us. It is by grace that Spirit God is reconciling all things. The Apostle Paul writes, "By grace you have been saved" (Eph. 2:5). Grace is a gift from God that helps us in all our daily struggles; it is abundant, and given to all those who seek it. God offers grace to help human beings accomplish good things that they cannot achieve alone.

Transforming the World

Spirit-led transformation is both a personal and a political process. Through claiming our erotic power in a dance of healing and hope, we can witness a verdant spring where lovers go and lovers come, the sky and sun become but one. Erotic power is the energy that produces creative synthesis and sustains us throughout life; this raw energy connects us with others. Erotic power grounds the concreteness and vividness of our experiences of empathy, creativity, sensuality, and beauty.[40] This erotic power of the Spirit resides and freely moves in and between us. It leads us to a path of dismantling destructive hierarchies. It is a powerful force that challenges and erodes damaging institutionalized structures that have held many people captive.[41]

Institutional racism and sexism have been so well integrated into our culture that they often go unnoticed. Society ignores their destructive realities and therefore does nothing to dismantle them. It becomes our Christian responsibility to work towards eliminating the structural evil that exists in our society, community, and churches. This can be achieved first by recognizing and then dismantling the white supremacy and racism and patriarchy and sexism that have loomed over our Christian tradition.

Erotic power is present in all parts of our being and energizes the struggle for justice, equality, and love. It inspires a desire within us that wants to drive away any form of oppression and injustice. Rita Nakashima Brock writes, "Through the erotic as power we become less willing to accept

40. Brock, *Journeys by Heart*, p. 39.
41. Grace Ji-Sun Kim, *Colonialism, Han, and the Transformative Spirit*, p. 76.

powerlessness, despair, depression, and self-denial. The erotic is what binds and gives life and hope. It is the energy of all relationship and it connects us to our embodied selves."[42] As Brock points out, erotic power fuels a new relationality that leads us to organize and work for a just and sustainable world. The erotic power of the Spirit of Justice transforms us to fight against institutional forms of oppression, whether it be patriarchy, sexism, classism, or racism. Eros connects us to one another. A longing for belonging, eros plays a vital role in community-building efforts. This erotic power will move us and stir us to change, empowering us to work for justice within our communities, our countries, and our world. Erotic power is fundamental to life and propels us to seek fullness in life. This erotic power energizes us to seek justice and live out our life in the fullest capacity of love. It is through love that we can achieve justice for one another and for the earth.[43]

Connection is the basic power of all existence. All that is comes to be by virtue of connectedness. Erotic power is the fundamental power of existence-as-a-relational-process. The root of life and the power of becoming is erotic power. Erotic power leads us, through the human heart, toward life-giving actions. As the foundation of life and the source of energy for human beings, erotic power compels us to search for the wholeness of life. This power affirms, creates, and is recreated in human existence by love. Erotic power compels us toward compassion, collective action, integration, self-acceptance, and self-reflective memory in our critical recollection of the past.[44] The Spirit-led life helps us stay connected to God and the Other in deep solidarity as we engage in the work of social transformation.

As we ponder justice, we need to be mindful of restoring broken and lost relationships. Lutheran theological ethicist Cynthia Moe Lobeda understands the importance of healing creation in social and environmental ethics. She states,

> The mystery of creation "is the indwelling of God within it." . . . We "mud creatures" are home to One who breathes through creation, healing, making whole, undoing injustice, and restoring right relationships, so that all might have life and have it abundantly. Having received God's subversive love, we are bearers of it.[45]

42. Brock, *Journeys by Heart*, p. 41.
43. Grace Ji-Sun Kim, *Colonialism, Han, and the Transformative Spirit*, pp. 78-79.
44. Brock, *Journeys by Heart*, pp. 41, 42.
45. Cynthia Moe-Lobeda, *Healing a Broken World: Globalization and God* (Minneapolis: Fortress Press, 2002), p. 133.

The Spirit is the source of "restoring right relationships." The Spirit keeps theological interpretations of life open for the future as well as sustaining the dangerous memories of the past.

This cosmic understanding of a communion between the living and the dead has been central in Asian, Latin American, and African religions, in which ancestors have significance for the present. Since the Spirit works in memory to access both the past and the future, both need to be treated not as predictable but as open to the mystery of God's transforming work. The memory as well as the future continually offer thresholds for the Creator to pass over into creation. The Spirit interprets the way we experience the anticipation of God's coming and the historical experience of remembering the God who has come. It becomes a gift flowing from the past and into the future, transforming our present reality.

The transformative Spirit of love has an internal and external dimension. When these two are fully integrated we can become advocates for justice in an unjust world. The world is unjust, and it always will be except in our dreams and the visions of our prophets. Life is full of complexity. Our problems are myriad. All individuals struggle with sin, and all institutions manifest social sin. Power imbalances exist. Some people simply decide they will break the rules because they can. Other people will always take God-given differences to state that they are superior to others. When these people possess a greater amount of power, they will shape institutions and societies to privilege themselves and take a greater share of the world's wealth and resources.

Since elite white males increasingly are in positions of leadership in our society, it is time to organize an alternative. As Jeffrey Stout argues in *Blessed Are the Organized*, if there is hope for democracy in America it will come from community organizers.[46] However, the problem with Stout's argument is that he limits himself to one style of organizing — the Industrial Areas Foundation (IAF), which grew out of the life and legacy of Saul Alinsky. Based on self-interest, this instrumental form of organizing has honed a method of organizing winnable victories within a community, but often through methods that are dehumanizing. It is vital that our organizing and advocacy appeal to the whole person, including their faith commitments.

Faith-rooted organizing is an innovative new model of organizing that gathers people for social change, from the deepest wells of their faith. Alexia

---

46. Jeffrey Sout, *Blessed Are the Organized: Grassroots Democracy in America* (Princeton, NJ: Princeton University Press, 2010).

Salvatierra and Peter Goodwin Heltzel argue that Christians have been great at gathering people for hearing the Word proclaimed and celebrating the sacrament, but think it's now time to gather people for faith-rooted social change.[47] It is only through building relational power through the depth of our faith traditions that we can truly trouble the waters and heal the world.

Jesus was an amazing faith-rooted organizer. While his public ministry was only three years long, he had a powerful impact on his society.[48] A poor carpenter from the northern Galilee, Jesus was called by God to inaugurate the Kingdom of God. He shared his vision with the people in his region, calling twelve disciples to follow him as a core team. When he turned his face to Jerusalem like flint (Luke 9:51), he was hyper-focused on his mission, engaging the powers and principalities of Jerusalem, both Roman powers and Jewish powers. As a result of Jesus' interrogation he was crucified on a Roman cross. Jesus' life provides a template of what it means to be a faith-rooted organizer today.

Faith-rooted organizing is centered in Scripture, theology, and spirituality and therefore faith communities find it easy to follow and make it a way of life.[49] It works for justice and moves towards social change for the good. It is a model that can be used to address poverty, racial injustice, affordable housing, education, immigration, police reform, health reform, environmental justice, sex trafficking, domestic violence, labor trafficking, and other global problems that result from racism, patriarchy, and neoliberal capitalism. Faith-rooted organizing offers a deep spirituality that can help sustain the community of revolutionary friends for the long haul.

Concluding Thoughts

Spirit God is the source and destiny of our erotic longing. The erotic power of Spirit God empowers us to be instruments of love, peace, harmony, and justice. Our Spirit-led erotic energy inspires us to work for justice where there is no justice and to bring love where there is no love.

We need to recognize the mystery of the Divine and embrace the living experiences of women with broken bodies who have claimed the erotic

---

47. Alexia Salvatierra and Peter Goodwin Heltzel, *Faith-Rooted Organizing: Mobilizing the Church in Service to the World* (Downers Grove, IL: InterVarsity, 2013), p. 11.

48. Salvatierra and Heltzel, *Faith-Rooted Organizing*, p. 12.

49. Salvatierra and Heltzel, *Faith-Rooted Organizing*, p. 12.

power of Spirit God. God's Spirit is a healing balm that restores the broken bodies of women into the body of Christ, which was broken for our healing and redemption (1 Cor. 11:24). As we cry out from our places of deepest sorrow and sadness, God hears our cry and brings healing and hope (Pss. 18:6; 34:17).

Many Asian American women experience psychological isolation through their silenced pain as victims of racism and sexism. Yet, as they surrender themselves to the Spirit, the Spirit intercedes with God on their behalf (Rom. 8:26). The *perichoresis* of the Trinity graciously bestows a love without limit that can bind up the brokenhearted and bring liberating light into dark places.

The persuasive power of love pulls us into the divine dance between Spirit-Chi and Christ-Sophia within the Triune communion of love. The *perichoresis* of the divine Trinity reminds us that God dwells among us and is our dance instructor. When we forget our steps or lose faith in ourselves, the Spirit as Teacher reminds us of the dance steps of the kin-dom that Jesus of Nazareth so persuasively performed (John 14:26). Through surrender to the Spirit we can sing and dance again.

The Triune communion of love embodies Sophia and Eros crossing boundaries to embrace us and make us whole. Spirit God brings wondrous wholeness to the lives of Asian American women who have suffered in the margins of society. Sophia and Spirit-Chi within the Trinitarian Godhead are poured out into the world, bringing forth new life and transformative justice.

The dance and erotic love within the Godhead allow justice to prevail and loving communities to exist on earth, as they dance to the rhythm of heavenly drums, joining angels and archangels in singing the praise of God. This musical and mysterious Godhead gives birth to empowered justice that seeks to spring forth in shalom justice. It is the mysterious bond of Sophia and Spirit-Chi's love that continues to shed divine mystery on our lives so that we can become more perceptive and open to the mysterious communion of love, which can only be experienced in the divine Godhead. The grace of God opens our hearts and allows the empowering Spirit to fill our hearts and lives, transforming our cities into spaces of healing and hope.

Spirit God is a border-crosser. The fluidity of God's Spirit moves into places that are bound and limited. God crosses boundaries and fills the margins with the Spirit of healing and hope. Led by the Spirit, we need to cross the boundaries of gender, race, class, and religion. What boundary is God's Spirit calling us to cross today? May we have the vulnerability to ask God, the courage to obey, the wisdom to walk rightly, and the creativity to overcome all obstacles as we seek to embrace the Other.

Embracing the mysterious grace of the Living God offers a pathway for possibility. A more just and sustainable world is possible, if we have the courage and creativity to join God in making it happen. As we open ourselves up to our erotic power, may we take each other's hand, delight in our differences, dance in harmony, and share Spirit God's open, all-embracing movement of love to the ends of the earth.

Conclusion

A long history of colonialism, patriarchy, and white supremacy marginalizes certain groups of people, especially women of color. We need to bring diverse theological voices into the conversation to help us understand more deeply the Christian message. We need to take steps towards understanding Asian Christianities, as they will ultimately help us understand our own North American Christianity as well as the Asian immigrants who call North America their home. Understanding history and culture helps us understand our past, our present context, and where we will be moving towards in the future.

Asian American Women and Model Minority

As we maneuver subversively around colonial structures, ideals, and consequences in a globalized world, we need to question our daily experiences of ourselves, each other, and God. As the world continues to marginalize the poor, women, populations of color, and others on the underside of history, we need to amplify their voices and challenge the status quo.

Asian Americans, particularly Asian American women, have been pushed into the category of model minority. This is a label placed on us by whites to compare us to other immigrant minorities and to pit us against other people of color. The term creates divisiveness among minorities and a false sense of righteousness among whites who use it. It is a term that needs to be discarded, first, because it puts a barrier between Asian Americans and whites. Asian Americans will always be kept on the fringes of society if we accept this falsely prestigious label. The model minority label brings the title of "honorary whites." This term implies that whites are superior and that we all need to strive to become like whites to qualify for this label and the status it confers. Perhaps we need to marry whites, as some Japanese Americans did, so that our children will begin to look white. But as we saw in *Madama Butterfly*, the fate of a Japanese woman who marries a white American man is often a tragic one. As we usher in a feminist, intercultural future, celebrating cross-cultural relationships and biracial children, we need to be honest about the shadow side of Western civilization, whose colonial past has lingering effects on our psyches and social order.

The term "model minority" is used to continually marginalize us and remind us that the white majority considers us inferior, but that it tolerates those inferiorities. It also demonizes us if we do not succeed. Since Asian Americans are a model minority, it means we are the best of the minoritized groups; other minorities need to strive to become like us. However, we are not really at the top of the hierarchy. We remain a marginalized people with the whites safely positioned at the top.

The model minority status prevents us from speaking out against the evils of sexism and racism. Since we are supposed to be model citizens, we are not to disrupt the peace in our society. This has kept many Asian Americans from protesting or claiming that we have been racialized and discriminated against in the workplace, school, society, and larger community. We know that we should be model citizens and therefore do not want to cause problems. So, in many ways we internalize our pain and never let it out either in a personal manner or politically.

Spirit God

The Spirit is powerful and can empower Asian American women to flourish. Asian American women strive to maneuver through the speed bumps present for minoritized groups. We are further marginalized in the church by patriarchal ecclesiology. In our existence in the margins, we come to meet the God who also exists in the margins. This is Spirit God who has always been part of our history, culture, religion, and ancestral heritage.

It is important to recognize that Spirit or Chi has always existed. It is our experience of the Divine who embodies Sophia and Eros and crosses boundaries to embrace us and make us whole. The mysterious and liberating reconstruction of God as Spirit can bring wondrous wholeness to the lives of Asian American women who have suffered in the margins of society. Sophia and Spirit-Chi exist within the Trinitarian Godhead and bring forth new life and transformative justice. The dance and erotic love within the Godhead allows justice to prevail and loving communities to exist. This Godhead gives birth to empowered justice that seeks to bring forth shalom justice. It is the mysterious bond of Sophia and Spirit-Chi's love that continues to shed divine mystery into our lives so we can become more perceptive and open to the mysterious bond of love, which can only be experienced in the divine Godhead. The grace of God opens our hearts and allows the empowering Spirit-Chi to fill our hearts and lives.

Spirit-Chi offers a new yet ancient way to speak about the Holy Spirit. We must use what we are familiar with to help understand God and to explain God to those around us. The concept of Chi has existed for thousands of years within the Asian culture and tradition. It is important to use this widely recognized term to help understand God within our present context.

Embracing an Asian concept or term may help us work towards some reconciliation and social justice. Racism fears the Other and builds prejudice and stereotypes of the Other or those who look different from white Americans. Using concepts and terms interchangeably among people may work towards dismantling the structural racism that is so deeply embedded in our culture.

The concept of Spirit-Chi is liberating and leads to steps to help the marginalized. Sexism and racism are demeaning barriers to overcome. At times, sexism and racism lead to death. To prevent such horrors, Asian American women turn to Spirit-Chi for assurance, comfort, and hope. It is in Spirit-Chi that Asian American women can encounter mercy, hope, and love. Spirit-Chi is the third person of the Trinity. The *perichoresis* of the Trinity exemplifies the love without limit of the Trinity. It is also the same love that Asian American women can experience in their silenced pain of racism and sexism. It is this love that I think can empower women's lives.

The erotic power of God (Spirit God) is transformative. Many downtrodden and weakened Asian American women can find renewed strength and power in Spirit God. Spirit God will transform our hearts and encourage us to transform our lives, communities, and society. A theological discourse that does not change lives is problematic and needs to be altered. This theology that understands God as Spirit God has transformative powers to change our world. It enables us to make it a just world for all.

Implications for Our Church Today

A theological reconstruction based on Spirit God will have important, lasting implications for the church. The contemporary church is dis-ordered through the diseases of racism, sexism, classism, and other "isms." Troubling the waters of the world, Spirit God heals the wounds of the church, so it can be a life-giving community of transformation. Through disrupting the closed circuits of powerful white men, Spirit God is descending to dwell with those who are excluded and wounded, especially women. Spirit God re-orders communities through fostering democratic decision-making, encouraging mainstream society to become accountable to communities of color, and supporting the faith leadership of women and girls. Through faith-rooted organizing, prophetic Christians are dismantling racist and patriarchal structures, while building a more just and equitable society for all. Healing between women and men begins as they work together to dismantle structures of exclusion and collaboratively build a more inclusive and sustainable life together. The transformative love of Spirit God heals broken relationships as wounded healers seek to heal the world.

Spirit God brings restoration to both the individual and the community through the active, collective struggle for justice, reconciliation, and peace. The community which has been broken by racism and patriarchy can find healing and wholeness as the most affected in the community, especially women, claim their God-given power as transformational change agents. We are called to be the change that we long for. Within the community, there are other sisters in the struggle who will comfort and encourage one another as they seek to build beloved community together.

Embracing Spirit God empowers all of us to work towards embrace rather than exclusion. Embracing the Other involves empathetic listening, overcoming differences, and being in solidarity with those who are marginalized and subordinated. It means sharing love and being loved. It involves increasing one's Chi to make one a healthier and fulfilled person. It may involve a hug or a spiritual embrace like Jesus and the Samaritan woman. We need to understand that we are connected through our Chi, and healing the brokenness between genders and people of different racial ethnicities can be achieved. Erotic power can bring a source of healing and a deliverance from suffering.

A prophetic theology of Spirit God will free us from oppressive notions of God and allow us to recognize the Otherness and holiness in God and in each other. The Spirit lends itself to a movement toward the de-centering of cultures and religions and toward equality. It is Spirit God who will give us life and sustain us as we maneuver through the complexities of immigrant life and embrace the foreign women in our midst. This is a liberating theology not only for Asian Americans who have experienced racism, prejudice, and subordination, but for the whole world.

"We love because God first loved us" (1 John 4:19). As God sent the Son and the Spirit to descend into humanity's darkness and despair, bringing the light of love and hope, we are called to descend into the places of greatest suffering in our communities. It is God's Spirit that guides us in our life-giving mission of mercy and justice, giving us the strength to love, the right words to say, and the power to heal. As Spirit God has embraced us in merciful love, we now warmly embrace the wounded and excluded in the world as a testimony to the merciful love of the Triune God.

Postscript

We began our journey with the story of *Madama Butterfly.* A beautiful and deep Japanese woman, Cio-Cio San (Butterfly), is commandeered as a sexual partner by Pinkerton, a U.S. naval officer. She is used and then discarded when she is no longer needed. The story ends in tragedy: when she is overcome with anger, fear, shame, and forsakenness, she commits suicide to maintain her honor.

If we are only left with tragic Asian women's stories, where is the redemption or the reconciliation? How can women gain liberation, freedom, empowerment when we are always left with tragic endings? Let us turn to Amy Tan's story, *The Joy Luck Club,* for another narration of the problematic and promising lives of Asian women. This is a fascinating story of four Chinese women who endured loss, tragedy, fear, and deceit to build new lives for themselves and for their daughters who were born in America. It is a story that goes back in time to share the tragic stories of their past and how they have overcome their pain for a better future.

All of the women's lives are blemished with traditional patriarchy, Confucianism, obedience, and honor. Within such a context, each woman is a heroine who has surmounted weakness to become who she is. The story of one mother and daughter, Waverly and Lindo Jong, is an intergenerational story of overcoming odds to become an independent, strong, and contented woman.

When Lindo was only four years old, her mother and the matchmaker made an arrangement for her to be married to Huang Tai Tai's son. So when she turns fifteen, her mother sends her to be married to Tai Tai's son, Tyan Hu. He is a young boy who has absolutely no interest in her, neither intellectually nor sexually. Lindo lives four years in a loveless and childless marriage, being continually abused by her mother-in-law. Winsome and wanting, Lindo uses her wit and sees an opportunity to leave an awful arranged marriage that is obstructing her growth from a girl into a woman.

One day, Lindo overhears the servant girl telling her lover that she is pregnant, and he abandons her. Lindo uses this as an opportunity to leave her awful marriage without dishonoring herself or her family. She uses this incident as a way to claim that she had a nightmare in which Tyan Hu's ancestors threatened to punish her, Tyan Hu, and the matchmaker. She goes on and says that the ancestors impregnated the servant girl with Tyan Hu's child. She states that the matchmaker intentionally paired the two for more money. Tai Tai becomes outraged and orders the matchmaker out of the family's life, telling the servant girl to marry Tyan Hu. This makes it easy for Lindo to leave her oppressive marriage.

This story becomes a source of inspiration and empowerment for young Asian women. A teenage girl uses her wit to overcome her circumstances to leave an oppressive relationship. It does not end in tragedy like *Madama Butterfly,* but rather ends with hope for her new life in Shanghai. Because she had the ingenuity and inner resolve to leave an oppressive relationship, she is eventually able to go to the United States, where she begins a new and fulfilling life with a loving husband, a son, and a daughter.

Stories like Lindo's remind us that women's lives matter and that their lives are important. The four mothers in this story overcame their collective trauma, despair, hardships, and patriarchal expectations through the connected erotic power of the transformative Spirit of love. These women's stories also remind us that women do not have to succumb to patriarchy, domination, and fear. Rather, women can break out of their confining pasts and soar into a new empowering future. Women do not have to be bound by their patriarchal cultural expectations, but can redefine and remake their own lives. Stories like Lindo's remind us today that even thousands of years of patriarchy and male domination cannot hold a woman's dream down and confine her to her own home. Instead, women have come a long way to freedom and will continue to be liberated from within.

Asian women's struggle for internal liberation is vital to their becoming fully engaged, loving liberators of those who are victims of external oppression. Our faith traditions provide important resources for this deep and difficult work of healing, reconciliation, and liberation. The Spirit of God is an important resource for women who are seeking to engage their pain in order to be healers of the world.

My theological reconstruction of the Trinity as Spirit God has vast implications for the church, especially for women, who make up the vast majority of our congregations. It will empower the taking of enormous steps toward the liberation of Asian American women, who are doubly bound by the racism and patriarchy of Western society and the cultural expectations of their own culture. That culture expects women to be quiet, subordinate, and submissive. Such assumptions become embedded in the immigrant culture and facilitate the model minority complex within Asian culture. These two cultural pressures prevent Asian American women from fighting back and reclaiming their full subversive moral agency. Prophetic faith can help them overcome the pain of marginalization and subordination, inspiring them to claim their power to be world-changers.

It is time to welcome women in all dimensions of their humanity, including their innermost souls. As women continue to tap into their soul strength, we are witnessing a new generation of strong women leaders, supported by loving male allies, lead a revolution of values. In 2014 the Black-LivesMatter movement led by African American women erupted onto the scene. It's time to open doors of leadership to women, especially young women of color, in all sectors of society. Women working together provide a sustainable soul force that is transforming the world.

Spirit God brings restoration to both the individual and the community through the active struggle for justice, reconciliation, and peace. Communities that have experienced difficulties stemming from racism and prejudice can instead build themselves up with renewed power from the Spirit. Within the community, there are other sisters in the struggle who will comfort and encourage one another as they seek to build beloved communities together.

This understanding of God within us as Spirit will not only comfort us but empower us to take steps in working towards a just society, a society which will not favor one gender over another or one ethnicity over another. Embracing Spirit God who embraces all humanity can lead to the flourishing of all people and can especially transform the lives of Asian American women.

A prophetic theology of the Spirit will free us from oppressive notions of God and allow us to recognize the Otherness and holiness in God and in each other. The Spirit lends itself to a movement toward the de-centering of cultures of oppression, moving us toward equality and justice for all. It is the Spirit of God who will give us life and sustain us as we maneuver through the complexities of immigrant life and embrace the foreign women in our midst. This is a liberating theology not only for Asian Americans who have experienced racism, prejudice, and subordination, but for all people who deal with estrangement in their own unique ways.

God's Spirit is within us and is empowering us to work towards the emancipation of all God's children. Embracing the mystery of Spirit God will move us toward articulating a more inclusive Christian theology that speaks to our growing global community. Spirit God is making a difference in the lives of communities, congregations, and individuals, building healthy ecologies of relation with and among each other. Spirit-led Christians need to become courageous prophets and lead the walk towards social justice, go to the mountaintop, and share the good news that Spirit God dwells in us all. As a sign of loving God and our neighbors, we need to reach out to the marginalized, sharing God's mercy through embracing the Other.

Index

Abjection, 15, 25-26, 78-79, 88, 110
Abominations, 22, 26, 86
Abraham, 83
Abuse, 87, 148
Affection, 110-11
Affirmative action, 50
African Americans, 42
Africans, 2, 63, 116; racialization of as
  "black," 3, 41, 59; on Spirit God, 133
Afrikaners, 2-3
Agape, 154
Ai kapu system, 40
Alienation, 1, 47, 110, 145; from invisible
  boundaries, 38, 57; of women, 77-79
Alinsky, Saul, 161
Aloha, 134
Althaus-Reid, Marcella, 118
Amazons, 89n86
Ammonites, 19
An, Choi Hee, 92
An-ae, 84
Ancient Near East, 92, 113
Angel Island, 7, 38
Anglo-Boer Wars, 3
Anima/animus, 141, 143, 143-44n7
Anti-essentialism, 112
Anti-Semitism, 44, 49
Aristotle, on women, 80

Asenath, 14
"Asian" (term), 35, 105
"Asian American" (term), 105
Asian American men, feminizing of, 89
Asian Americans, 31, 33-38; assimilation
  into whiteness of, 50; and the civil
  rights movement, 50-51; educational
  and cultural achievements of, 50; encounter of racism by, 12; loss of Asian
  language among the second generation of, 55; as "perpetual foreigners,"
  17, 48, 51-53, 54; segregation of, 37; as a
  silenced minority group, 57; subordination and marginalization of, 42; as
  unassimilable, 51-53. See also Asian
  American men, feminizing of; Asian
  American women
Asian American women, 6-7, 8; casting
  out of from society, 57; as double
  bound, 172; exile between cultures of,
  12; and han, 39-40; leadership in the
  church of, 53; marginalization of, 30,
  53-54; oppression of, 31; as orphans,
  107; as perpetual foreigners, 107;
  pitting of against other immigrant minorities, 165; psychological and legal
  handicaps of, 38-39; silenced voices of,
  87, 163; social, religious, and cultural

174

diversity of, 106; on Spirit God, 138-39; understanding of self, 79
Asian Christianities, 165
Asians: gendering of as feminine, 45; immigration to America of, 7; and male children, 83; as migratory people, 8; on Spirit as Great Mother, 145-46. *See also* Asian women
Asian women: as colonial fantasy, 89; as exotic Other, 64; as expendable commodities, 69; as the Other, 65-66; romanticization of in the Western imagination, 93; struggle of for internal liberation, 171
Assimilation, 42, 57, 60
Australian Aborigines, 134
Avatar (film), 78n49

Barbarians, 45
Barrenness, in the Old Testament, 14
Barrie, J. M., 33n4
Basileia, 100-101, 123
Beauty, Western norms of, 54
Beauvoir, Simone de, 82, 84
Belonging, 55, 160
Bhabha, Homi, 8, 57, 74
Bible, the: as against colonialism, 97; androcentrism of, 101; as a colonizing text, 74-75; and the gendering of biblical language, 15, 16-17; misuse of, 74, 92, 98
Binaries, 76, 93, 112
"Blaming the victim," 119
Bloch, Robert, 78
Boaz, 94, 96
Body and spirit, 130
Bonding, inter-ethnic, 95, 98
Boundaries, crossing of, 76, 88, 97, 132, 157-58, 163, 166
Brainerd, David, 118n5
British Empire, 66
Brock, Rita Nakashima, 92, 141-42, 159-60
Buddhism, 107, 137
Bulgakov, Sergei, 147, 154-55
Bullying, 1
Burma, 36

Butler, Judith, 99n17, 154

California Gold Rush, 34
Calvin, John, 2
Calvinism, 2-3; Dutch Calvinism and racial discrimination, 2
Capitalism, 67, 68-69
Cappadocian theologians, 147
Carter, J. Kameron, 41
Carter, Jimmy, 37n19
Caste system, 48, 59
Center, and margins, 73, 112, 116-19, 157
Cherokee women, 97
Chi, 5, 115, 125-26, 133, 136-38, 142, 152, 166-67
Chin, Vincent, 51
Chinatowns, 55, 56
Chinese Exclusion Act (1882), 35-36, 63
Chinese labor, importation of to America, 34
Cho, Seung-Hui, 12
Christianity: the egalitarian vision of early Christianity, 102-3, 113, 125; perpetuation of racism and sexism by, 138; in the religious experience of Korean women, 107; as a replacement for Judaism, 44; Western Christianity, 10, 71-72, 85, 135
Christology, 9
Chung Hyun Kyung, 108-10, 114
Church, the: as constantly reforming itself, 104-5; dis-ordering of from racism and sexism, 168; in the global South, 105; inclusive character of, 101; patriarchal structure of, 104
Circumincessio, 153
Civil rights legislation (1965), 37
Civil rights movement, 50
Class system, 48
Coakley, Sarah, 154-55
Coleman, Monica, 92
Colonialism, 41, 58, 66, 68, 72-73, 75, 90, 111, 112, 165
Color, fluidity of, 52
Columbus, Christopher, 59
"Comfort women," 29-30, 65, 150
Common good, 138, 152

Index

Communism, 73n36
Community organizers, 160-61
Compassion, 160
Confucianism, 53, 79, 82, 107
Connectedness, 160
Conquest, 60, 70-71, 72
Conversion, 70
Counter-language, as resistance, 73
Creation care, 127-28
Crusaders, 62
Culp, Kristine A., 100
Cultural hegemony, 63
"Culture wars," 69
Cultures, de-centering of, 168-69, 172

Daly, Mary, 103n28
Decolonizing, 8
Defilement, 15-16, 18, 86
Deliverance, 71, 72
Depression, 141
Despair, 141
Developing world, 88
Difference: celebration of, 104; Jung on, 144
Dionysius, 131n26
"Discipleship of equals," 101-2
Displacement, 60, 75, 78
Divinity, as transformative Spirit of love, 140
Divorce, 24, 83, 86, 102
Domestic violence, 13
Domination, 6, 27, 46, 47, 171
Dualism: of men and women, 84-85, 89; movement away from, 146; Western dualism, 88, 130, 143
Dube, Musa, 92
Dussel, Enrique, 69

East, the: Eastern religious traditions, 48; as the Other, 62
Ecofeminist theories, 81
Ekklesia, 101
Election, distortion of into exclusivity, 3
Elijah, 143n7
Ellis Island, 7
Embracing, 151
Empire, 90

"Enfleshing freedom," 116
"Engendering cultural hermeneutics," 93
Entertainment culture, 119
Equality, 82, 101-2, 104, 169, 172
Eros, 10, 139, 141-49, 154, 162-63, 166-67
E.T. (film), 78n49
Ethnic cleansing, 27
Ethnic erasure, 48
Ethnicity: as multiple, 76; purity of, 20-22, 27; and race, 40-41, 42
Europeans: colonization by, 59; distinguishing of themselves from Asians, 45; gendered as masculine, 45
Evangelism, 72
Eve myth, 26, 81
Exclusion, 151-52, 168
Exclusionary Immigration Act (1924), 35
Exile, 18-19, 60, 77-78
Exodus story, 70
Exogamy, 20
Exotic, the, as erotic, 64
Exploitation, 41
Ezra, 5, 7, 14-15, 16, 23-25, 30

Faith, prophetic, 172
Faith-rooted organizing, 161-62
False consciousness, breaking the chains of, 103
Family, 80
Farley, Wendy, 146, 148
Father, as dominus, 80
Fear, of the unknown, 151
Fee, Gordon, 158
Feminine, the, rejection of, 21, 25-26
Feminism: faith-rooted feminism, 99-100; postcolonial feminist biblical interpretation, 6, 92; transforming power of, 98-100
Feminist theology, 8-9, 91-92; Asian American feminist theology, 105, 109, 136; on erotic power, 142-43; intercultural feminist theology, 92; and intercultural studies, 93-94, 98; as not universal, 77; white feminist theology, 91-92, 100-104, 113-14; and women of color, 103-4, 113-14
Fertility cult, 28

First World, 76, 88
Ford, John, 131
Foreign nations, 14
Foreign women, 66; as expendable, 19, 29; in the Hebrew Bible, 5-6, 13-16, 21, 23-26; as invisible, 94; and Israel's "whoring" after foreign deities, 16; objectification of, 38; as the Other, 19; as pawns, 32-33; in the twenty-first century, 6; vilifying of, 96-97
Foreigners: as defiling, 15-16, 86; as distant from the white norm, 151
Foucault, Michel, 56, 154
Frazer, James George, 85
"Free spirit" (of Nietzsche), 128
Fundamentalisms, religious, 69-70

Gaia, 137
Gays and lesbians, as the Other, 22
Geist, 126, 128, 129, 136
Gender analysis, 92
Genocide, 27, 42, 70
Global South, 103-4, 105
Globalization, 23, 69, 72, 92
God: as Almighty Father, 116; breath of God, 144; of the center, 116-17; of the Christian West, 33, 85, 135; compassion of, 108-9; conception of in creative, nonhierarchical, non-Western ways, 9, 33; continuity of with the world, 127; dance of, 154, 163; de-centered perspective of, 9; desire of for loving relationship with humanity, 99; dwelling of among us, 132, 163; economy of God, 121; as faithful husband to Israel, 27; fire of God, 135-36; God of deliverance (liberation theology), 71; immanence of, 127; knowing God by experiencing God, 109; limited understandings of, 136, 146; manifestation and dwelling of in the material world, 127; of the margins, 115, 116-17, 122; masochistic understanding of, 9; Otherness and holiness of, 172; presence of God, 132; reimagining of, 92, 131, 146; as Spirit, 5, 9, 167. *See also* Spirit God; Trinity, the

Golah community, 19-20, 21, 24
Goliath, 96
Gomer, 27
Gospel, the, and liberation of the oppressed, 101
Governmental entitlements, 50
Grace, 39, 159
Great White Father, 33
Greek ascetics, 143
Green, Rayna, 96

Ha, 134
Hagar, 6, 14, 17, 19, 24, 32, 83
Han, 39-40, 57, 111
Hara-kiri, 65
Hate crimes, 42
Hawaii, and sugar plantations, 34-35
Hawaiians, on Spirit God, 134
Healing: and wholeness, 158; between women and men, 138
Hee, Choi, 107
Hegel, Georg Wilhelm Friedrich, 115, 126-27, 128, 129
Heinlein, Robert A., 78n49
Heltzel, Peter Goodwin, 41, 117, 121, 125, 162
Heritage, loss of, 55
Hermeneutic: intercultural hermeneutic, 120; multifaith hermeneutic, 107-8, 138
"Heteropatriarchical American" ideal, 77
Hierarchies, dismantling of, 159
Hinduism, 69, 137
Hippocrates, 45
Hispanic Americans, subordination and marginalization of, 42
History, 126-27
Ho Chi Minh, 73n36
Holiness, 15
Holmes, James, 12
"Holy seed," 15, 19, 21
Holy Spirit, 158, 167. *See also* Spirit-Chi
"Homeplace," 73
Homogeneity, 77
Homophobia, 148
Honor, 28
"Honorary whites," 1, 12, 52, 166
hooks, bell, 73-74, 87

Hopkins, Dwight, 134-35
Hosea, 27-30
Hospitality, 152
"Household Code," 102
Human flourishing, 172
Hutchison, William R., 71
Hybridity, 8, 20, 22, 26-27, 74, 76, 95
Hypostases, 147

Identity, 85; contestation of in the post-colonial context, 76; fluidity of, 154, 158; search for, 67
Immigrants: Filipino immigrants, 34; hyphenated reality of, 47; Japanese immigrants, 34; Korean immigrants, 34; South Asian Indian immigrants, 34
Immigration, 6, 23, 67-68; and anti-immigration sentiment, 36, 67; the quota system in Asian immigration, 36; worker immigration, 67-68
Immigration Act (1917), 35
Immigration Act (1924), 63
Immigration Act (1965), 36, 38
Immigration law, 35-36, 48, 63
Imperialism, 60, 61, 63, 64, 66, 84, 90; classical imperialism, 67n19, 68; economic imperialism, 67; modern imperialism, 68
Impurity, 15-16; "ritual" impurity, 18
"In-between," 55-57
Incarnation, 130, 145-46
India, 133-34, 149, 151
Individualism, 144
Industrial Areas Foundation, 161
Inheritance, 28
Inipi, 134
Injustice, 17-18, 25, 29, 121-22; gender injustice, 92
Inside person, 84
Intermarriage, 18, 20, 22-23, 52, 86
Intimacy, 111, 141
Isai-Díaz, Ada María, 92, 101
Ishmael, 17, 83
Islam, 52
Israel: adultery of, 28-29; conquest of Canaan by, 75n40; exile of, 15; injustice

of, 122; suffering of, 75n40; xenophobia of, 95

Japan, occupation of Korea by (1910-1945), 149-50
Japanese, on Spirit God, 134
Japanese Americans, internment of during World War II, 36-37
Japantowns, 56
Jennings, Willie, 41
Jeong, 110-11
Jesus: on embracing the Other, 150-51; as a faith-rooted organizer, 162; identification of with the marginalized, 123-24; as Jewish, 44, 49; as marginalized, 116; racialization of as white, 49; resurrection and ascension of, 125; as a supporter of empire, 116; teaching on the kingdom of, 100-101
Jezreel, 29
Joh, W. Anne, 9, 92, 110-11, 114
John Damascene, 153
Jong, Lindo, 170-71
Joy, 148
Joy Luck Club, The (Tan), 170-71
Jung, Carl, 136, 143-44
Jung Young Lee, 117
Justice, 115, 126, 168, 172; economic justice, 99; gender justice, 138; Jubilee justice, 123; shalom justice, 121-23, 125, 138, 147; social justice, 10, 104, 167, 173; transformative justice, 142

Kang, Namsoon, 92
Kapu, 40
Keller, Catherine, 92
Khayelitsha Township (South Africa), 2
Ki, 5, 134
Kim, Jean K., 11n2
Kim, Seong Hee, 93n4
Kin-dom, 101
"King" industry, 34
King, Martin Luther, Jr., 4, 44
Kingdom of God, 100-101, 124
Knowledge, as power, 89-90
Koinonia, 125
Korean American women, 30, 40

Korean culture, 114

Korean emigration, as social and spiritual death, 35

Korean War, 65

Korean women: as "comfort women," 29-30; experience of religious pluralism, 107-8

Koreatowns, 56

Kristeva, Julia, 15, 21, 25, 78, 85, 110

Kung San, 133

Kwok Pui-lan, 92, 93

Kyung, Church Hyun, 92

Lacan, Jacques, 79n53

Land ownership, 75, 79-80, 86

Language, loss of, 55

Leadership, 161

Leah, 14, 83

Lee, Hyo-Dong, 155-56

Lepers, 149

Levitical purity and holiness system, 21

Life energy, 134, 137-38

Life force, 143

Lilith myth, 26

Lobeda, Cynthia Moe, 160

Logos, 143, 146

Love, 110-11, 144

Mad Men (TV show), 13

Madama Butterfly, 11-12, 17, 64-65, 166, 170-71

Majoritization, 47

Male domination, 171

Mandela, Nelson, 2

Marable, Manning, 41

Marginality, 55-57, 73-74, 116-20, 122, 172; as empowerment, 157

Marginalized, the: hearing of, 87; Spirit's movement among, 132; theologizing from, 116-20

Marriage, 22, 28, 82-84, 113. *See also* Intermarriage

Mass murderers, 12-13

Matriarchy, 81, 98

Matter, and spirit, 130-32

McFague, Sallie, 129-31

Merchant of Venice, The (Shakespeare), 78n49

Michener, James, 12

Migrant workers, 67-68

Migration, 8, 66-67; forced migration, 60

Military brides, 29

Minh-Ha, Trinh, 88

"Minoritized," 47

Mirror stage, 79

Mishpat, 121-23

Missionaries, 70

Mixed marriage. *See* Intermarriage

Mixing. *See* Hybridity

Moabites, 19, 95

"Model minority" myth, 1, 12, 37, 50-51, 57, 116, 165-66

Moi, Toril, 89

Montaigne, 81

Mother, as passive role, 80

Mother Goddess, 81

Mother Teresa, 149

Muslims, 69

Mystery: as engulfing the being of God, 157; in theological discourse, 147

Nadis, 133

Naomi, 94, 96, 97

Nationalism, 48

National Origins Act (1924), 35-36, 63

Native Americans, 131; harming of by Christians, 70; Native American women, 96; racialization of as "Indians," 3, 41, 59; on Spirit God, 134; subordination and marginalization of, 42

Nehemiah, 5, 25

Neoconservatives, 50

New Testament, the, as postcolonial, 75

Ni, 134

Nietzsche, Friedrich, 115, 128-30

Num, 133

Obed, 95

Oduyoye, Mercy Amba, 92

Oikonomia, 121, 156

Oppression, 141, 160; dismantling of,

158; freedom from, 168-69; of women, 92, 120
Orient, the: feminizing of, 8, 89; as the Other, 62
Orientalism, 7-8, 37n22, 45, 60-61, 65
Orpah, 92, 94, 96-98
Other, the: Asian women as, 65-66; embrace of, 4-5, 149-53, 164, 168; foreign women as, 32-33; the Orient as, 62; as racialized, 57; racially non-whites as, 64; women as, 7, 21, 84-90, 113
Otto, Rudolf, 12
Ousia-Sophia, 155
Overman (of Nietzsche), 128

Page Law (1875), 35
Palmer, Aaron, 34
Pandora legend, 81
Panentheism, 131
Panikkar, K. M., 61
Patriarchy, 3-4, 13, 20-21, 25, 28, 73n33, 80-81, 97, 117, 148, 152, 159, 165, 171; in the Ancient Near East, 92; in Asian American households, 53-54; in Asian culture, 57, 107; in the Christian West, 85, 135; in the church, 104, 166; dismantling of, 103; oppression from, 132; resistance of, 100; as thriving on dualism, 84; in the United States, 107
Patriotism, 48
Paul, on women in leadership roles, 102
Pax Romana, 73n33
Peace, 168
Pentecost, 125, 135
People of color, as deviant, 113
Perception (TV series), 144n7
Perichoresis, 153-59, 163, 167
"Perpetual foreigners," 17, 32, 38, 48, 51-53, 54, 107
Peterson, William, 50
Philios, 154
Philosophy, continental, 126
Plastic surgery, 54-55
Pluralism, religious, 107-8
Pneuma, 5, 137
Pneumatology, 9, 10, 108, 125
Pocahontas Perplex, 96

Pollution. *See* Defilement
Polo, Marco, 62
Poor, the, 69, 120, 124
Popular culture, 119
Postcolonial studies, 8, 60, 72
Poverty, 119
Power, 41, 119-20, 152-53, 161; erotic power, 139, 141, 152-53, 157, 159-62
Powerlessness, 141
Prana, 5, 133
Preferential option for the poor, 120
Private property, 80-81
Privilege, 41
"Promiscuous wife" metaphor, 28
Promised Land, 2, 17, 70, 95
Prophets of revolutionary love, 157
Prostitution, militarized, 65, 150
"Psycho" (story and film), 78
Puccini, Giacomo, 11
Puritans, in New England, 142-43
Purity, as a myth, 95

Qi, 5
Queen of Sheba, 89

Race: blurring of by hybridity, 22; as a category used to isolate, dominate, and subjugate groups, 45; and the creation of cultural barriers, 41-42; and the trumping of culture, 42
Rachel, 14, 83
Racialization, 43-44, 46, 47
Racism, 1, 4, 27, 39, 42, 119, 148, 152, 159, 166; against Asian American women, 38; against Korean North American women, 40; as based on the color of one's skin, 13; covert racism, 47, 51; and the disordering of the church, 168; and fear of the Other, 167; institutionalized racism, 1; as leading to death, 167; legacies of, 4; nondeliberate racism, 47; and the promotion of domination, 45
Rahab, 95
Reagan, Ronald, 37n19
Reconciliation, 111, 152, 167, 168
Religion: and distinctions between "us"

and "them," 59; and the subordination of women, 81, 88
Religious studies, as colonizing discourse, 72
Resistance, 73, 87
Ressentiment, 47, 128
Righteousness, 122
Roman Catholic Church, male leadership in, 60
Ruach, 120, 133, 137, 138
Ruether, Rosemary Radford, 91, 103
Russell, Letty, 91
Ruth, 92, 94-98

Sabbath, 121
Sadiqah, 122
Said, Edward, 7, 60-62, 63, 65
Salmon, 96
Salome, 143n7
Salvatierra, Alexia, 161-62
Samaritan woman, 124, 168
Sarah, 83
Sayonara (novel and film), 12
Scapegoat/scapegoating, 14, 22, 82, 87
Schüssler Fiorenza, Elisabeth, 8, 91, 100-102
Scripture. *See* Bible, the
Self, 93
Self-denial, 141
Sex trafficking, 65, 152
Sexism, 4, 106, 111-12, 148, 159, 166, 167; against Asian American women, 109; against Korean North American women, 40; as disordering the church, 168
Shakespeare, William, 78n49
Shamanism, 107
Shekinah, 121
Silence: as betrayal, 4; from displacement into a new language foreign to one's mother tongue, 78; of women, 87
Skin tones, hierarchy of, 13
Slavery, 6, 42
Smith, John, 96
Social Darwinism, 63
Solitude, 129
Solomon, foreign wives of, 5-6

Sophia, 143, 146-48, 155, 158, 166-67
Soul, as an aspect of the body, 129
South Africa, racism in, 2-3
Space, 56, 70, 73, 78
Spielberg, Steven, 78n49
Spirit-Chi, 9-10, 142, 155, 158, 163, 166-67
Spirit God, 9, 120-26, 166-67, 172; and compassionate care of the Other, 9; and the empowerment and liberation of the marginalized, 115; global understandings of, 133-36; as Great Mother, 145-46; as heart and soul of Christian theology, 4; as helper, 151; liberation of from Western colonial captivity, 131; as life-giving energy, 5, 126; love of, 140, 145, 168-69; and matter, 130-32; movement of, 132, 172-73; at Pentecost, 125; as the source of erotic longing, 162; as the *telos* of history, 126-27; transformative power of, 132, 158-60; as vital and elusive, 134-35; Western colonial captivity of, 115
Stout, Jeffrey, 161
Subordination: of Asian American women, 172; of foreign women, 38; of women, 79-82, 93, 99
Succession, the exclusion of women from, 83
Suffering, 39, 111; unjust suffering, 39. *See also han*
Sugirtharajah, R. S., 67
Suicide, 65
Superiority, positional, 6, 92
Supersessionism, 44

Takahashi, Kemechiyo, 7n6
Tamar, 14, 94
Tan, Amy, 170-71
Taoism, 137
Theism, classical, 116
Theology: black theology, 50; and cultural context, 99-100; discrimination and marginalization in, 109, 119-20; from the margins, 120; globalization of, 136; as inclusive, 173; liberation theology, 50, 69, 70-71; liberative theology, 155; *minjung* theology, 50;

as not "timeless truth," 99; prophetic theology of the Spirit, 172; Reformed theology, 99; reimagining of to help the marginalized, 69; replacement theology, 44; womanist theology, 50
Third Reich, anti-Semitism of, 49
"Third Space," 57
"Third World" (term), 56
Thurman, Howard, 44
Tommy (opera), 79n53
Townes, Emilie, 92
Townshend, Pete, 79n53
Tradition, and modernization, 69
Travel, 66, 76
Trinity, the, 9, 140, 147-48, 163, 172; mutual indwelling of the three persons, 153, 156-57, 167; mutual love in, 147-48; reimagining of, 154-55

Urban space, 56
U.S. legal system, "colorblind" approach to, 49

Vietnam War, 65
Violence, 6
Volf, Miroslav, 151-52
Volk, 41n32
Voyager, 78

Walter-McCarran Act (1952), 38
Waniya, 134
War Brides Act (1945), 36
Warrior, Robert Allen, 70-71, 72
Waugh, Evelyn, 78n49
Way of negation, 146
Weber, Max, 3
West, the: "civilizing" mission of, 68; and the definition of Eastern history, culture, and religion, 62-63; social constructs of, 112; superiority of over the East, 63-64
"White masculine" ideal, 3-4, 59
White power, 9, 42, 49, 112
White privilege, 1, 43, 49, 64, 112

White supremacy, 43, 44, 47, 79, 112-13, 132, 159, 165
"Whiteness," 43, 47-50; and the erasure of differences, 48; exposure of as racialized, 43; as the norm, 41-42; as a social construct, 49
Wilderness experience, 17
Wisdom, 144
Women: alienation of, 77-79; bodies of, 21; as the cause of evil, 21; as commodities, 29; compelling of to be against one another in patriarchy, 97; as expendable, 24; experiences of, 77, 91, 112; fidelity required of, 83; as guardians of tradition, 69; identity of, 76; as inside persons, 84; "insider" women in the Old Testament, 14; in leadership, 88-89, 92, 98, 102; liberation of, 82; and the lost paradise, 81-82; oppression of, 3, 6, 92, 106; as the Other, 7, 21, 84-90; and the performance of traditional chores, 84; as property possessed by men, 85; reimagining of as embodying a hidden wholeness, 90; rights of, 4, 22; subordination of, 3-4, 25, 79-82, 93, 99, 120; as subversive, 97-98; virginity of, 83; as the weaker sex, 80. *See also* Women of color
Women of color: as at the bottom of the new-world hierarchy, 60; as commodities for the military, 29; as deviant, 113; marginalization of, 165; in theological discourse, 91-92
Woodley, Randy, 131
World War II, 29, 36-37

Xenophobia, 95

"Yellow peril" myth, 37, 51
YHWH, 16, 24, 28
Yin and yang, 137

Zarathustra, 128-29
Zipporah, 14